MW00340269

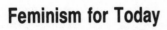

Feminism for Today

General Editor: Teresa Brennan

The Regime of the Brother

After the Patriarchy

The Regime of the Brother
After the Patriarchy

Juliet Flower MacCannell

London and New York

First published 1991
by Routledge
11 New Fetter Lane, London EC4P 4EE

Simultaneously published in the USA and Canada
by Routledge
a division of Routledge, Chapman and Hall Inc.
29 West 35th Street, New York, NY 10001

Typeset in 10/12pt Palatino by
Mayhew Typesetting, Bristol
Printed in Great Britain by
Clays Ltd, St. Ives plc.

British Library Cataloguing in Publication Data
MacCannell, Juliet Flower
  The Regime of the Brother: After the Patriarchy
  – (Opening Out).
  1. Society. Role of women, history
  I. Title II. Series
  305.4209

Library of Congress Cataloging in Publication Data
MacCannell, Juliet Flower
  The regime of the brother: after the patriarchy
  /Juliet Flower MacCannell.
    p. cm. – (Opening Out)
  Includes index.
  ISBN 0-415-05434-6. – ISBN 0-415-05435-4 pbk
    1. Women – History – Modern period, 1600–   2. Social history –
Modern, 1500–   3. Women in literature. 4. Feminist theory.
I. Title. II. Series.
HQ1150.M33   1991   90-8982
305.42–dc20   CIP

ISBN 0-415-05434-6
ISBN 0-415-05435-4 pbk

Contents

Series preface

Feminist theory is the most innovative and truly living theory in today's academies, but the struggle between the living and the dead extends beyond feminism and far beyond institutions. *Opening Out* will apply the living insights of feminist critical theory in current social and political contexts. It will also use feminist theory to analyse the historical and cultural genealogies that shaped those contexts.

While feminist insights on modernity and postmodernity have become increasingly sophisticated, they have also become more distant from the *realpolitik* that made feminism a force in the first instance. This distance is apparent in three growing divisions. One is an evident division between feminist theory and feminist popular culture and politics. Another division is that between feminism and other social movements. Of course this second division is not new, but it has been exacerbated by the issue of whether the theoretical insights of feminism can be used to analyse current conflicts that extend beyond feminism's "proper" field. In the postmodern theory he has helped build, the white male middle-class universal subject has had to relinquish his right to speak for all. By the same theoretical logic, he has also taken out a philosophical insurance policy against any voice uniting the different movements that oppose him, which means his power persists *de facto*, if not *de jure*. Currently, there are no theoretical means, except for right sentiments and good will, that enable feminism to ally itself with other social movements that oppose the power networks that sustain the white, masculine universal subject. *Opening Out* aims at finding those means.

Of course, the analysis of the division between feminist and other social movements is a theoretical question in itself. It cannot be considered outside of the process whereby feminist theory and women's studies have become institutionalised, which returns us to the first division, between feminist practice and feminism in the academy. Is it simply the case that as women's studies becomes more institutionalised, feminist scholars are defining their concerns in relation to those of their colleagues in the existing disciplines? This could account both for an often uncritical adherence to a postmodernism that negates the right to act, if not speak, and to the distance between feminism in the institution and outside it. But if this is the case, not only do the political concerns of feminism have to be reconsidered, but the disciplinary boundaries that restrict political thinking have to be crossed.

Disciplinary specialisation might also be held accountable for a third growing division within feminism, between theoretical skills on the one hand, and literary analysis and socio-economic empirical research on the other. Poststructuralist or postmodern feminism is identified with the theoretical avant garde, while historical, cultural feminism is associated with the study of how women are culturally represented, or what women are meant to have really done.

Opening Out is based on the belief that such divisions are unhelpful. There is small advantage in uncritical cultural descriptions, or an unreflective politics of experience; without the theoretical tools found in poststructuralist, psychoanalytic, and other contemporary critical theories, our social and cultural analyses, and perhaps our political activity, may be severely curtailed. On the other hand, unless these theoretical tools are applied to present conflicts and the histories that shaped them, feminist theory itself may become moribund. Not only that, but the opportunity feminist theories afford for reworking the theories currently available for understanding the world (such as they are) may be bypassed.

None of this means that *Opening Out* will always be easy reading in the first instance; the distance between developed theory and practical feminism is too great for that at present. But it does mean that *Opening Out* is committed to returning theory to present political questions, and this just might make the value of theoretical pursuits for feminism plainer in the long term.

Opening Out will develop feminist theories that bear on environmental degradation, ethnocentrism, neocolonialism and escalating aggression. It will do so through general cultural analyses of modernity, and particular studies which, amongst other things, dissect the displacement of African women's oral traditions, offer a psychoanalysis of antifeminism and antisemitism in Eastern Europe, deconstruct environmental polemics in India, and follow the traffic in bodily organs from the South to the North. *Opening Out* will draw freely on the various contemporary critical theories in these analyses, and on social as well as literary material. *Opening Out* will try to cross disciplinary boundaries, and subordinate the institutionalized concerns of particular disciplines to the political concerns of the times.

Teresa Brennan

Acknowledgements

Dean MacCannell has contributed as much to my understanding as to my well-being in the course of my writing of this book. To him, all my love.

Teresa Brennan and I first met on the shifting grounds where feminism and psychoanalysis attempt to construct a relation: the compatibility of our views on this subject, as well as Teresa's editorial genius, provided me with rare and wonderful support. To her, my deep gratitude and friendship.

To the many people who have gone into the production of this book, especially those whose readings gave me perspective on what I was doing, my thanks. Avital Ronell, Elizabeth Wright, Judith Pike and Lollie Groth each read part or all of the manuscript in ways that were especially helpful to me. Thanks also to Ellie Ragland-Sullivan and Joan Copjec for their encouragement on this project.

Intellectual debts can never be adequately assessed, but among those whose work has been of great importance to me, I do not wish to forget my graduate students at the University of California, Irvine, who have studied the Enlightenment with me over the years, as well as my undergraduate students who invested their credit in such experimental courses as "Psychopathology and Narrative", "Women and Empire", and "Women and War". Without their collective inter-locution much of this would have lain fallow. I also regard the collegiality of the Members of the Focused Research Program in Gender and Women's Studies at Irvine in this light. Eric Halpern was responsible for several readings which resulted in the refinement and improvement of the manuscript. Daniel MacCannell and Jason MacCannell have also been material to the process, offering both insights and detailed knowledge of imperial matters and for bringing a side of George Orwell to my attention that I had overlooked.

Material support was provided by Irvine's Graduate Studies and Research Office, and the President's Humanities Initiative of the University of California, which funded the Focused Research Program and Initiative on Women and Gender that I direct. I am also grateful to the Dean of Humanities for granting me a summer fellowship to work on the manuscript. Cornell University's Department of English generously offered me accommodation while I was on sabbatical, and the interchange with that faculty and also the faculty in Romance Studies was invaluable.

Note on passages translated

I have supplied the French originals for Rousseau and several other authors (Duras, in particular) I use extensively because my arguments depend on close analysis of their prose, and the available translations do not always carry the full complexity of what they say.

For the Rousseau quotes, I have cited the standard reference on Rousseau, the *Oeuvres complètes* published by Gallimard, Pléïade, which use the original spelling and orthography.

Page numbers following French quotations refer to the French editions of the relevant work, those following English quotations refer to the English edition. Details of these editions are to be found in the notes section.

Superscript letters following English translations indicate that the original French is given in the Passages translated section at the end of the book.

Introduction: the structure of the book

You must be father, mother, uncle to yourself.
(Anna Howe to Clarissa in *Clarissa*)

In this book I argue the necessity of employing a combination of psychoanalytic and rhetorical methods to criticize the central concepts (liberty/equality/fraternity) produced at the birth of the Enlightenment version of modernity – in order to reach a structural and formal understanding of the failure of modernity. Attention to the woman as one of the means of decoding this failure is mandatory. It is not just a matter of studying how the myths of Enlightenment became ideologies in the service of bourgeois rationalism, imperialism, racism, and sexism – Arendt, Adorno, Horkheimer have done this. My intent is both more grounded and more general, more "anthropological": my interests lie there where myths, metaphors, and ideologies touch the human heart (often in the form of an attack), striking at the roots of the human community – its biological, familial, and erotic roots – in ways specifiable by psychoanalytic theory, and the methods of rhetorical, literary, and semiocritical analysis.

While such an endeavor may permit us eventually to restructure certain relations in a more positive way (especially, but not exclusively, sexual relations) two key issues need to be couched (perhaps in the practical psychoanalytic sense). The first is a question of the ego. To answer it has implications for the structure of what is the "ego ideal" in modern culture, its "superego."[1] It is no longer an unquestioned "Father": for, when I say the familial root has been attacked, I am speaking not just of the maternal relation, but also of the paternal one – the ego stands alone, or so it imagines, after the patriarchy.

The second is a question of the woman, and it is more disturbing, yet more fundamental: what is the value of woman in modernity, after the patriarchy? It is perhaps most important to the empowering of the modern, nontraditional society that we studiously avoid noticing its consciously artificial, made-up character.

The political ego

It takes some effort even to recognize that there is a superego, operating without check, in a modernity whose cardinal feature is "la mort de Dieu" (at least from the eighteenth century on).[2] The Enlightenment decided upon the construct of an ego rather than an obvious superego as the synthesizer (not creator) of all social and political forms. As Georg Simmel put it, "[The ego] stands so much on itself alone that even its world, *the* world can stand on it."[3] That that ego, which stands upright, and bears the weight of social, political, juridical, and other cultural forms on its fictive persona, is now coming to be seen as gendered (or gender-biased) – a male ego – and as exercising the powers of sovereignty (Freud's "his majesty, the ego") provides preface enough to the analysis that follows. To point out its imaginary-fictive character does not get us off the hook: it works or stands in as a symbolic ordering principle, one not overtly labeled "I" but "It". *It* is thus free to exercise power – without responsibility, without accountability to the ego's relations.

Despite its burgeoning numbers of members, the roots of the collective *it* have narrowed considerably in modernity: we know, at least that the root model of difference, sexual difference, has been left out. This book asks why.

The brother

We can no longer beg the question the modern ego refuses to be asked: its familial status. "Whose ego" is being privileged in modernity – privileged by modeling a superego whose existence it denies? My answer is – the Brother's. By placing this modernized ego into the center of its kinship network we can ask the question we moderns have been loath to ask – "Who and what is the superego in modernity, and who are its relations?" The time has come to subject the hidden superego to a radical critique: the society formed by it and which it forms is not one of fathers, not one ruled by elders, but by sons. Unfortunately they have managed to act as sovereigns (like the *père jouissant* of *Totem and Taboo*, or Rousseau's *Second Discourse*) rather than "well-meaning" Oedipal patriarchs. Their privilege is the freer in modernity, where we claim an absolute right brought about by the death of the tyrannical "father" to self-governance and an absolute equality for everyone. I by no means want to imply that same-generation self-governance – the logical political outcome of the death of a tyrant – is never more than a utopian dream, or a useful lie. We have not only not exhausted the possibilities of democratic self-governance – the absence of the tyrant – I would say we have not even begun to do so. What we have in the place of the patriarchy is the Regime of the Brother.

The woman

The actual history of woman under this regime has accelerated and exaggerated the defects of the patriarchal evaluation, and withdrawn whatever was positive from it. Her fictional history tells us another story, in anamorphosis perhaps, but one worth reading. When an "other" woman makes her appearance in Rousseau, Stendhal, James, Duras, Rhys, Prawer Jhabvala, and Cixous she is both familiar and strange. In selecting these texts, my eye has been on tracking the equations in which the woman is set and which enhance rather than diminish her value specifically in postpatriarchal terms, inside the fraternal empire. These authors are marked by the double sense they have of how the Regime of the Brother attacks and negates the woman, and further by a special effort to redeem that value even under his reign. Rousseau looked to Madame d'Houdetot for a feminine desire that could act as a model for her lover; Stendhal, the fond brother of Pauline, gives us women imagined as in equal partnership with men; James provides us, in his Maisie, with a proto-woman who makes an ultimate strength of her ultimate weakness (her absolute lack of a given identity) and Duras grants us a mother who plays perfectly the negative role her first-born son, "the Brother," assigns her, while formulating several effective kinds of rebellion against it. The failures are also here, the feminine victims of brotherly "love": Antoinette Cosway in *Wide Sargasso Sea* by Jean Rhys, Elizabeth in Jhabvala's story, "Two more under the Indian sun," and the women of Cambodia in Cixous's *Terrible but Unfinished Story of Norodom Sihanouk*. But even in these the triumph of the Brother is incomplete: Antoinette (a.k.a. Bertha Rochester) ends a madwoman, yes, but she nevertheless manages to burn down "cardboard England"; Elizabeth's presence exposes the greedy imperialist roots of her "do-good," morally superior English compatriot in India, and Cixous's powerful play gives us pause to reconsider the aggression against the traditional society that her old women face, first in the saturation bombing of their country, and then in the regime of Pol Pot.

Because Jean-Jacques Rousseau was one of the first to detail this process, to lay out its implications for the form of the social whole, and – I will argue – to remodel it, I have laid out the relations among his fiction, political theory, and his analysis of the ego. After outlining the theory of the Regime of the Brother in Part I of this book, Part II, chapter 3, "Egomimesis," concentrates on the ego for which

Rousseau is so famous, and on fraternal eros in his work. While he invented the form of modern love in his fiction (the new Héloïse), he also provided an extensive analysis of the ego – and of modern, post-patriarchal society.[4] His work, taken as a whole, sets up a relation of the ego to Narcissus and the democratic collective in terms of the relation to the other and to sexual difference: he writes of onanism and homoeroticism in his *Confessions* as well as of his other *amours*.

Rousseau's significance for understanding the Regime of the Brother should be plainer after the discussion of the "Primal scene of modernity" in chapter 1, and of "Modernity as the absence of the Other" in chapter 2. In the remainder of Part II, I first, in chapter 4, "Feminine Eros: from the bourgeois state to the nuclear state," locate Stendhal's reading of Rousseau in sociocultural and political terms, and mark the difference between the courtly paradigm for the role of woman and her modern "love-life." The transformations of the woman orchestrated by the bourgeois state under conditions of total war and the nuclear state are then examined in a study of *Hiroshima, mon amour*, whose heroine "Riva" is "cured" of her madness by identifying with the narcissistic aggression of the soldier-male-lover she has watched die in Nevers. Her madness is to be contrasted with that of Lol, the heroine of *The Ravishing of Lol V. Stein*, who submits to every version of "the woman" offered by the bourgeois order – but not totally. Her slight deviation makes all the difference.

In chapter 5, "The end(s) of love in the western world," I draw out the globalization of the western denial of sexual difference as a societal base, and read four narratives where the role of the "brother" is made to appear in the strongest political and economic analytical light: issues of race, class, and empire surface in *The Lover*, *The Seawall*, *Wide Sargasso Sea* and "Two more under the Indian sun."

Finally, I look in chapter 6 at how reconstructing the mother – imagining her loving and relating to someone other than her first-born son (for example, her daughter) – offers a new way of recalling the parental relation. Duras's text harbors no nostalgia for a return to the good old dad of all times, or for good old Mother Nature. She sees the "mother" in all her destitution in the post-Oedipal situation, under the regime of her eldest son: "their mother never knew pleasure." But Duras shows us the mother through different eyes from those of either the father or the brother – those of the daughter. Her daughter is luckier than the motherless Maisie of Henry James's *What Maisie Knew*, who creates a feminine identity literally from nothing, but also differently from her artificial construction by the pseudo-patriarchy.

The book charts a progression from the "savage" society as seen in Rousseau's *Second Discourse* to the developing "neo-savage" society of today. The expansion of the ego center on which modern society constructs itself, with its alibi of fraternal love, is first seen in Rousseau's *Reveries of a Solitary Walker* and traced through *The Confessions, The Social Contract, The New Héloïse* and *The Letter to D'Alembert on The Theatre* (*Politics and the Arts*) to Stendhal's *De l'amour*, which he called a study of "ideology" in contemporary Europe (1828). Stendhal understood Rousseau, and his text aims to retrieve the catharist version of courtly love for remodeling "the woman," while ironizing the tyranny exercised over her by the bourgeois order. Duras's *Hiroshima, mon amour* is then read as a demonstration of the progress that has been made, under the bourgeoisie and the brotherly regime, in "perfecting" the woman as a negative value.

The work of Duras is pivotal. For Duras is uniquely able to depict woman at her most highly prized in the regime (that is, her worst): witness the bored, tortured Riva, the artificial woman, entirely programmed by male desire – a pure product of a male imaginary, completely identified with it in its aims, goals, and desires, but one who "acts as if" and "looks like" a woman. But Duras gives us an "other" woman, too. That is the mother, daughter, sister who fight against the pseudo-patriarchy and in some cases (e.g. *The Lover*) the actual regime of a tyrannical elder brother. *The Seawall* has "Ma" as an alternative to a mother modeled on nature; *The Ravishing of Lol V. Stein* combines the storybook heroine, the daughter, wife, mother, and other woman roles in one central figure – with a vengeance; and *The Lover* grants us one of the first mother's daughters to appear on the stage of world fiction.

In this book, then, I confront the cardinal implications both of eliminating the woman (or more exactly, sexual difference) under the Regime of the Brother, and of erroneously equating the modern order with a patriarchy. But I also want to raise the question of what a potentially post-Oedipal community might look like, free of the distortions of nostalgia for the past (the patriarchy or the primitive), exoticism, and fear of imagining the future. The problems to be analyzed, minimally, are the following:

– The occupation of the "superegoic" position not by a neutral, third person, but by a "He," the Brother, who must be recognized as such and whose tendency to exercise power without responsibility must be examined critically.
– The suppression of the "sister" who replaces the mother as the primary other whom the new "man" must reject in order to become a man. This denial is an effect of the secondary deprivation of a symbolic paradigm for the woman's identity: neither mother nor father model her identity and desire. Is it possible for either

brother or sister simply to support the identity of the other without incorporating one into the other, and, if not, what third term, parental or communal could be the ground of such a support?
– The emergent understanding of the artificial patriarchy, which is beginning to yield to a postmodern arrangement, the "neo-totemic," in which the death of the father is made clearer, as is the taboo on the mother and sister, than it was in the nineteenth and early twentieth centuries, with their ideology of the "traditional" family.

This should open the door to new thought on the subject of women in this situation: what is the value of the woman in the post-Oedipal condition?

The brotherly "general self" is, after all, the one that advanced the causes of European "civilization" through imperialism and war and it bears strong scrutiny. Until only very recently it was the unquestioned focus of social and cultural, but especially economic, value. Now that its principal activities and accomplishments – economic exploitation and domination, colonialism and empire-building, the arts of war and the construction of the powerful, centralized nation-state – are being questioned, the "symbolic" prestige of that particular (male) image is waning. Concomitant shifts in the "figure of the leader" and the configuration of the "superego" or the Other are also necessary. Surely the woman will soon be seen as an untapped natural resource for revising these forms. That she has not yet been called upon to act as a model for this new society indicates that she is still subject to a fundamental taboo in the post-"Oedipal" order, one which forms the modern community by varying and altering significantly the set of equations framed by the patriarchy.

Part I

The theory and history of the Regime of the Brother

Chapter 1

The primal scene of modernity

> The super-ego performs the same function of protecting and saving that was fulfilled in earlier days by the father and later by Providence or Destiny.
>
> (Freud, *Ego and Id*)[1]

It is not accidental that Freud makes culture a parent: it is supposed to start something and keep it going. Fundamental to all human societies is an unquestioned desire to reproduce itself in some form – any form, material, substantial, spiritual, etc., in the next generation. Yet we are unmistakably marked by a notable reproductive anxiety, a fear of fathering. What was once the keynote of psychosis[2] is a general cultural mode today. The central question of this book is whether the contemporary human community, especially but not exclusively under nuclear conditions, desires to perpetuate itself? Such a question is unaskable, but it is also serious and necessary.

Let me reframe the question in linguistic and rhetorical terms. Freud's last texts deal with a crucial displacement: the unconscious, the id takes over from the father-superego as the model for the collective. In these late works the id becomes the equal and rival of the superego for defining the form of the human collective: the "It." Ever since the Enlightenment the "It" has seemed to be the embodiment of a principle of impartiality. Neutral, the impersonal third term is necessary, as Benveniste reminded us, to found every discourse, to set up every relation of "I" and "you," and to speak every general will. The very figure also of judgment, the neuter is neutral: supervisory, the umpire chaperons between players who cannot speak to each other in its absence. Theorists are understandably reluctant to think about the form of the "we" – its shape, gender and number – that has been summed up and overcome in the invention of the "It": to ask the sex of the *collective person* would be impolite now that we no longer assume the traditional third person is modeled on a He

(God, the Father) or She (Mother Nature). For, while it is easier to picture the collective body as iconically a him or her, the thought is deeply repugnant to modern social forms. We find gender designations strangely inappropriate to the modern democratic collective. Mother countries and fatherlands are associated with radical political variants, and the great emblem of democracy, the United States, has settled on the "primitive" solution, the figure of the mother's brother, Uncle Sam, who can fill in for a parent without needing to be one.

It is even more impolite to ask what *It* wants, to suggest that *It* desires.[3] But it is less out of politeness than out of fear: as an unconscious, the *It's* silence indicates a potential alliance with unnameable instincts.[4] Unconscious desire violates the notion of a neutral third party: *It* was a device invented to counter the blatant monarchism of a patriarchal superego, the irrationality and death-orientation of a maternal id. Yet, can an unconscious be beyond or above desire? Yes, if *It* is satisfied. But, then, what is *It's jouissance*?

Perhaps the collective id Freud adumbrates changes when it is no longer simply a fact of and within the individual psyche. There it engulfs and ensnares, even seduces, the hapless ego, whose function, at its best, is to "broker" between the commands of the superego and the instinctual demands of the traditional id. But Freud does not seem to credit the notion of neutrality in the *It* any more than in the id. Attributing the growth in the collective of a fundamental death-wish to *Its* disconnection from sexuality ("Eros") in the widest possible sense, Freud writes: "It would . . . be possible to picture the id as under the domination of the mute but powerful death instincts, which desire to be at peace and (prompted by the pleasure principle) to put Eros, the mischief-maker, to rest" (*SE* XIX, 59). He thus perceives an alignment of the death-drive and the magnified "id": Death is *Its* unconscious desire. What *It* wants is the opposite of sexuality with all its attendant conflicts: *It* wants to die. *Its* desire is the well-known desire for death as peace, repose, the cessation of tension and conflict. And *It* therefore desires our death in us.[5] The function of the collective, once it is framed as an unconscious freed from an Oedipal symbolic, is equally free (though it need not be so)[6] to promote death over life. This is Lacan's insight, too, that a collective death-wish seems to organize more of the human commonality, human culture than we have – traditionally – been willing to admit.

The Ego and the Id can be read less as Freud's mourning the waning of Oedipus than as an expression of fear – for and of a collective which operates in the absence of any parental – fatherly or motherly – relation at all. We might think that Freud's evident terror of the *It* in this late text (harboring "mute but powerful death instincts") is of a deadly maternal unconscious (as in Kristeva's analyses of abjection which point toward the displacement of the paternal superego by a maternal id) where our collective death-wish is a desire for a return to the maternal body (womb = tomb). But something new, non-traditional, lies in the character of this collectively unconscious form. *It* does not function as we imagined the superego did, i.e. either as a father ("protecting and saving") or a mother. Its essence is not parental at all – neither paternal nor maternal.

It is less a matter, that is, of a "feminine id" opposing a "masculine ego" and superego than of a previously unknown form: an unconscious that, though liberated and *jouissant* like the pre-Oedipal mother and child, is also a ruler, a sovereign. *It* demands; *It* commands us to "pursue happiness." That *It* is telling us to "Enjoy!" has obscured its imperative nature. We have thought ourselves to be "self-governed" and no longer, with our rights of "man" intact, fulfilling the desire of an Other, the commands of a king (the evident gender of this formula is now fully exposed). Our "collective" logic – our naive belief – is that we no longer have a superego, that *It* wants nothing. If we look more deeply, however, we find that, in the wake of the democratic revolution in governance, what has been done away with is only the recognizable parental function of the superego, and its best part. *It* is not Hobbes's "neutral" Leviathan, but an interested party. For the *It* seems to have become a new tyrant as well as a new form of liberation. We must ask: who or what is *It*? The question sends us back to the family, where we will unmask which of its members is acting as the superego without admitting it. The family portrait has to be repainted to fit the modern frame. To complete the portrait of what is now an artificial group in modern life, we have put not the father but the Brother at the center.

The modernization of the superego

Technically, the Enlightenment dispensed with the patriarchy: it gave up the cult of the ancestor in the particular way it defined its turn toward modernity (more formally and openly, perhaps, than in the "modern" turn in the Renaissance). Sociologists have suggested that modern, as distinct from traditional, culture is marked by a double relation to the past, to the ancestor: Ferdinand Tönnies defined the modern as one who feels free to forget the dead.[7] Or, rather, free from a forced intergenerational legislation of his activities. He is relieved from the cult of the ancestor which marks all traditional societies. Since the Enlightenment "traditional" society has been supplanted by what Freud calls an "artificial group" (*die Masse*)[8] making its patriarchal ideals at best a charming fraud, at worst an ideological cover for another kind of exercise of power, the command to conformity in mass society. In the modern "artificial group" the "leader," according to Freud, is just like the members of his group – only greater. He is not necessarily Other, in the manner of a father, not an ego-ideal, but an ideal ego. To become a "leader" requires only an arbitrary or fictitious distinction between him and his fellows: he claims no special right, he is not the privileged son and heir, but only one among brothers. As such he acts as the father without being him, and can draw on reserves of a now simulated affect (paternal love). Retaining the "name" of the father he embodies a misnomer (or a metaphor), for he is really only first among equals. As mere metaphor he is not obligated to exercise the paternal/parental function of "protecting and saving" – a metaphor incarnate is too weak a figure to sustain real community, embracing diversity. It can only mirror the same. But it is not too weak to found the group as a kind of simulacrum or art form. Another way to put this is that by occupying the father's (empty) place, playing his role, the Brother can simulate a symbolic order – imaginarily: he is the paternal metaphor of the artificial, modern collective. In this sense he bears comparison less with Oedipus than with the cannibalistic sons in *Totem and Taboo*.[9]

Now we know that, sometimes, he is not very nice: a spoiled brat, a father-child, who has never needed to grow up. We also know that it is precisely at that moment when an actual liberation takes place (when the tyrannical ancestor is overthrown and the power falls to the younger generation – to the brothers) that both self-governance and repression (as taboo) really begin.[10]

The Enlightenment (at least its narratives) made clear that, like it or not, the patriarchal household was to be made subject to a political state shaped by a new, non-patriarchal egalitarian norm – fraternity. But, as Montesquieu warned, democracy had to fear two things: extreme inequality and extreme equality. The construction of a political state around liberty, equality, and fraternity is indeed the very essence, the real hope and glory of modernity, the heart of democracy. They free us from irrational hierarchies (equality), from arbitrary repression by a despot (liberty), and permit us to recognize the common humanity of all members of the species (fraternity). Had it fulfilled all its promises a democracy so founded might have provided a new form of human community, and definitively displaced the Oedipal model and its malevolent clones.[11] It did not. Instead, it retained the Oedipal form, but not its substance (to moderate the ego-centered passions, to civilize and foster communal aims, to support sexuality through difference). Under the "name" of the father another and sadistic Other – unconscious, superego, *It* – has begun its reign of pleasure and of terror. The Regime of the Brother begins.

What is the law of the Brother?

It ought to be a law of liberation, one recognizing that, with the death of the father, everyone is in the same condition: without the despotic authority of the father, we are literally all equals. Instead, a new "No!" rises to the lips of the leader in imitation of the father: the brother utters a prohibition, or rather acts it out silently. Like the primary Oedipal intergenerational incest taboos which are the basis of family, it is still directed against familial relations: but its focus is changed, widened, to work at the level of the group or society. "Taboos still exist among us . . . they do not differ in their psychological nature from Kant's 'categorical imperative', which operates in a compulsive fashion and rejects any conscious motives" (SE XIII, 14) and also p. 22: "the obscure origin of our own 'categorical imperative' . . . ."

Regrettably, his regime may finally cause us to long for a return of authentic Oedipal patriarchy[12] – it seemed much safer under Oedipus than after his death. The dream of an equitable patriarchy has, none-theless, been definitively supplanted by a different form, now seen as neo-totemic in character, whose potential – for good or ill – we must face. That we can as yet do so only uncertainly, without the faith that its commands and restrictions ultimately serve life-yielding aims (those Freud first aligned with "Eros") makes the situation urgent. Disillu-sioned with the failures of patriarchy under modern conditions (global war, for example)[13] we have not found a substitute, preserving and protective, power in our contemporary communal forms.

Oedipus is one of the most elementary of human formations, but its second coming in human history has been as farce – so far. The brother's version of the "Oedipal arrangement" has managed to be entirely compatible with national, economic, and political order, especially in their aggression against traditional societies. And so we have arrived at a political impasse which will require substantial theoretical initiative and imagination to overcome. Despite our efforts to re-form and re-evaluate Oedipus, and despite all evidence to the contrary, we cannot help but feel that both it and the bourgeois order that seems to embody it, are more attractive, homier, safer than what is now in the making: the familiar bourgeois-Oedipal household seems preferable to any alternative pre- or post-Oedipal condition we dare to imagine. Nevertheless, that home was always a fantasy, and now has, objectively, no sure existence. So, while it appeals to us as it does to Antoinette Cosway in Jean Rhys's *Wide Sargasso Sea* ("safe") and to Mrs Wix in James's *What Maisie Knew* ("nicely tucked in"), many writers have also revealed the truth of that fantasy: Antoinette is utterly destroyed by the allure of patriarchy as her brother sells her to the sadistic Rochester; Maisie ends by prefiguring the street urchin, the proto-homeless woman, as one natural and artificial parent after the other abandons her to her own devices. There is ample proof, that is, that the home of Oedipus is in shambles.

In the long run, the question has to be asked of the Brother as of the *It*: what does he want? Because the erotic programme of the regime of the brothers has never made itself clear, it has left the field to Narcissus. Traditional Oedipus, providing for sexual pairing and the perpetuation of the group, cannot compete with Narcissus. At least once this century a deadly narcissistic group threatened to triumph over all other varieties of the modern social relation. It presents the strongest and most insistent challenge for us to devise new ways of thinking that relation, of achieving equality of condition without reduction to mirroring the same.

Post-Oedipus: the historical destruction of the parents

The Holocaust is the key historical event that forces a re-vision of the modern symbolic as a post-Oedipal frame. That is the fact of the calculated, planned disruption of the civilizing and protective side of Oedipal order effected by fascism. It is clear that the resonance, in the symbolic, of the rationally planned destruction of a community, a species, a tribal and above all, perhaps, a familial relation – artificial "Oedipus" at its darkest – is by no means limited to those who were its direct victims.[14] What it did not intend, however, was the transformation of Oedipus and a certain renewal of its powers to strengthen communal, familial, and intergenerational ties. I stress transformation because things are different now between our parents and ourselves, and this transformation acts as a model.

Members of my generation did not spend our childhoods dreaming the terror of an all-powerful totemic father as the Wolfman did. Instead I had the nightmares parents are supposed to have: how to save, how to protect those who cannot protect themselves. I was born in the last days of 1943 in the midst of the war period, but to parents whose existence day to day, in America, was in no wise immediately threatened. Yet fascism had stubbornly demonstrated the fragility of the parents, their vulnerability, their powerlessness. The Holocaust structurally reversed the parent–child relation. It did so to serve fascism's aggressive narcissistic ends: to be itself the survivor and the master, replacing the weak and feeble parents for good. In our dreams, the children were the "parents." Our parents never came close to being the royalty, the kings and queens of the old family romance – we knew them as potential victims, knew they were barely able to survive without our help.

It may be for this reason, then, that what happened to my generation, what assaulted and neutralized the traditional Oedipal form, had an unintended effect, different from the vicious desire that prompted it, in the collective psyche. It unwittingly enabled us to do away with our wish to do away with our parents and thereby "freely" enjoy. It did so by undoing the stricture that the sexual drive is never open to consciousness, the Oedipal stricture. The aggression against the parental relation was so fierce on the part of fascism that it could not help but open our eyes to that parental relation – that it was a relation to us. Which is to say, that theirs was a sexual relation to each other, what made them our "parents." It opened our eyes, or gave us to "see" the one relation our language, our narratives, and our culture had never permitted us to see before.

We came to know that they were what they were by virtue of their roles in the sexual production of human life, not by virtue of their magical and elevated power. Now it is living sexual difference (the relation between the parents as well as to the parents) that Narcissus, the aggressive ego, and the sadistic superego they model, so furiously and emphatically deny. Obeying this superego's (*Its*) own commandment to "enjoy" himself, Narcissus set the death-drive in motion for others as well as himself. But by unwittingly disclosing to us what the traditional Oedipus had genteelly barred from our knowledge and which the pseudo-Oedipus greedily hoarded for itself – the sexual relation of the parents with each other – we entered a new state of mind and soul, one we have to contend with for better or for ill. At least it gives us a way of looking at the artificial "sexual relation" which is really the only relation that seems to exist now: symbolized, marked in the drama of events in human life, in its fantasies, nightmares, and illusions, hysterical headlines, collaged couples in tabloids, it is emerging as the primary form of the social tie – one rapidly knotted and as rapidly undone, at a manic pace of fission and fusion. Like the absence of the parental relation, however, the omnipresence of the imaginary couple is a symptom of group narcissism – the failure of real relation to the other, the actual loss of sexual difference. And it, not the Oedipal patriarchy we so often imagine we oppose, is the dominant form of contemporary social relations.

Pseudo-Oedipus and the Regime of the Brother

Although we have nostalgia for the patriarchy we have to face the challenge of the Regime of the Brother, of modernity. That we can now see that the "patriarchy" is a "pseudo-Oedipus" divested of its symbolic, law-giving, life-preserving function requires us to use new critical tools. The pseudo-Oedipus must be read from a new vantage point, as deserving of as much or more blame than the good old Oedipus. We cannot keep replaying the winless war between the ancients and the moderns, fathers and sons, old and new (or Third World and First World), wasting our analytic energies on demands that the father be done away with – that process has already been well launched. We must instead ask that whatever or whoever has taken his place be called to account. We should require a review of whether or not It is doing a good enough job – which means we should analyze the Regime of the Brother as a distinctive variation on patriarchy or "traditional" society. In post-Oedipal society, the "patriarchy" is not a symbolic but an imaginary function and it must be criticized with different analytical methods from those that presume an Oedipal symbolic.[15] We might turn, I suggest, toward the totemic paradigm.

The son who replaces (killing and eating him) the greedy father in *Totem and Taboo* does not exactly bear his guilt as a debt toward his progenitor the way Oedipus does, internally. And why should he? His father was a tyrant, after all: the one and only possessor of goods and of all libidinal – especially sexual – claims. Eating his father, the son assumes his powers; but, though he enjoys them, they undergo a displacement via a "guilt" that is projected outward: in the form of denying himself relation to his family members, especially of the opposite sex. (See Freud's discussion of the splitting of man's libido into "affectionate" and "sensual" feelings where "women of the family who have been tenderly loved since childhood" are separated from "strange and unloved women" who satisfy the sensual needs of men under totemic exogamy.)[16] That his mothers and sisters and daughters are the ones for whose sake he had killed his progenitor makes no difference to the form atonement takes. He can no longer relate to them after the murder: they are subject to a taboo which takes the positive form of the rule of exogamy.

What then does this son enjoy in replacing his father? Well, he gets to act *as if*, without having to take any action. A father-figure, he mimes, selectively, the father's features. But he also gets to imitate and mock up relations to all other family members, too: not only is he the "father" (but only metaphorically) he is the mother's lover (the object of her love, but only in her dreams) and he is his brother's lover (but only rhetorically – the brotherhood of man). But most of all he is his sister's boss, and really so. It seems that what he "enjoys" is the power to distort and center all familial relations on himself alone, warping the world into a fiction of fraternity, the dream of a universal, which becomes the nightmare lie of the family of man. Agent and sole heir of patriarchy's most negative features, he creates as many false leads and artificial ties as he needs to cover his destruction of his real familial roots and relations. And he thus absolves himself of any obligation toward them. He does not have to fill the father's role any more responsibly and positively than the tyrant had: he is only acting, after all. It is he who is a pro forma father, without a communal or global species-saving goal, a despot, a mute sovereign, the (only) one who really enjoys.

Thus, far from being a paternal moral lawgiver or a self-governed liberated self, the modernized fraternal superego is both ego and *It*, changing roles whenever it suits him. The *It* becomes – narcissistically modeled – a mute, destructive sovereign; the ego the fixed center (as distinct from the "shifter" I of linguistics and of the kinship system) of a kinship network from which it is pleased to cut itself free, not, as Christopher Lasch argued in his *Culture of Narcissism* (New York, W.W. Norton Inc., 1979, 82–4) – a deeper attachment to the maternal superego. And we know that the life-instincts, the self-conserving forces are never ultimately served by a narcissistic Eros: Narcissus wants to mix love and death. In dedicating ourselves to the ego as the principle of the collective, then, we have unconsciously pooled our desires and created in *It* a collective death-wish. *It* seems to want to die in the service of its own pleasure principle, the plenitude of its romance with its own image.

Can we afford any longer to allow *It* not to speak its desire? In questioning the neutrality of the *It*, exposing *It* as a family member (the Brother), the full range of his arrogated powers can be seen – and analyzed. We have yet to find how democracy would function if its center were not the narcissistic ego, but its relation to the other. For the democratic conception to survive the narcissistic assault (always so alluring), "Eros, the old mischief-maker," has to be called up – even in the form of the anxiety of sexual difference, the critical difference the law of the Brother disavows.

The *It* is revealed to be familiar, after all, only our brother. That the phallic father, the *père jouissant* of *Totem and Taboo*, is the role the brother not only covets but is playing out is what we have not understood before: he seems to be so "above desire." But he has really only separated, radically, need and love – the material and ideal ends of the erotic spectrum – from desire, and he has assigned all desire to others: they are left wanting. His role is obscured by our collective logic, our naive belief, that we no longer have a superego, that we tell ourselves what to do. In the wake of the democratic revolution in governance, however, what has been done away with is only the recognizable parental function of the superego (protection) and the (re)appearance of the parents in the id, where desires are turned away from them and toward the same generation, brother and sister.

Collectively, modern society is a fraternity – the "universal" brotherhood of man.[17] Its desire, we have been told, is *hommosexuel*: homo-, homeo-, and man-sexed (which makes it, technically, anal-sadistic). According to Lacan, "social feeling" is rooted in the period of "infantile homosexuality" when "fraternal objects" are eroticized: this is the period when "the social instincts form." (Lacan bases this on Freud's analysis of the fraternal love-object in infantile homosexuality.[18]) But it is a modern social instinct insofar as its desire is neither for the mother nor the father, but the brother. In this way, the heated opposition in the positions of Lacan and Irigaray can be partially reconciled, seen now as two sides of the same critique of what is less a psychocultural constant than of the same historical situation, remarked by both from two different sexual vantage points.

Even at its most general – the family of man – modern "humanity" excludes the "sister-function"[19] as the constitutive or foundational part of its genre (and of its gender), as forcibly as Oedipal patriarchy ever excluded the matriarchal function. This exclusion, under terms of same-generation self-governance (modern democracy), vitiates its claims to being a civilization founded on justice, equality, and freedom. Furthermore, this exclusion paves the way for a narcissistic superego.

In the end, the Enlightenment has to be dealt with for its programme: to forget the dead, to install the rule of the contemporary, the same generation, over the rule by the dead, the elders. Modernity's two central resources are to raise the merely spectral symbol of a dead ancestor to privilege one contemporary figure (who steps in to represent the law in modernized form) and to exorcize the dead, sublimating its relation to them.

But can the "historical subject" afford not to remember what it "forgot"? We are, after all, linked with and inhabited by the dead. Recent writers like Hélène Cixous have reminded us that the positive need to remember the dead is an integral part of our humanity as a community; Freud did so, too, in his contrast between the individual and the narcissist who denies his libidinal ties to and dependence on the other. To remember the dead is to remind ourselves that our individuality is dependent on and linked to the other. But remembering that we are joined with, linked to, the departed – that we are, like them "victims of the same condition and the same disappointed hope"[20] – is also to resist the hegemony of "capitalist"/"masculist"/ "western" culture (or any of the other mythic epithets we might choose for civil(ized) life). Horkheimer and Adorno wrote:

The respect for something which has no market value and runs contrary to all feelings is experienced most sharply by the person in mourning, in which case not even the psychological restoration of labor power is possible. It becomes a wound in civilization, asocial sentimentality, showing that it has still not been possible to compel men to indulge solely in purposeful behavior. That is why mourning is watered down more than anything else and consciously turned into social formality. . . . In reality, the dead suffer a fate which the Jews in olden days considered the worst possible curse: they are expunged from the memory of those who live on. Men have ceased to consider their own purpose and fate; they work their despair out on the dead.[21]

To suppose the absolute departure of the parent is to empty the communal treasury of any libidinal sacrifices we once had deposited willingly in it. But it is also to imagine that we are debt-free. Among the many conflicts experienced by the ego as it defends itself against (taboos) a relation to the other is that it is compelled (by a necessity it is the first and loudest to deny) to attach itself to something outside itself – primarily the mother. The ego finds itself in a position of having to depend on another's love and care, whose good deeds, as the old saying goes, will not go unavenged. Attachment, love, in this maternal model, depletes and overcomes the ego.[22]

No longer a benevolent parent, the superego can make no valid claims on our libidinal energies under conditions where we can with assurance deny it exists. Except that, of course, it does. We are simply unconscious about the process. The post-deist, post-paternal, post-monarchic self imagines itself free from necessary sacrifices, imagines itself entirely free to "Enjoy!" The imperative form of the phrase retains the symbolic, ordering function of the father, but with perhaps less justice than he. For It is evidently not saving (us) but moving (us) toward (its/our) collective extinction. The sorry condition of modern love reflects the embattled condition of Eros in what is now, materially, a nuclear state: Its "love" is not unequivocally opposed to a death-drive. Any reflexive faith that It is a parental form in modernity (a mother or father who never fails to keep a promise and in whom we can invest libido in perfect confidence) is a patent absurdity when the cultural, cultivated "ground" we stand on and for is ground zero and when our civilization seems bent on assaulting traditional societies first and then mourning them afterwards.

Its "diversion" of libido – and all that is culturally called up by that term, from recreation to art – persists and must be thought as a new form of obligation. Even though we "know" we need no longer divert our individual libido to an "Other" who is ourselves – we are liberated, self-governed – we continue to direct our energies to *It*. We have now named the model for this new libidinal structure, this dangerously sacrificial and death-oriented one: Narcissus, the only object of our collective desire.

Here the crucial contradiction of the modern, artificial collective, founded on the ego, appears in the starkest light. Oedipus was intended to overcome primary narcissism through a castration that is the price of full citizenship in group life. Instead, it has not prevented the triumphal return of Narcissus, the same who imagines himself to be an other. And, in contrast to the classic Oedipal patriarch, this fellow lacks for nothing: he does not desire, but fully enjoys – himself. His longing is always being satisfied.

Something has gone wrong; "Oedipus" now serves as a cover for what it was intended to overcome and excuses abuses in its name: we reach the limit of idealization, imaginary identifications, the processes started by Oedipus, reaching their logical contradiction in the final reduction of plurality again to the one. The particularity of the other is elided in a mythic-metaphoric "Oedipal symbolic" – one that is imaginary. The pseudo-symbolic, formed exclusively around the male signifier, the phallus, fails to ground the community or civilization it is supposed to: it founds instead a group of male egos – a fraternity.[23] As Irigaray has made painfully clear, the sexually different partner is always lost.[24] Her loss is not incidental but integral to the economy of the modern group.

The desire not to desire

The historical turning point for the woman is indicated by the change in the definition of "desire." Pre-revolutionary libido marked with a male sign (what Baudelaire called "fucking and the glory of fucking" in his description of *Les Liaisons dangereuses*)[25] is the "heroic" form of desire, don juanism. It yields to the categorical imperative of taboo on desire, the desire not to desire: Valmont is no more, and Merteuil, the woman who desired like a man, loses her *oeil*/I. Yet the eighteenth century had also seen the revival of an alternative principle – catharism and the feminine side of courtly love – which threatened to compete with the male libido for defining and directing desire's energies. It is this alternative that is brutally cut short by the new regime: where Richardson's Clarissa had absolutely refused to marry the odious Solmes, to whom "fear and terror looked pretty in a bride,"[26] Rousseau has his Julie's passion submit to Wolmar's less candidly violent domestic order.[27]

Unfortunately, the presumed "loss" of conscious desire was ascribed to the death of the aristocrat. A nostalgia grows for a time "before the revolution," for the positive desiring-power of the noble classes, a nostalgia that accuses the bourgeoisie, but offers no alternative model except a reversion to a mythified (and completely distorted) image of the past when "desire" was not alienated.[28] But what are the real politics of this perceived disturbance in "desire"? Was it really the "loss" of aristocratic power, or something not recognized in the bourgeoisie's self-constitution? Stendhal, astutely, attributed to the bourgeoisie's inability to enunciate its desire the expansion of its economic and political power: its rebel poets sing their desire for "a bicameral legislature and a budget" (*La Chartreuse de Parme*'s Ferrante Palla), reserving the right to tax themselves. Such desire-power is absolute, and it never needs to experience desire, want, or need. Nor does it need to tolerate its signs in others: women and those extraneous to its bureaucratic forms and rationalizations.

Thus the first, the bourgeois, economy of the fraternal displacement of the familial model makes the denial and obscuring of desire critical. It is also a symptom and a cause: it permits the capitalist programme to employ desire at loose ends, so to speak, and to ignore the other model – feminine, courtly[29] – that once contested the dominant male one. By not admitting the alienation inherent in any form of desire, the brother allows alienation to go unchecked. Under Oedipus, "desire"'s alienation is open:[30] always split between its primary aim – satisfaction – and the object which appears to be the means to its satisfaction – or at least to enjoyment or pleasure. There are desires we must not satisfy without risk to ourselves and to the collective: instinctual needs, incestuous desires, death-wishes, etc. The father demands that object and aim be kept apart. (Before Freud, Rousseau was distinguishing the aim of desire from its object, which he found to be as much an "obstacle" to the aim as a means of obtaining it.[31])

Lacan, too, sees desire as fractured into three factors: need, demand for love, and a "desire" which is condemned to insatiability. Alienating and splitting, "desire" was once primarily an Oedipal mediation, integrating "man's desire" with communal aims. But the way Lacan couched the question of the desire of the Other, intimating his suspicions about its sadistic character, rewrote the concept fundamentally: the relation of need and love to desire, twisted under the patriarchy, is more radically separated, severed, in the new stage of the development of civilization, where the "Other" is not only or even generally the well-meaning if harsh Oedipal father, but instead the "phallic" father of *Totem and Taboo*. The process of fragmentation accelerates under the Regime of the Brother, where the original split of desire from material needs is also cut off from the need for love in all its range of meanings.[32]

The consequences for identity are profound and as yet unknown. When we thought we could identify with the father's "desire," our identity was secured. His is a "good" alienation, partly relieving us of our desire for ourselves (narcissism) and leading us into a relation to the other. But in the absence of a parent, the use of a father-figure may merely displace or disguise narcissism, empowering the "Other"'s desire while failing to quell egotism, and denying any need for another. In this schema, we found our "own" identity, as well as the fiction of the Other.

Anthony Wilden has reminded us, however, that, in our society, all our supposedly "individual" desires are "coded" by an Other who is only a transposed ego. Consequently, it is no longer merely a matter of one's own identity, but the evaluation of others, political, sexual, and economic others, that is at stake:

> The paradox of identity and autonomy which this involves – identical to or identified with what? – puts us in the position of desiring what the Other desires: we desire what the Other desires us to desire. (Consider the situation of the ethnic minorities in England, France or the United States, for whom all desires are coded white.)[33]

The affinity between this understanding of alienated desire and Marx's perception that "under capitalism (symbolic) relations between people are reduced to the status of (imaginary) relations between commodities or things" should be clear.[34] Desire is not only a sexual but a social and economic term. Under current sociopolitical conditions, the more we are tied to the ego/other/It for our identity through our alienated desire, the less we are related to each other. Relations with the other beyond the sexual are increasingly shaped by proliferating and even contradictory codes. Can we end the link between desire and alienation?

It might be possible to revise the concept of desire fundamentally in relation to identity, sexual difference, and needs, in the emotional as well as economic and social senses, but it might also be time to drop the concept. If Oedipal desire is the bedrock of civilization, we are understandably loath to tamper with it. Yet it has already changed under the pseudo-Oedipus, the Regime of the Brother, and it has yet to respond adequately to the charges feminism has brought against it. At the same time, feminism must take care not to become an unwitting ally of the Brother's programmatic attack on anything that smacks of Oedipus. It may be that the end of alienation, of employing desire as a power-source for extracting and using vital energies, is at hand, and that we are returning to that "cold" society, the Lévi-Straussian "neo-savage" world of parsimony, limits, and the end of exploitation of man by man.[35] Some alternative to the progressive life-threatening death-drive now apparent everywhere is clearly in order: but the question is, at what price for women and sexual difference?

The apparent absence of desire is not proof positive that alienation is overcome: that its drives and energies have diminished and have not merely gone underground, into the *It*. While the ahistorical, neo-totemic, synchronous world looked to by analysts from McLuhan to Jameson may be the best we can yet imagine, I suggest that this is not – yet – a viable option. The variety of guises and disguises in which the patriarchy and its mutant, the fraternal order, are now miming and mining the "pre-Oedipal" to exploit its images of equality and ecological balance to the real detriment of genders (feminine), classes (those whose desires and energies are fully engaged in labor), and races (generally non-white) have to be fully exposed. Until we have looked deeply into the heart of the new totemism we should not be entirely ready to adopt it, or to accept the absence of desire as an unambiguous sign that the old order is being reformed.

Might it not even be more useful to work at remodeling desire by looking at those whose desires have been most completely alienated, and whose needs are never met in the Regime of the Brother – the sisters? While there has been an evocation of "feminine desire" in some feminist discourse as an alternative model it has been without sufficient attention to how that desire is framed not only by Oedipus but by the Regime of the Brother. Oedipus identifies woman's desire with maternal desire; the brother assumes she has no special needs or desires – he might be obligated to fulfill them (as she fulfills his). Woman's "desire" should be useful as a resource for bringing need–demand–desire together again. But the overlay of maternal, daughterly, moral, social, and political encodings under Oedipus mutates and re-forms under brotherhood and remains only partially analyzed. The result is that only glimpses of another kind of "woman's" desire are available, several in the authors I treat here – Duras, Rousseau, Stendhal, James: but they remain only glimpses without a complete critique of the system in which they are inserted.

The sisters

When the brother calls on the figure of a departed parent he makes insupportable claims to legitimacy through it, and denies those with equal claims. Locke saw this as the potential weakness of the new society he could see taking shape, when he inveighed against primogeniture as a bad substitute for the old monarchical form of governance.[36] (In the section entitled "Who Heir?" of the *Treatise on Filmer* Locke interprets God's words to Cain that his brother Abel shall "be Subject unto thee and thou shalt Rule over him" by pointing out that the words are "conditional" – "if thou dost well."[37] Those with equal claims are, of course, his brothers and sisters. But the sister is particularly important to the brother, as we shall see, in the construction of his own identity, and it is perhaps for this reason that she is most adamantly denied any value, place, identity – or desire. Negating the relation to the past is not the only feature of the Regime of the Brother. It must also deny the sister.

Why denial of the sister?

If "sexuality" as the substitute for the parental relation seems to be everywhere, and its fundamentally narcissistic structure (in which one "couples" with a fantasmatic projection of oneself) is revealed, its basis is not yet clearly understood. It is primarily a rejection of Oedipal "symbolic sexual difference" – wherein gender constructed as opposition is (ostensibly) to serve reproductive ends, but also to control and render socially appropriate the forms of desire. (Oedipal desire does not in itself recognize the need of each gender for the other.) This structure changes under the Regime of the Brother, becoming the pivot on which the brother's empowerment depends, even though, as we shall see, rejecting the Oedipal patterning of desire could also have empowered the sister equally. Let us examine the situation of sexual difference in the modern, post-Oedipal frame.

We will compare the encoding of sexual difference (through the fiction of the "desire of the Other"), first under traditional patriarchy and then under the Regime of the Brother: both are detrimental to the status of woman, but the latter may in some ways be worse, as long as it goes unexamined and unchallenged. Freud felt that the notion of the "sexual" should be limited to "whatever has to do with the distinction between the *sexes*." Yet, as he put it in his *Introductory Lectures* XX, "We are, at present, not in possession of a generally recognized criterion of the sexual nature of a process."[38] Not only does this mean that Freud extends "sexuality" well beyond genital distinction (beyond and disconnected from the reproductive frame), he also leaves us with the question of gender difference: its value, origins, consequences in a new non-Oedipal frame. Under a widened notion of sexual process the *raison d'être* for sexual difference remains unresolved. Whenever or wherever a sense that sexual difference is somehow critical appears, its rhyme and reason, so to speak, remain so puzzling that theory has effectively put it aside, permitting this difference to be absorbed or modulated under one dominant form, that of the male. Women are coded men, and lesser men at that, and so are their "desires," which are, therefore, strictly speaking, alienated.

The way it works in traditional Oedipus is that the woman is the living embodiment of a deficient male identity: wanting physically and emotionally. The girl-child is supposed to assume an identification with the father and then to be left with/as nothing[39] – unless or until she becomes a mother, her only acknowledged relation to sexual difference. But the mother is precisely what Oedipus rejects and is designed to reject, so the cycle begins anew.

The girl under patriarchy is faced with an inhuman choice: to do without an identity, or to identify with what she is not (it amounts to the same thing). She can accept that she has no symbol, no way of expressing her special needs, and thereby identify with what is "only an absence," as Lacan puts it.[40] Or she can identify with what she is not: her father, a man. Under Oedipus her "identity" is either absent or the reverse of her reality – and her "desire" is always a misstatement: her lack is seen as a quite literally unsatisfiable desire.

Now, a "missing" body part is a terrible model for her "identity": the woman is set up from the start as one who cannot have one. Thus, as Irigaray[41] has made plain, women cannot afford to rely on a body part for identification without falling into the Oedipal trap, which masks the reality of sexual difference while putting it to use. For while the presence or absence of a penis is the root of the problem, what makes it significant is its use in depriving woman of identity: we never learn, she never learns her desire, her needs[42] – she can demand no special love – except according to a male agenda, set by a father, a husband, or a son. She is, of course, granted a certain "place" under patriarchy: limiting her "desire" is the privation exacted so she can keep that place, that of being a crucial if unacknowledged link in the most highly valued relation – of father to son. This mother desires only a phallus (a baby, a son, power) and forgoes other options for her desire. From the daughter's standpoint this means that Oedipus stops her mother from acting as a model subject – a subject and not an object of desire, one with a positive identity, expressing her needs and her loves.

Under the modernized Regime of the Brother, however, the father/son relation ceases to have centrality. Woman potentially comes into her own. (It was only with "castration" that Freud came to be interested in feminine sexuality – even though he may have inflected it incorrectly.) The question is whether the new post-patriarchal Oedipus, the Regime of the Brother, still requires that the girl, as Lacan puts it, "follow for some time the brother's path" (*Séminaire III*, 198, i.e., identifying with a father-figure she can never become), even though the father is gone and the brother is in charge. In the modern situation, it seems, an alternative path to identity (sexual difference and then desire) for both boy and girl is a real possibility.

A diminished paternal/parental pattern for both makes the central event in the formation of sexual identity the relation of sister to brother. Neither objective identification with an ideal Father nor with a phallus "desired" by his Mother would be primary in constructing identity for the boy, who would have to turn to a same-generation *different* or *similar* "other" for a model.

Now while he may have some hope of finding his "like," Freud tells us that the little boy never succeeds in acknowledging the female genitals as different:

> Children . . . (or, at any rate, boys) attribute the same male genital to both sexes. If, afterwards, a boy makes the discovery of the vagina from seeing his little sister or a girl playmate, he tries, to begin with, to disavow the evidence of his senses.
>
> (Freud, *SE* XVI: 312)[43]

This brief passage provides us in effect with a scenario that I would call the "primal scene of modernity." It is the chief mechanism which empowers the brother over his sister. It is the discovery of castration, but read completely at odds from the way it is under Oedipus. The thought that he becomes a man only by comparison with and difference from his equal but different "other" is never admitted. He suppresses his sister's specific desire – for equal access to identity – making it the basis for his law, his rule. The brother seizes the sexual "symbol" in a power grab rooted in his own inability to accept a mere genital difference as the foundation of his "identity" – and of hers. He sacrifices his sister's or girl playmate's genitals in this primal scene: two who are recognizably different are rapidly reduced to one, as under Oedipus, but this time the woman, and the real other, the sister, is absorbed into a general brotherhood, and is granted no special place just because she is the key figure, the sole real basis of the brother's identity. That the boy is quick to deny that he is bereft of a positive means of identification does not mean that he is any more secure on that point than the girl: he simply asserts otherwise, denying it, her, and any responsibility he might have in this condition for constructing *her* identity.[44] He disavows any material obligation to her for his "identity." He also relieves her of (or bars her from) the need to be active in co-creating that identity.

At this point the full poignancy of the situation becomes evident: not only the girl-child, but the boy has no clear means of attaining identity in the post-Oedipal frame: the "patriarchy" in modernity is less a symbolic than an imaginary identification of the son with the father he has completely eliminated even from memory. He has thrown off the one – God, the king, the father – to replace it with the grammatical and legal and emotionally empty fiction of an I who stands alone and on its own: "his majesty the ego." Self-created, however, he is only a figment of his own and not the father's desire. This is the dilemma he simply refuses to acknowledge: he makes the law.

But we know, after Lacan, that every law is the repression of a desire, and it creates a drive; the brother's desire to deny his real dependence on his sister's difference operates as a new fundamental fantasy (incestuous relations with her)[45] that must be disavowed, fuelling a drive to forget her, to taboo her – or do away with her altogether. When Hegel said that the community could never recognize what is fundamental for its existence, he intended the mother; I am arguing that the modernized community "needs" to misrecognize the sister.

The brother denies his sister her identity, affirming his own. This is not just in the abstract, no mere question of repressed instinctual desire. Because the brother cannot recognize his absolute reliance on her for his identity, her place and her desire are "not there." While the mother of Oedipus might want her son and the phallus, the post-Oedipal sister is permitted to want nothing. To regulate woman's desire – and thereby her identity – was always the way of the patriarchy; to outlaw it and to do away with her identity is a cardinal feature of the Regime of the Brother. The Oedipal mother's specific desire has a central object – her son; the post-Oedipal "sister" has no such identifiable desires – at least not yet. We accepted (far too long) the patriarchal power to define, shape, and twist woman's identity, woman's desire, at will, and to go without fulfilling her claims to identity, her demands for love, or even meeting her minimal material needs. But what about now, during – and after? – the Regime of the Brother?

There is thus a strategic and political reason to speak of desire. Certainly desire is an overused concept and subject to abuse; it is not at all clear that simply silencing it is not one more way of reinforcing a taboo. Just as we have had to reinvoke, more powerfully than before it was criticized by Derrida, the power of speech, only this time with a political accent, we may have to do the same for the power of desire, again with a renewed political nuance. The object would be to relink need, love, and desire. If we do not, we lose sight of the human need for love in all its forms as a primary aim in and of human existence. We also risk being or seeming to be completely satisfied with things as they are, de-historicizing our lives too soon. And we risk prematurely telling those whose basic needs are not being met that they, like Rameau's nephew,[46] have no right and no need to desire.

The "original" site of desire (the null, the lack, the empty set) can literally be anywhere in the world. If we are what Deleuze and Guattari call "deterritorialized," properly "nomadic" inhabitants of a world which both radiation and the electronic media have rendered quite literally boundless, how will our fantasies of the nuclear "state" emerge?[47] As a condition of absolute internationalism, where, like the inhabitants of Zones Three, Four and Five in Doris Lessing's fable,[48] one can establish intercourse with anyone else? Or as a reterritorialized, recentralized world – a gigantic ego-formation? It is a real question.

The reproduction of brothering

Although Freud placed the problematic of the modern symbolic under the sign of Oedipus, we must conclude, especially after reading *The Ego and the Id*, that he found it dysfunctional under conditions of modernity. For in modernity group life – both "mass society" and a re-modeled family – is self-consciously artificial. Like the good old "God", the good "father" is only a name, one that is now clearly no more than a figure. While it seems therefore freer, it licenses many abuses, especially sins against "natural" groups (families) and communal forms (tribe, clan, ethnicity) it was supposed to symbolize, enable, and endorse. The appropriation of his symbols, transformed into figures, may once have appeared as a liberation from tradition, but the technology of the figure proves – as in the instance of the paternal "metaphor" and religious fundamentalism – to be a two-edged sword. If we fail to confront the technical base of (post-Enlightenment) Oedipus in the exchanging figure, we falsely equate the "patriarchy" with the "symbolic." And we provide an alibi for the Regime of the Brother and its aggression against all others, just as Jane Eyre's aunt alibis for her wretched, egotistical – and ultimately suicidal – son for his reign of terror against her destitute niece.

After all, the brother has not shown much family feeling, either for his same sex or his sister: Cain and Abel are more appropriate models for modern "brotherhoods." In Marguerite Duras's account of the "reign" of her despotic elder brother in *The Lover* the author terms him a "child killer" responsible for her younger brother's death. Not literally, however. Her younger brother, she writes, was "immortal" – and no one noticed. What the elder "kills" is the reality of the son as child, the ethical promise of the real equality of brothering. He deserves to be replaced by a more care-full sister. The brother who plays (and plays at) the paternal role has only partly learned his lines.

I first came to the question of how the Regime of the Brother needed to diminish even the relatively meager value placed on woman under the patriarchy while analyzing Samuel Richardson's *Clarissa*. Clarissa is a figure of great prestige and favor in the traditional patriarchal household, beloved by parents, grandparents, and uncles. She begins to suffer only when power passes from the parental to the same generation: her brother James exercises tyranny over her, and her sister Belle envies and maligns her. It is they who restrict Clarissa's field of play within the home (she is literally imprisoned in the house). Her loveless would-be lover, Lovelace compounds the situation when he repeats James's gestures with a vengeance, immuring Clarissa in a brothel disguised as a respectable middle-class home, and, eventually, rapes her.

Why the drive to negate Clarissa, who, pictured by early twentieth-century critics (including women) as a silly prude defending her virginity,[49] is in truth an astute, observant and conscientious woman? The motivation is as much her relatively high value under the patriarchy as her willed resistance to having her desire decided for her by her brother. She inherits from her grandfather (lopping off "one branch" of James's expectations) and so her siblings fear she will go on to "*out-uncle* us, as she has *out-grandfathered* us" (*Clarissa*, 24). As a "favored" child, she has provoked many readers to feel a certain satisfaction in taking her down a peg or two: Freud describes this motive, in what is a new kind of modern moral code, as based on the competitive nature of

> children's relation to their parents, . . . a reaction to the initial envy with which the elder child receives the younger one. The elder child would certainly like to put his successor jealously aside, to keep it away from the parents, and to rob it of all its privileges. . . . If one cannot be the favourite oneself, at all events nobody else shall be the favourite. (*SE XVIII*: 119–20)

Clarissa's is thus a struggle not against the patriarchy *per se*, but for her value and identity in the new regime. Her initial recourse – her only hope – lies in a romantic partner: brother-like, but not a brother, Lovelace. He indeed "values" her, preferring her to her sister Belle: but this only makes his aggression toward her the more tragic and the more deeply symbolic, for in the long run he destroys any real value she might have. In her rape, she is drugged and in the dark; her perceptions, intelligence, and feelings are entirely eliminated, and these were her finest features. She can thus take on "infinite" value (what is the difference between zero and infinity?) – the "love" she inspires in Lovelace after her death, and continues to claim even from readers today. That is clearly not good enough, as Richardson's readers – Goethe and Diderot, Prévost and Rousseau, and we ourselves – all have felt.

What is finally significant about the Harlowe family is that it is essentially behaving not like the biologically based family group, but like Freud's *Masse* built on the (pseudo) identicalness in its members. It resists the desire for relation to anything other than itself on the part of its members. It quashes the Clarissa who can really recognize that the passions are the same in both the sexes (*Clarissa*, 187). And it gives us a way of reading the so-called love-life of the modern group, Lacan's "erotomania," as rooted in this enforced desire for the same. Freud points out that even groups formed quasi-spontaneously around a romantic object, such as the women who "crowd around a singer or pianist after his performance," and who are unified by the spirit of love "for the same object" are acting out an enforced identification with each other which, while it prevents one of them being preferred over the others, is nonetheless rooted in envy and competition:

> What appears later on in society in the shape of *Gemeingeist, esprit de corps*, "group spirit," etc., does not belie its derivation from what was originally envy. No one must want to put himself forward, every one must be the same and have the same.
>
> (*SE XVIII*: 120)

Identification as a member in a group (even a family) such as these might appear to take place in an Oedipal triangular fashion, but the occupant of the "third party" position (the singer, the leader, the brother) is no father, but a mere pretext for enforcing identicality and identification. He reflects and refracts only one self-image so that symbolic three-dimensionality is illusory. Since the figure reflects this selfsame image (he is an ideal ego), he is fundamentally "like." The artificial "group" is therefore technically a form – imaginarily extended as in a hall of mirrors – of the ego. And that ego works as the brother's does, binding the group libidinally by negating difference: that is its moral and social contract.

As we re-think the family romance, transformed by the advent of the modernized attitude, we also come to another point. The modern symbolic has been displaced and modified by an increased power in the imaginary. If the brother is a variant on and an intensified mimesis of selected paternal features (they are not his best ones), to read the "laws" of the brother in the constitution of the modern social contract is not just to read his repressions (i.e. his desire) inside the family but his power and influence outside the family circle as well.

Chapter 2

Modernity as the absence of the other: the general self

Walter Benjamin suggested that "the social" is firmly rooted in the egoistic imaginary: his description of the *flâneur* is a vivid exemplification as well as critique of what we might call the Kantian (or possibly Rousseauesque) ego supposed to be the final base on which both the "general self" of humanity and the production of fiction are formed. For Kant, the ego is itself the producer of all objectivity: the bewildering variety of sense impressions reduces their heterogeneity to formal unity only because the ego is a unit that makes synthesis possible. As Georg Simmel put it, the Kantian ego is "the ultimate legislator of the cognizing mind" because it is the only unshakeable basis on which the world could be known.[1] The world is thus a production of the ego, which is identical in all men, and it is the basis of their homogeneity. But in Benjamin this synthetic quality is stated such that the full disaster of its narcissistic potential stands revealed. He writes:

> The *flâneur* only seems to break through this "unfeeling isolation of each in his private interest" [Engels] by filling the hollow space created in him by such isolation with the borrowed and fictitious isolations of strangers.[2]

This structure provides no obstacle to the narcissistic option, the narcissistic pathology: enter "his majesty, the ego." A critique, then, has to be made of the "individual" and of the "group" modeled on it.[3] In the artificial modern group the process of symbolizing the individual is obscure, much more complex than when the ego is a merely virtual center of a *parenté*, kinship relations: on the one hand, the individual feels all-powerful, alone responsible for the creation of a whole society. On the other, he desires to be fully absorbed in the collective body.

Benjamin extended Freud's insights as to the imaginary basis of modern society, likewise linking it to the ego's powers for synthetic projection: how else could the idea of "society" or "the city" appear as a phenomenon at all? The person who imagines himself the center and synthesizer, the producer of all collective forms, is not its child either; he was born of no parents, his children are his in name only. No one is more than a bit in a circuit of imaginary exchanges – organized economically – that scramble simple generative or parental relations (father–son, producer–product).

In assessing the Enlightenment as being where such literary and aesthetic decisions are made, possibilities opened, and options foreclosed, we need to take full measure of its being the site of modernity, that frame of mind that takes the attitude of freedom from tradition, the past, and the ancestor, and places fraternity over paternity. Its imaginary re-forms the relations among men, women, and children into the ideological figures with which we are familiar – of "love," the "romantic couple," "home and hearth," "the woman," "the child," and "the natural" all encoded in regularized national languages – and re-forms the nation-state along lines that simulate the patriarchy.

Civil, urban society, that is, resembles Freud's "artificial" group, crowded with egos and their imaginary projections. And, so Diderot tells us, with fictional figures as well. Both populate and produce the new *polis*. Its imaginary, which permits identification with the other (the ideal of sympathy, pity) and the exchange of places with the other (the ideal of democracy), results in "freedom" – but of a limited or special sort: the freedom to set an exchange value on oneself. With brotherly love and industrial capitalism, he/she/it – all free to sell their labor-power – are technically commodities.[4] This is a freedom and bondage both. Benjamin saw the commodification of the person dialectically, as potentially a new form of human being, just as Lacan saw that the "symbolic" murder of the "thing" in us was at the same time a kind of liberation, permitting a certain "objectification" to act as a subjective resource. The commodification of love-for-sale (Benjamin's prostitute is "saleswoman and wares in one") embodies both the betrayal of personhood and an odd form of potential self-determination as well.[5] A society composed of such commodities is new on the world stage. And so are its narrative and literary forms.

With the opening of modernity, fictional figures, displacing what might be thought of as "real" others, are powerfully constituted as means of exchange: Pamela is "real" – more real than real.[6] As Pamela becomes a leading figure, relationships form around her; if Diderot is to be credited, the same holds for Clarissa, and indeed all of Richardson's writing.[7] They are gossiped about, they organize new social groupings; Diderot reports he has often stumbled upon a heated argument, only to find the participants taking sides in the endless wrangle between Clarissa and the Harlowe family. The suggestion is that society is adding new members, fictional relations.

These new relations are not always welcome. They crowd the growing urban landscape, the modernized mind. In his account of late
eighteenth- and early nineteenth-century laments about urbanization
which appear in such writers as Blake, Benjamin highlights Engels's
perception that such complaints had an ironically imaginary basis.
The city is indeed a vast accumulation of people, a "crowd," but this
crowd is far more apparent than real: it is the product of a mirror-
effect. Benjamin comments:

> Next to Engels's clear description, it sounds obscure when
> Baudelaire writes, "the pleasure of being in a crowd is a mysterious
> expression of the enjoyment of the multiplication of numbers." But
> this statement becomes clear if one imagines it as spoken not only
> from a person's viewpoint but also from the viewpoint of a
> commodity.[8]

"The multitudes" or masses are mere multiplications of a singular,
private self dominated by an "unfeeling isolation" and maintaining
"each in his private interest."

Freud has noted, in his "Group psychology", that the "artificial"
group of today is fundamentally structured by the inherent appeal in
a mirroring of the "same." If *die Masse* is not formed by a set of relations to others (a kinship network at whose purely provisional center
stands an ego defined solely on the basis of those relations – "I am
wife, son, nephew," etc.) it can only be formed by an extension or
expansion of the ego, multiplied and endlessly reflected. Indeed,
Freud tells us, the group demands uniformity, conformity, so that the
ego at its root finds no opposition. So it is that a major feature of this
group is, not surprisingly, an aversion to sexual difference (the root
paradigm for difference-in-relation). The group, Freud explains, binds
the libido of its members wholly to itself as a unified entity:

> In the great artificial groups, the Church and the Army, there is no
> room for woman as a sexual object. The love relation between men
> and women remains outside these organizations. Even where
> groups are formed which are composed of both men and women,
> the distinction between the sexes plays no part. . . . [Such groups
> are] not differentiated according to the sexes, and particularly
> [show] a complete disregard for the aims of the genital organization
> of the libido.
>
> (*SE XVIII*, 141)

The positive quality in this is evident: not only is one freed from irrational ties (sexual, familial) but one is apparently freed from
divisiveness. But this seeming liberation is only for the few: in fact,

Freud reports (and our contemporary experience corroborates), such groups have an unlimited aggressive narcissism: though they brook no internal difference, they also know only aggression and hostility against those who are not fully incorporated into it – outsiders, non-believers, other groups, and, of course, the other sex.

Benjamin provides further insight into the peculiar character of modern society when he analyzes how "mass" society appears in Baudelaire's writing.[9] Noting the poet's simultaneous attraction to and struggle against taking a "bath in the multitude," Benjamin finds in Baudelaire's ambivalence the secret of the special appeal in the crowd: the allure of indifference – in all senses of the term. If the crowd coldly passes one by, it also displays no evident internal differentiations – divisions of class, sex, race are never perceived features of a "mass." (The question of the place of woman in societies whose constitution has been framed by opposition to bio-logically based groups is rarely asked, mainly because sexual difference plays no part in the artificial group. As "crowd" the character of the urban mass appears to be classless and sexless.)

A fictional dimension is interpolated in a process of literal exchange. Once fiction-as-exchange becomes involved in filling the empty heart, it has already taken the place of the other. And it has also prepared the way for what Lacan calls the imaginary (not symbolic) Other; or what Freud more concretely, more politically and somewhat more ominously names the Leader.[10] The symbolic function becomes narrowly defined as quantification and economic evaluation, and the domination of use value by exchange value accelerates as the pro-cesses of commodification extend to one's person and one's work.

It is no surprise, then, that Benjamin found his best analytic material less in empirical observations than in literature – a not illogical source, when we think about it. By reading Baudelaire in the light of Freud (but also of Engels), Benjamin attuned himself to the psychic and emotive as well as the economic registers on which his poems are deployed. It is to Benjamin, indeed, that credit must be given for being one of the first to discern the arrangements among fiction, the image, exchange, and the loss of the "other" – and to express them in a way that is adequate to their indirect yet omnipre-sent force in modernity. More importantly, he also found residual resources in fiction (as in the commodity) when it is not considered exclusively from the viewpoint of the imaginary (i.e. exchange): but only when the root narcissism involved is profoundly challenged.

Under narcissism, the (use) value of narrative (i.e. for forming a specifically human being; instructing us in codes) yields to its exchange value: we can literally produce and do away with others at will, make them do our bidding. As exchange, fiction clearly had some part in the commodification of the person. At least the so-called private "sphere" – the empty heart of each individual – is, like the "cityscape" around him, subjectively experienced not as empty (though it is) but as "filled" – with the absent other. Or, rather, with the absences of others. The so-called "emptiness" of the heart is thus an "encrypting" of an other who is missing, who has been done away with, and/or lost in the exchange. "Human being" is therefore marked as the driving of exchange values into the very heart itself. "Love," "sympathy," and "identification" (or their opposites, hate, cruelty) are all made part of a mirror-effect, losing their connection with life: the relations contracted with fantasmatic others (who stand in for the real others that have been lost in the process) are no longer serious (mothers, fathers, laborers). Critique must henceforward develop the role that fictional figures now play in the constitution of society – they are no mere adjuncts, but integral components. We will need to analyze fiction's role using a dialectical critique which includes both its drawbacks and its positive potential.

Fiction and the social order

For some time, the novel held much promise of providing a model not just of what has been denied but of what is general, communal (*noa* as well as *tabu*): that it failed to picture for us the form (as value and process and not just the already constituted structure) of the modern collective is a puzzle and a challenge. Heidegger tells us that art was displaced from the center of modern life by technological production.[11] I want to make the case that, even when art fails to "give men their look" and "outlook," to do so under the Regime of the Brother is pathological, since the "society" it models is egocentric and narrow and its claims to generality are always projections of that ego. Predictably, where our art has tried to model the cosmopolitan, polyglot community, rather than a unified, single-sexed, or single-ethnic one, it has been highly resisted: where Bakhtin sees the novel as the first genre that attempted such a modeling, he is writing at the same time as people like Denis de Rougemont are condemning the literary contamination of occidental cultural cohesion.[12] And while Bakhtin and Medvedev condemn the act of reading as a solitary pursuit[13] they also see it as linking the individual to the value horizon of his social world, providing the focus Heidegger says is impossible. They are to be compared with Roger Caillois, whose critique of the novel in the early 1940s[14] also centered on how the novel privatizes (the definition of "private" differs from the Russian one): reading prevents the kind of union a strong "virile" (the term is his) society demands. What he means by "private," however, turns out to be "the bedroom" which is at the heart of the novel, and where "society" speaks the least (he means, of course, a society of men).[15] Nevertheless, to continue to imagine the novel as "social" because it is "Oedipal" is to subscribe to Barthes's thesis that "all narrative returns to Oedipus;" we have to blind ourselves to the waning of Oedipus in modernity,[16] or content ourselves with working over material that is no longer important or central to our own cultural life – the symbolic life of the collective. We could only claim that narrative is the site of unconscious libidinal investments which (through various relays and transformations) become vehicles for social consensus.

If I am right, however, literature became not a mere adjunct to serious social life, but a major player in the creation and ongoing maintenance of the modern social order, the one which proscribes but cannot prescribe relations. In the heart of fiction a certain battle was fought between the imaginary and the symbolic, masculine and feminine versions of libido, over certain primary symbolic (in the sense of collective) forms. If modern literature has not been understood as a symbolic, this has more to do with the structure of modernity (its political relation to art, the Brother and his superego) than it has to do with any inherent incapacity on the part of literature or art to be recognized as socially symbolic forms. Fredric Jameson has recently reopened the question as to why we cannot use literature as a socially symbolic act.[17]

Calls for linking narrative to the contemporary symbolic without limiting it to a distorting ideological function have been made not often but with enough frequency to be meaningful.[18] But we lack good models for this. Our chief example of how social and aesthetic functions are integrated is myth (in Lévi-Strauss's sense of a compromise construct that bridges contradictions and divisions) which only works in the case of the small or bounded society, not a modern one. In modernity, myth takes on pathological form, as Barthes amply illustrated.[19] Or rather, myth only works positively where the "group" it forms and informs faces nature as its opponent. When, in modernity, the opponents are other groups, myth serves political ends.

The possibility of a society composed of diverse, recognized relationships – the realization of democracy – remains the unimagined, unthought alternative to whatever is not yet right in democracy itself. The art forms – like the multivocal novel – that might have articulated democratized social models were often rejected because of this possibility. Caillois, for example, preferred a large-scale work that would sum up as well as inaugurate or give birth to the kind of unified society (anti-individual, but also anti-democratic) he admired:

useless monuments (like cathedrals or what he thought Tenochtitlán's architecture was) created by contributions of anonymous collectives, a whole society in concert.[20] His attitude toward the novel (private, bourgeois, sexual, and too diverse in character, a totality of fragments rather than a unified whole) is shaped by his desire for synthetic unity in communal forms.[21] Fascism, recognizing the "artificiality" of the modern human group,[22] found in political theatre and mass rallies a spirit of festival and a unified experience of the sacred which the everyday comedy, the romances of bourgeois life never provide: transcendence of the artificial by means of artifice. This is the wrong answer, but it is based on asking the wrong question: how best to mirror in art the already artificial projection of the ego that society is – a dream of wholeness and unity?

In this book, I am looking at how narrative not only reflected but analyzed the dialectic of the absence of the other, the presence of the fraternal superego, and indirectly showed how the structural denial of the woman related to the more general absence of relation to the other in modern, neo-totemic or post-Oedipal society. Let me end with a simple model. Fiction often provides thinkers like Freud with their critical analytical material.[23] One short story is cited by him in *Civilization and its Discontents*. In a poignant footnote Freud gives us to understand that "civilization" demands the sacrifice of the simple love of two people for each other, not just individual instincts.

> Among the works of that sensitive English writer, John Galsworthy, who enjoys general recognition to-day, there is a short story of which I early formed a high opinion. It is called "The Apple Tree", and it brings home to us how the life of present-day civilized people leaves no room for the simple natural love of two human beings.
>
> (*SE XX*, 105, n. 2)

We rarely consider Freud a sentimental heir to the belated topos of the romantic couple battling the laws of industrial capitalist society, but there it is, embedded in one of the most general of Freud's texts, where he claims that all of "civilization" and not just a specific moment has a serious stake in repressing this particular relation. He asks how benevolent is a superego that suppresses a love (Freud includes the sexual) relation. What Freud's attention to the superego's ("civilization's") demand for this disconnection does, in the face of the commandment to universal love, is discredit the command as naive (no ego ever really sacrificed itself to another) and to discredit the high morals of *Kultur*: it masks the class, race, or economical interests we are heeding by acting reflexively, unconsciously.[24] Galsworthy's "Apple tree" concerns, after all, a quite passionate sexual relation, unmarked by moral reflexions on either side, between a peasant girl and a university student who is resting at her residence while recuperating from an injury to his foot (!) incurred on a walking tour. They plan elopement and marriage. When, preparing for the elopement, the boy goes into town to buy the girl a dress, he runs into some pals from his own social class: and one of them is a young girl. She is not described as having any special allure. But in the end the boy reflexively, absentmindedly reintegrates himself into this bourgeois world, marrying this nonentity, who is a proper girl from his own urban class. And he forgets the uninhibited peasant girl. Thus the boy obeys an imperative instead of his desire, but it remains unpronounced: his father does not have to say or do a thing to divide the lovers. But the only grounds of this imperative/"moral" order, this "symbolic," are economics and class, not communal in the most general sense. Who benefits from a superego of this nature?

If we assume a "moral imperative" here (a commandment to quell wild sexual passions) we miss the point that Galsworthy's couple violates no grandiose ethical plan but only threatens an established economic and class order. "Civilization" is merely "symbolic," its superego less an entity "above it all" than one who serves the ends of a particular lordship over others, whose intercourse *It* prevents not for the benefit of the whole group, but for only a certain class or segment of it. This is the part about the superego (in its sham form) that Lacan did not miss. *It* is enjoying the advantages of Oedipus to make a secondary "cut" in the social field (here, in the relation to the other). The silent "superego" the lamed lad obeys in Galsworthy is a middle-class concern about a figurative father, a dad – no real patriarch – who has granted him identity only as a member of a class, not as a sexual identity. This superego cuts him off not from the natural and the maternal, but from a girl his own age, a sisterly figure.

Conclusion

This book, then, is my effort to answer certain questions that have haunted feminist theory (and me) for some time: how have the Oedipal, post-Oedipal, and even postmodern arrangements of the sexes, with their corresponding evaluation of women, been formed in relation to the political, cultural, and theoretical revolutions produced since the Enlightenment – the era where modernity was born, so to speak, of itself? We have seen one attempt – that of Lévi-Strauss – to assess the exchange value of woman in the pre-modern case – and we have seen that attempt criticized roundly and soundly by Gayle

Rubin[25] and others when its model is transposed to "our time." Despite innumerable critiques we have managed to avoid a key question: what is the value of woman in the modern (by which I mean only the post-Enlightenment) social and sexual arrangement? It is no longer controversial to suggest that there has been a failure to integrate the woman. Now it is time to move the question: has this failure played a key role in dashing the promise of modernity, and how is this to be altered in the postmodern, neo-totemic condition: the mass society, "global village," or "artificial" group which is becoming the primary form of our collective lives?[26] As modern society becomes self-consciously postmodern, recycling bits of pre-modern group forms, feminism needs to raise the question of sexual difference, in particular, whether the new totemism will truly be beyond gender or the mask for one tyrannical gender's rule. By proceeding both historically and formally I try to look back to the Enlightenment for important models, particularly to a different Rousseau, and to modern narrative and film to find the track of contemporary, hidden relations of production.

What would the modern – or even postmodern – democratic collective be like, one not modeled by the elder brother's seizure of the father's place and role? In what form would democracy take on its fullest aspect, one that did not subvert but sustained its liberation from patriarchal governance? It might – and this is just a hypothesis – look different from the way it looks when it installs itself, unconsciously and repressively, in power, along the lines of the brotherly superego.

If we ever manage to get a glimpse of a really democratic form it will have had to do, certainly, with recognizing the loss of sexual difference and the absence of relation to the other that dominates the imagination in the Regime of the Brother, not the presence or absence of the imaginary or the symbolic in themselves. I see literature as analyzing the symbolic, and taking, potentially, a hand in reframing it, a process that would involve uncoupling the symbolic from the "patriarchy," but more important from the pseudo-patriarchy, the hegemony of the imaginary in the Regime of the Brother. And, in this, literature is ahead of theory. All the more so if my reading of Freud's "Group psychology" is correct, and that it is indeed the "fraternity of men" – universal brotherhood, male bonding, "homo-social desire," the "virile" group of the "college of sociology" – that is the truth of that imaginary, of patriarchal ideology. It is far less the father than the brother that modern literature calls to account; less the mother than the sister who must be recognized and given her due as the real rather than the imaginary "other" necessary to found male identity and group life; less the son than the younger brother, the son-not-heir who can appear in a new symbolic.

In the face of the possibility of a more honest set of representations of the now-withered patriarchy, new and more hopeful versions of the neo-totemic have been produced – by men (Lévi-Strauss, Wilden, McLuhan, Jameson, Eco, Baudrillard, Freud, MacCannell)[27] as models of the post-patriarchal world. Yet, with the exception of only a couple of these, the relation between the structure of such new fundamental fantasies as "mass society," the "urban crowd," and so on has not yet been explored. They may be close relatives. The initial appearance of the neo-totemic has often been disastrous (Fascism, fraternal orders, etc.) for those in minority or marginal positions.[28] The key is to get it right this time. For, while we might hope that the postmodern is a revival of the ideals of equality, fraternity, and freedom as modeled by the ideal "cold" ahistorical, non-exploitative, ecologically parsimonious "savage society," a less sanguine reception of this image, put into the service of ideology, gender supremacy, and the bourgeoisie has to be faced. Especially by the women, the real tribal peoples, the real ecosystems that are being "preserved" only in fantasmatic fashion, and excluded from any say in the matter by the Regime of the Brother.

Part II

Readings in the Regime of the Brother

Chapter 3

Egomimesis

Ces deux Messieurs qui sont absens
Nous sont chers de bien des manieres
Ce sont nos amis, nos amants
Et les péres de ces enfans

(Rousseau's mother's song[1])

The weaker the individual becomes, from a societal perspective, the less can he become calmly aware of his own impotence. He has to puff himself up into selfness, in the way the futility of this selfness sets itself up as what is authentic, as Being.

(Adorno, The Jargon of Authenticity[2])

Egomimetic desire: Rousseau and the modernization of the ego

If in modernity (the time of self-governance, self-begetting, no fathers) formal arrangements – social, personal, aesthetic – are no longer laid out or programmed Oedipally, they must be rethought. Alternatives to Oedipus are not necessarily attractive: the sadism of the superego, a group psychology formed on the model of fraternal homosexuality and/or narcissism, the revenge of the sister or the mother. These are all in Rousseau – in *The Second Discourse*, *The Reveries*, *The Social Contract*, *Julie*, and the *Confessions* – and more. In many ways he anticipated Freud and Lacan, and an affinity is most apparent in the linkage all three perceived, in different ways, between the structure of the ego and the sociopolitical body. Freud's central thesis concerning the artificial group is already partly foreseen in Rousseau: for both, modern society as a form does/did not require at least two persons to give it birth. Alone among his contemporaries, Rousseau questioned strongly the assumption that "more than one" had (ever yet) been the origin of human society, insisting on the primacy of egoism and narcissism in the construction of human society as we know it.[3] Like Lacan, though, he also found the ego to be the source of aggression under certain conditions.[4] In these issues he prefigures psychoanalysis; we have not seen the extent of the parallel because of the way the peculiar logic of his beliefs about the self–other relation was seized upon by those who were politicizing individualism. The extent of the connection needs to be fully explicated and will affect the way we understand even his political thinking. In the Anglo-American reading of Rousseau, for example, the systematic side of his thought, when recognized, is insistently distilled or filtered through the mirror-staging of the self (and its linguistic correlate, metaphor) before other dimensions of class or collective identity are treated.

As I have noted, Freud showed how tenacious the model of the single self (the ego) is – even at the most seemingly collective or general level. The narcissistic ego arises by repressing recognition of the other as other, withdrawing its libido from others and focusing it on itself. While narcissism is always a feature of the full range of human love, it is not always dominant. The recognition – and acceptance – of difference is what the narcissistic ego does not tolerate: recognizing the other is as difficult as admitting one's infantile dependence on the mother. An imaginary solution, in which "I" am the origin of a fictive otherness, permits the "I" to remain in the scope of Narcissus's mirror without openly recognizing how much it wants to be alone.[5]

Nevertheless, Freud describes rare, fleeting, fragile – almost impossible – moments where the self or ego is able to face a relationship to an other: when "conscience" as such appears. I am thinking here of his sensitive and powerful "Thoughts on war and death" (*SE XIV*). Freud frames this essay as a study of how the ego is modified or transformed under the influence of what he calls "erotism," i.e. love for the other. This "erotism" utilizes the narcissistic moment as a means of relating to the other. Freud first distinguishes a pre-amorous attitude toward death on the part of "primaeval man" from one formed "beside the body of someone he loved." Like Rousseau, he marks the birth of conscience as an affair of passion, born of equally powerful love and hate, so much so, that its primary feature is a marked ambivalence of feeling. Unlike Rousseau, who depicted his *sauvage* as a site of a genteel primary narcissism which he knew to be a pure fiction, Freud posits the "savage" or "primitive" man (as original egoist) as a real, historical entity, a true brute: "He had no objection to someone else's death; it meant the annihilation of someone he hated, and primitive man had no scruples against bringing it about" (*SE XIV*: 292). He continues, "In my view, primaeval man must have triumphed beside the body of his slain enemy, without being led to rack his brains about the enigma of life and death" (293). However, to love is to have made the other a part of one's much-loved self: when the loved one dies, that self, which is for us so immortal, cannot admit even this much of its death. It is thus that "spirit" is invented; remembrance, and also dread of the slain enemy arise – as alternatives to believing in the death of the self.

Such is Freud's original myth of the birth of conscience. He makes it quite plain that this primeval brute is to be distinguished absolutely from the contemporary peoples we call "savages": we recognize him only in certain stages of our own ego's development, stages to which we seem, collectively, to be regressing in our pursuit of global war. The hard-won prize of conscience, requiring so many twists and turns of mind and heart, is for Freud fully developed in so-called savage races of today. In a move not unlike Rousseau's in *The Second Discourse*, Freud portrays an egotistical primitive man, but only to show how the ostensibly "civilized" persons of today are the ones who replay his role. By comparing the "savage," from whom the "civilized" races pride themselves on being distinct, with the deepening brutality of modern "civilized" peoples, Freud engages in an unprecedented critique of what he, finally, names as a modern evil: "the nations of the white race upon whom the leadership of the human species has fallen" (*SE XIV*: 276). It is the very presumption that we are "civilized" (with civilization narrowly conceived as leaving the instinctual needs, including need and love for the other, unrecognized) that invites a viciousness in us not to be found in any known "primitive" today. Even the savage warrior, Freud tells us, must atone "for the murders committed in war by penances" (295) whereas no such constraints are placed on our aggressiveness as long as we are pursuing "legitimate" wars in the name of the state. Our soldiers return from the battlefield (if they survive) to a home untroubled by the thoughts of dead enemies. This amounts to allowing our unconscious ("murderously inclined toward the stranger" (299)) to operate entirely unchecked under modern state law, to become a narcissism without limits, grounded in an (unconscious) wish to do away with the other, to do without the other.

It is on anthropological grounds that the Freudian unconscious meets the thought of Rousseau, as both decode the modern ego's reproduction of a really savage id: one no longer capable of being contained by an Oedipal guilt that allows us to civilize our aggression by sublimating and repressing it, but not to recognize it. When Oedipus' authority wanes, it has no residual power to counter narcissistic love and the aggression it incites. Only another kind of "erotism" could supplement its loss, one that functioned like the body of the "dead loved one" once did, but can no longer do under modern conditions, where the dead are so freely forgotten (or "live" on, as in Poe's crypts and mausoleums). Yet what element is there, incorporated into ourselves, whose loss would renew the conceptual act – consciousness and conscience – and act as a check on the narcissistic drive? Such is the critical question: how to contest the hegemony of the law of the Brother, which is to deny the relation to the other. For Rousseau, the answer lay in the arts.

Now, after Freud, the arts can be understood as the site of restitution, remembrance, and reparation of the aggressions made against the body of the mother – art is her "sublimation" and reflects a more or less "simple" unconscious.[6] But in *Séminaire VII* Lacan explicitly distinguishes a primal artistic sublimation (which takes ritual form) from what occurs with and for the modern "historical" subject. In modernity, art sublimates not merely the mother but the father as well. Art's ritual role in structuring, forming the social group virtually disappears with the advent of the "law" as the root form of society.[7] Thus, if art in the modern setting is to be placed under a sign of primitivism, neurosis, or psychosis (where it indeed often uncertainly resides under Oedipus), its power to effect and renew the act of conscience seems virtually nil.

Linking Rousseau to Lacan, however, unexpectedly yields a new perspective. While Rousseau is associated with an apologia for *amour de soi* and the innate goodness of the ego, it is Lacan who shocked the analytic community by insisting on the aggressiveness inherent in the ego. Nevertheless, Lacan is invaluable for dealing with the historical and literary implications to be drawn from Rousseau's thought for our time. It is the reflection on art that joins his analytic to Rousseau's. It is a question of a specifically modern art (one not rooted in timeless ritual). Lacan says that artistic "production" as we know it is "historically dated,"[8] which makes it possible for us to ask, "What does society find in its art that is satisfying to it?"[9] While art may continue to be (*à la* Freud and Klein) restitutive in character, its restitutions (of the mother, for example) only appear as such with the modern historical subject, the one "free" of the obligation to restore – the one who forgets.

> Our subject has, in relation to the functioning of a signifying chain, a completely solid and pinpointable place in history. The function of a subject *at the moment of its appearance*, of the original subject, the subject detectable in the chain of phenomena, is susceptible to a new formulation, an objective locating. What a subject represents originally is nothing other than this: he can forget. Suppress this "he" – the subject is literally in its origin, as such, the elision of the signifier, the signifier *sauté* in the chain.[10]

(Lacan adds that this constitutes the "in the first place," or the "first person" of the historical subject, or what I call the "modern" subject.) Rousseau's complex insight on the relation of art to conscience and to the dead beloved, becomes in the light of Lacan, newly powerful as a counter to the post-Oedipal Regime of the Brother, more effective than Freud's Oedipal reading of the arts can be.

For Rousseau, the play of the arts in modern society "restores" not a maternal but another body, not a dead parent or bride, but something alive and unrecognized: the primordial object which Lacan, like Kant, called *das Ding*. (The thing is the transformation of the object – the means of satisfying an aim, as unattainable as it may be – into the site of satisfaction itself: the woman's desire or "want", for example, becomes thingified as her "thing," her sexual part, a "hole.") *It* is what cannot be sublimated, therapeutically, by the *beaux-arts*: the general or political unconscious. For Rousseau, the arts "restore" the wholeness of the social body as a thing, not as a traditional set of relations. They stage the "desire of the brother" – which is his desire not to desire, to hold the position of the "full" or satisfied superego, the morality of *das Ding*. This is what the critical function of the arts must make clear (as Rousseau does in the *Letter to D'Alembert*).

Pinpointing the problem of who – which missing "he" – takes the "first place" in modern "historical" society, filling the father's missing chair *in absentia* in modern political life, means demonstrating that he can be uncovered. Through art, we uncover the id-entity: the *It*, the modern superego, the one that suspends all claims a "traditional" or restitutive, obligation-driven art has, but without offering an alternative form of positive conscience, or tableau of obligations toward the other. It is therefore not only that art must now reveal the hidden "he," but it must provide such a tableau of the forms of relation to the other. What art would make it possible? Hegel felt the novel was the model of art for modernity, but it is perhaps less the novel, which obviously critiques and projects modernity, than the theater that became the form of choice for a *theatrum analyticum*, at least in regard to the unconscious. Re-staging the body, the mother, the family, the pastoral in a non-primitive, anti-nostalgic mode, Rousseau permitted the critical reading of modernity as a time of their absence, one part of a programme of resistance to the narcissistic regime of the actor-brother. The first play Rousseau wrote was *Narcisse, ou l'amant de lui-même*.

But it is the other side of the coin, the way in which the arts alone, in modernity, could provide the means of forming conscience and consciousness, that is most crucial and most complex in Rousseau's vision. It is not a matter of "aesthetic education" but of providing the necessary supplement to the ego's denial of relation to the other, the supplementary other whose lack alone permits the birth of conscience. The arts must be prevailed upon to offer a paradigm of the desire of the other. To model this "otherness" Rousseau elected the woman.

Rousseau's critique of the ego

Rousseau is the "first person" of modernity – the supremely modernized ego, he who labored at the birth of modern society, and he has always been considered a prime example of the modern ego, at its best and at its worst. At least, so the history of Rousseau criticism tells us. His "self" – both real and conceptual – has been understood in two distinctive ways. The first is as a classical broker-ego, mediating between, in Kantian terms, the transcendental and empirical egos (or superego and id).[11] The second is utterly pathological – Rousseau as narcissist, paranoiac, homophobic. Thus, while, for Ernst Cassirer, Rousseau was first to uphold the ethically fine Kantian transcendental ego (which, he argues, Kant derived from him) as standing apart from and above his fallen empirical self,[12] other readers have judged Rousseau as quite a case. Jean Starobinski pointed out the vast narcissism in him that undermines his theories of individualism and self-love.[13] Jacques Derrida anatomized his onanistic imaginary, vitiating whatever is "general" in his will and his desire.[14] And his smug male supremacist posture (Allan Bloom) betrays, it seems, a deep misogyny.[15] The picture of pathology culminates in Lacan's pronouncement that Rousseau is a classic paranoid, latent homosexual:[16] the repeated appeals he made to "humanity" are as many symptoms of his extreme narcissism and egotism. They tend to miss his whole game, which is to restructure our concept of the modern self as a psyche, one specifically not founded on repressing the mother, but on repressing the father – for the benefit of the son.

While defenders of Rousseau's social and political thought have had to assert that it stands apart from his personal pathological condition,[17] there always lurks a suspicion that his aberrancy might undo his finest theoretical work, especially his attending of the birth of modern democracy.[18] The thought that he himself might have planted such doubts is rarely ever considered. My question is, why single out Rousseau? Has not Lacan taught us that narcissism, specularity, misogyny – pathologies at the level of the individual – haunt not only Rousseau, but the very structure of bourgeois and modern society?[19] Rousseau has provided such a convenient summation of so much that is pathological in the modernized political psyche that he has perhaps over-deflected attention from the political to the clinical and prevented us from looking more directly at the structure of his "general" self: his formulation of the "historical" subject, the forgetful superego.

Our "insight" that Rousseau is "narcissistic" is a blockage, a resistance to reading his work as more than a set of symptoms (although it is that too), i.e. as a complex analysis of the flawed relation of self to society. Again, before Freud and Lacan, Rousseau discovered that the most critical paradigm for both the recognition and the misrecognition of difference and the other is the sexual one. Locus of passion (the love or hate or love–hate which binds one self to an other), it is where difference (or the failed consciousness of it) takes on the particularly restrictive and repressive form of gender.[20] In what follows I will situate Rousseau within a framework of sexuality as it is crucially linked to the symbolic forms of the social order as well as where it remains exclusively defined by the imaginary, or egoistic, domain.

Egomimesis: *The Second Discourse*

> Love is impotent, even though it be reciprocal, because it does not know that it is only the desire to be One, which leads us to the impossible of establishing the relation of them. The relation of them who? two sexes.[a]
>
> (Lacan, "Encore"[21])

Repressing the recognition of the other as other rather than as the same is figured as mimetic doubling, or more precisely, as egomimesis. It produces the effect of eroticism, love of the other, but it is only an effect – a mirroring, narcissism. Rousseau's *Second Discourse* showed that the cultural transformation of bodily needs into "desires" (new needs) and of familial love into love as a "mad" passion is the result of forming culture on the model of self-love or egotism (*amour propre*). The definitive shaping of the collectivity, whether it accommodates a relation to the other, or only the all-consuming "one" is rooted in the egomimology of exchange.

As I indicated, Rousseau, who gave the first precise descriptions of the process, was also its first critic. In part II of *Le Discours sur l'origine de l'inégalité parmi les hommes* Rousseau takes the "savage" out of the paradisal situation – where his exclusive feeling was of his existence – that framed his ego-solitude in the first part. In part II, it is the preservation of himself – and not only his being, but his *bien-être*, his well-being – that counts. Well-being implies the satisfaction of primary needs, freedom from necessity. It also carries connotations of a higher good. What Rousseau had depicted as a pleasant and satisfying sensuality in the first half of the *Discourse* ("le fruit ne se dérobe pas à la main") is revalued and devalued in the framework of "civilization": the immediacy of satisfaction of needs is now given the epithet of "animality," implying that a negative comparison between higher men and lower beasts structures man as a being superior to his needs. All primary needs, so easily satisfied in the savage state, are defined as "animal" appetites: hunger and lust, devoid of any sentiments of the heart.

Rousseau terms this foundational comparison or distinction man's first "enlightenment" ("nouvelles lumières"[22]), and it is: his first act of judgment. That the judgment is flattering to his self-esteem is significant, since all his relations to his fellow men (including, Rousseau lets us know, his female ones) are modeled on this first comparison. Even when he goes on to "identify" himself with others, it is within the limits of his desire to secure his well-being, defined as "advantage" over others, and safety for himself:

> Although his fellowmen were not for him what they are for us, and although he had hardly anything more to do with them than with other animals, they were not forgotten in his observations. The conformities that time could make him perceive among them, his female, and himself made him judge those he did not perceive. And seeing that they all acted as he would have done under similar circumstances, he concludes that their way of thinking and feeling was in complete conformity with his own. And this important truth, well established in his mind, made him follow, by a presentiment as sure as dialectic and more prompt, the best rules of conduct that it was appropriate to observe toward them for his advantage and safety.[b23]

The egomimetic model of identification and sympathetic introspection is a flawed or fraudulent foundation for human association, because it denies, from the beginning, its roots in the relation of greater and lesser, higher and lower, superior and inferior, and because its model is exclusively singular. Rousseau makes the drawbacks of egomimesis abundantly clear (the maddening circularity of specularity in his Neufchâtel preface to the *Confessions*, where each person projects his own self-understanding on to others he imagines to be just like him; the problem being, of course, that no one ever knows himself).[24]

In "paradise" there had been no need of labor or of communal effort to satisfy needs; but, in the reality frame which dominates the second half of the *Discourse*, material and practical difficulties multiply to the point of exhaustion: Rousseau catalogues in rapid succession differences in soils, climates, seasons, barren years, long winters, hot summers, cold, etc. Man really does have to work, but it is less for satisfaction of elemental needs than to maintain his advantage over nature, animals, others and to ensure safety for himself. In the second part of the *Discourse* self-reflection is not a mode of experiencing the feeling of being, but a resource in the now paramount motives of securing advantage and preserving the self. In another anticipation of Freud the pleasure principle is used to identify the (similar) motives of the other: "Taught by experience that love of well-being is the sole motive of human actions, he found himself in a position to distinguish the rare occasions when common interest should make him count on the assistance of his fellow men, and those even rarer occasions when competition ought to make him distrust them."[c25]

The process of masking (with metaphor) the primary egoistic passions is also the process of re-forming them as social (but still egotistic) passions.[26] The "first word" used to designate the other ("giant" in the *Essay on the Origin of Languages*) is a monstrous trope ("figuré") since it indicates absolute distinction from the other. But its monstrosity at least conveys something of the primary ego-passion – rejection of the other. When the trope itself is hidden within the conceptually "neutral" term "man" – a universal implying equality – difference between self and other is buried further, and placed in a condition where an archeology is required to retrieve its passional (hostile) base.

We can begin to see what was claimed in chapter 1: human interaction is thereafter freed not only from recognizing the other but from recognizing the ego-passions that shape it. The model is metaphor, or transference. Identification (equating the self with the other) stays rooted in the self, so that an alienated form of self-identification (metaphor) permits one to be identified by one's properties, which are equally rooted in the figure. What it is important to emphasize is that, be it in the mode of "equalizing" the difference between self and other (i.e. denying that what relates you to him is a *distinction*, an implicit hierarchy) or an acknowledgment of superiority or inferiority in ranking, all distinctions/indistinctions are likewise egotistic in origin, that is, a denial of difference and a reduction to the same, to the one.

So it is that the *Second Discourse* ultimately pits the "souverain" – as a vast, mute, and ever-open mouth – who narcissistically satisfies its own appetite, against its own society.[27] The repressed fantasy of the other as a monster (the "giant" of the *Essai*) returns in the form of the *It* without restraint, an unbounded fund of desires suppressed and misrecognized in and as the foundations of human "society." This is no society at all, but the product of smoke and mirror, of the egomimetic process.

En route to human history – which is created, Hegel wrote, by blocking the satisfaction of animal desire through the process of idealization – something has taken a wrong turn. The communitarian structure – supposedly built "outside" the family circle – is also a nostalgic/screened memory of the family circle itself which is encrypted and incorporated in the human heart: a complex. The foundations (on one gender base, one figure) of the city are laid over a pit – of passions.

In the *Second Discourse* the first relation is familial, and Rousseau places "familial" love at first outside the legitimate-patriarchal structure of "fathering" (metaphor), though not outside the conjugal and parental:

> The first developments of the heart were the effect of a new situation that united the husbands and wives [women], fathers and children in one common habitation. The habit of living together gave rise to the sweetest sentiments known to men: conjugal love and paternal love. Each family became a little society all the better united because mutual attachment and liberty were its only bonds, and it was then that the first difference was established in the lifestyle of the two sexes.[d28]

The family generates sexual difference, but it does not preclude – to the contrary it requires – incestuous relations. "The first brothers had to have married their sisters. In the simplicity of the earliest mores this custom was without drawback" and "They became husbands and wives without having ceased to be brothers and sisters" is how he puts it in the *Essay on the Origin of Language*.[29]

This familial, familiar form of loving association predates, for Rousseau, the elaboration of group or tribal speech, which only developed as each contribution to the well-being of the human "degenerates" into a new need. "This first love" with its "little society" yields to extrafamilial love when an exchange occurs between a number of such "little societies" or families. The "metonymic" form of love-link, the random association of people because they happen to be nearby cedes to a "metaphoric" form. Propinquity is now programmed as a function of the distinction between families (households), not by chance:

> Eventually a permanent proximity cannot fail to engender some intercourse among different families. Young people of different sexes live in neighboring huts; the passing intercourse demanded by nature soon leads to another, through frequent contact with one another, no less sweet and more permanent.[e30]

As it becomes "permanent" it develops systematic values, codes modeled on those of the household or patriarchy – the family communal dwelling becomes the city, civilization. The problem comes only with the denial of its relation to the other in its roots,[31] its dependence on and desire of the ego as an imaginary structure. It conjures away the other as it conjures him up.

The imaginary city, the artificial crowd has cost a great deal. Rousseau's *Discourse* delineates what Freud leaves largely unspecified. The ideologization of "society" acts, through imaginary "exchange," to wholly absorb the aim and objects of desire: this ideologized image perverts an aim, a wish, or a desire. Not only is the early family, in which the degree of narcissism is moderated and lessened by love – lost amidst the welter of new passions and new needs generated endlessly through metaphoric production, but the metaphoric mode becomes the sole means of gratifying desire, providing the substitute for what has been lost definitively. The impasse is shaped. The "lost" associative structure – body, family, pastoral – remains encrypted, buried, forming and shaping the unconscious heart. Absorbing the libido the crypt, in the ego has the power to prevent the movement (in the psychotic) from family to "polis": but at the same time dwelling in the imaginary city is paranoic.

Rousseau's *Rêveries*: The political critique of egomimesis[32]

Because we consistently read Rousseau as caught unconsciously within the ego-frame he challenged, we take him as paradigmatic of the dilemma of modern life: he is the model of paranoia, i.e., of the unresolvable antagonism between the individual and society: "Often the advantage of one is to the prejudice of the other, private interest is almost always in opposition with public interest."[f] He always seems to place the self in an economy of loss *vis-à-vis* the collective. But that is true only if we assume the "collective" is more than a gathering of fantasmatic others who are in reality projections of the self. The "whole" social body, like the mirror-staged ideal of his personal body collected by the infant in Lacan's discourse, turns out to be no more than a disguise or return of the ego. For Rousseau, that is exactly what it is. His insight is that the self is the unconscious root of the social "whole."

Keeping to the direction of the reading of Rousseau I have outlined, that is, a dialectical and proto-psychonanalytic reading, we can now see how Rousseau challenged the ego and its political economy of loss (which disguises itself always as a ["metaphoric"] surplus or gain). The entrance into "society" or civil life as a "mutilation" is read as the "acquired power of the whole" as an imaginary which castrates us in order to regulate and govern all social or sexual intercourse. But more readily or more rapidly perhaps than Freud, he questioned the "Sovereign" (the superego) remaining alert (paranoic-ally?) to the danger run by the (oxymoronic) "unconscious ego." "I" fantasmatically doubles itself as "we," which then becomes he (the tyrant) and finally *It* (the mute and all consuming *It/*id, who demands an *absolute* investment with no return to the other).

Castration-mutilation – the source of the "power of the whole" – is to be read in Rousseau in terms of another question which radically implicates the structuring of society in general.[33] If what we "sacrifice" to join the human community (our sensual body) is only a relay and disguise of narcissism and *amour-propre* (the high estima-tion of the self and its new value) then there is no true loss of self involved. In fact, the only thing lost is the real other. Human (if only "figurative") sacrifices – of the erotic family, of the other – are now to be seen as what is required, disturbingly, by the very process of our civilization.[34] The question of sacrifice in Rousseau is more than the version of castration we have learned from Freud and Lacan in so far as the other is involved in the process. This then illustrates the shift from patriarchal to fraternal Oedipus as a historical shift that ironically predates the discovery of Oedipus in classical mythology. Rousseau was first to find that what is mutilated or damaged by a civilization formed exclusively on an ego-base is the intersubjective, especially the sexual, relation. The "self" and "society" join in commanding the expulsion of the "other" from the individual/collec-tive psyche. The corollary of a negation of otherness then, is an act of sacrificing the other to the benefit of the self, a self staged as an ethical sacrifice to society, and a society which is only a disguised form of the ego.

It would also be possible to sacrifice the self rather than the other, that is to withdraw the libidinal investment in the self (disguised as the Other) and offer it to someone else. Castration (the cutting off of the body) is a reinvestment in the self, since the "nobility" of this sacrifice reinforces our tendency to overvalue ourselves. (And Rousseau is quick to point out that one never really sacrifices the self – nobly – without really committing the "ignoble" act of victimizing or sacrificing the other.) Yet he does hint at the possibility of a self-sacrifice that is not a ruse of the ego: an absolute "loss" of ego in a relation to the other. Thus when sexuality (as desire for the other) is renounced it is considered meritorious in a "society" which is merely a generalized form of the ego. The slightest inclination toward the other – preferring her or him to one's own self – is therefore dangerous to self-preservation.

Let us now turn to Rousseau's analysis of how the ego's self-love becomes aggression toward the other, and then to the elaborate denials of this aggression perpetrated by modern forms of "community." Rousseau's *Fourth Reverie* is justly renowned and yet it has never been fully analyzed. Perhaps this is because it provides the clearest example in his writing of his recognition of the aggressiveness of the ego as it recounts tales of brutality in children. Moreover, he relates ego aggression to the moral and social values the bourgeoisie is developing along (pseudo)patriarchal lines – lines which allow aggression to flourish while "disavowing" or "disapproving" it. Moreover, the text as a whole is framed by a prior narrative (Book II of the *Confessions*) which is essentially that of a sexual failure (the affair of blaming his theft of a silver ribbon on the girl who admired it and who was the intended recipient of it).

Rousseau is sensitive to the passing not only, as most critics have believed, of the mother (Nature, his mother, etc.) but of the father, the post-Oedipal condition. More significantly, Pateman excepted in part, Rousseau has yet to be fully credited for his analysis of the advent of the fraternal regime.[35] It pervades and frames even those of his texts that appear the least political. The two following passages, from the *Fourth Reverie*, are usually read in the context of philosophical discussions of truth, lies, and the realm of fiction, and as far as I know these particular texts have never been given a political or social framework. In my view they illustrate Rousseau's sense of the "cost" of the social contract of modernity – founded on same-generation ("Lockean") as distinct from intergenerational codes and patterns (the patriarchal household). It is a matter of how we relate to those who are our peers, when out of the house of patriarchy we are free to do without traditional constraints and proscriptions. This liberty is not absolute when it means the formation of libidinal ties to the other – but it also risks becoming so when these ties to the other are not made and narcissism triumphs. We have begun to see how the role the "brother" has assumed (his "father-act") perverts the promise of the distinctively modern symbolic order, alters the "contract" to favor one self over the other(s). The ego, in all its aggressiveness and as it is unleashed rather than moderated by modern social arrangements in favor of "absolute liberty" and freedom from (=power over) bond(age) to the other.

The pair of narratives in the *Fourth Reverie* concerning Fazy and Pleince have evoked very little separate commentary, and what there is inevitably deals almost exclusively with the question of truth versus fiction. Both passages concern childhood aggression and sympathy; and, taken together, they show the structure of two entirely different if incipient moral orders – each rooted in a different traditional gender paradigm (father and mother). But these social dimensions are rarely remarked. As we would expect, Rousseau locates the power (in word and deed) in the order of the masculine gender and grants the feminine a weak and silent, if beloved role: Rousseau's mother, after all, died at his birth. But we might be surprised that Rousseau, "father" of the rather vapid Emile, is depicting children as engaging in physical brutality. By comparing these two passages we are forced to think the relation to the other in the fraternal or same-generation frame outside the paternal moral order. What Rousseau is doing, in a way, is to rewrite Cain and Abel, making a critique of "brotherhood" for our times.

The first passage could be called "a child was being beaten: or Fazy in the paternal household." Rousseau recounts an incident in which he suffered a permanent injury, a scarring due to a malicious trick played upon him by his cousin. He locates his description very clearly in time, space, and the social order: it occurred on a Sunday, in the workshop of the home of M. Fazy, his uncle by marriage, etc., and it is very real-seeming.

> I used to spend nearly every Sunday at Les Pâquis at the house of a Monsieur Fazy, who had married one of my aunts and had a calico works there. One day I was in the drying room where the calender stood and I was looking at its cast-iron rollers; my eyes were tempted by their shiny appearance, I touched them with my fingers and was moving my hands up and down over the smooth cylinder with great pleasure.[g][36]
>
> *(Fourth Reverie, 77)*

Rousseau's sensuous pleasure – symbolically homo(auto)erotic (rubbing the shiny cylinder) is shattered by his cousin:

> when Monsieur Fazy's son, who had got inside the wheel, gave it a slight turn so neatly that it just caught the ends of my two longest fingers, but this was sufficient for the ends to be crushed and the two nails to be broken off.[h]
>
> *(ibid.)*

He now tells us that his cousin Fazy, alarmed not by the pain he has caused, but by the one he himself will suffer – with all due moral rigor – when his father hears about it, begs Rousseau to suppress the cause of the crushed fingers:

> Young Fazy cried out in alarm, got out of the wheel, threw his arm round me and begged me to be quiet, saying that it would be the end of him. At the height of my own pain I was touched by his, I stopped crying and we went to the fish-pond, where he helped me to wash my hands and stop the flow of blood with moss.[i]
>
> *(Fourth Reverie, 77–8)*

Despite his own extreme pain his cousin's clear terror of his father's justice "touches" him ["Au fort de ma douleur la sienne me toucha . . ."], and he offers, generously, to lie: "He beseeched me in tears not to give him away; I promised, and kept my promise so well that more than twenty years later no one knew how two of my fingers came to be scarred, for so they have remained"[j] (ibid., 78)

Further evidence of his own magnanimity is brought forward when he mentions that the injury coincides with a parade, "when the citizens were to perform their military exercises,"[k] where he and his cousin, along with three other children, were to have formed a rank. While he lies abed in pain he hears the company's drum pass beneath his sick-room window, "avec mes trois camarades."[37]

This loss of a body part – sacrifice or castration in later idioms – will be compensated: it becomes narrative capital, and Rousseau is able to use it on several occasions, including this one, to his own profit. It is reminiscent of Sir Arthur Conan Doyle's story of "The engineer's thumb." Watson and the engineer grope for some possible way of accommodating the engineer's absolute loss in terms of how critical it has been to his escape, etc., when Holmes interrupts their poignant discussion with the interjection that the engineer will be paid with "experience" and with material for hundreds of after-dinner conversations.

For Rousseau keeps the secret of his cousin's misdeed – but only for twenty years ("plus de vingt ans aprés"): promises, like contracts, bear implicit dates, and are evidently not for ever. We are free to be completely cynical about Rousseau's self-professed magnanimity toward his cousin, but as a narrative which would not exist outside the structure of credit (truth, lie, faith, good or bad), the Fazy episode is a miniature "realist" novel, an ideological or imaginary story *par excellence*. It is not, however, a good fiction. For Rousseau, good fiction has to operate independently of an economy and a power politics of loss and gain: one man's profit is another man's loss. The lie always operates at the expense of the other: Rousseau's "lie" on behalf of Fazy (and later on behalf of himself) means that one must suffer for the well-being of the other. What makes fiction different from this structure should become clear when we look at the second episode. In contrast to the Fazy episode, no one would be anxious to comb through it looking to catch Rousseau in a lie or self-aggrandizement: it has an air of unreality.[38] Let us turn to the next episode.

Rousseau describes another scene, which we could call "another tale of aggression: Pleince and the mother's garden." Its place in his life is marked by Rousseau as subsequent to the Fazy incident: "My other story is very similar, but comes from a later period in my life"[l]

(*Fourth Reverie*, 78). It is extremely important to emphasize the temporal position Rousseau assigns to this second incident: it post-dates the Fazy episode, Rousseau is older, etc., and the "innocence" of this narrative is thus disconnected from any associated illusions of a real or primary, childhood innocence.[39] Consistent with Rousseau's thought elsewhere, the "corruption" of social or symbolically ordered man here antedates his "innocence." The story is also strangely neutral; not only indifferent to matters of truth and lie, it lacks the color and drama of the Fazy tale.

Once more we see the child Rousseau suffering an injury at the hands of another boy, Pleince, with whom he has played and openly quarreled in a public square:

> I was playing a game of mall at Plain-palais with one of my friends called Pl[e]ince. We got into a quarrel over the game, and in the fight he gave me such a well-aimed blow of the mallet on my bare head that if he had been stronger he would have cracked my skull. I fell instantly. Never in my life have I seen anyone so distressed as that poor boy when he saw my blood flowing down my hair. He thought he had killed me. He flung himself on to me, embraced me and hugged me, weeping and uttering piercing cries. I too embraced him with all my might and shed tears in a state of confused emotion which was not entirely disagreeable. Finally he set about staunching my blood, which was still flowing, and seeing that our two handkerchiefs would not be enough, he took me off to his mother, who had a little garden close by.[m]
>
> (*Fourth Reverie*, 79)

Rousseau's iteration of a similar incident is puzzling. There is a certain symmetry in the events – tales of wounding both – but for all their surface similarities, the two incidents are not, in fact, "*toute semblable*," and their differences should be remarked. To begin with, the quarrel here is public, linked to the inherently competitive antagonism of the game situation; Fazy's malignant intentions are closed to reader and victim alike and therefore open to all kinds of (psychological and other) speculation, like Eco's "open work." The engine of destruction is not only simpler than in the first description (a wooden club versus a metallic machine), but it is frankly wielded by the assailant, whereas Fazy acts as a *deus ex machina* offstage, with several layers of mediation between him and his victim.

Beyond these significant but still superficial contrasts between the whys and hows of the child's maiming, the scenes differ in their moral, rhetorical, and performative aspects. Once again it is the perpetrator of the injury who cries the more over what he has done. Yet Rousseau carefully depicts Pleince as weeping in an uncalculating, unreflective way, while Fazy is playing for his victim's sympathies with all the melodramatic and sentimental means at his command ("il étoit perdu," "il me supplia avec larmes de ne point l'accuser," etc.). Pleince weeps rather in the manner of Lacan's "primary transitivistic child." In this mode no clear demarcation between self and other yet exists: one child hits another and then cries himself because "someone" (anyone, everyone) has been hurt. Pleince weeps not for the staged sentimental advantage it will give him. Rather, he seems to be displaying the ambivalent character psychoanalysis will later ascribe to all interpersonal acts involving death and loss.

We can now see how closely Rousseau's description of the scene with Pleince coincides with Freud's later treatment of the birth of conscience for the primitive, a conscience that is like yet different from either Oedipal guilt or the pseudo-guilt of the son in *Totem and Taboo*. The chief difference is the identification with the other, even to the point of death, which means recognizing what the unconscious will not recognize – one's own mortality. For Rousseau stresses the incident's resemblance to the scene of a fatality ("il crut m'avoir tué," coupled with Rousseau's emphasis on the severity of the blow: "d'une main plus forte il m'eut fait sauter la cervelle").

As I have shown, Freud assumed the existence of "primeval man," who, like Rousseau's *sauvage* is not already what Rousseau called "reflexive" (his term for the narcissistic self-conscious man of today): his "original man" or primordial self does not yet conceptualize because it has not yet experienced guilt. What Freud created here is no less than a genealogy of the concept, of thought being born with conscience. This is not unlike Rousseau's evocation of pity (our natural aversion to seeing another being suffer) at a similar moment. The sequence goes as follows: the "triumph" over the other is complicated by the simultaneous birth of love and guilt:

> what released the spirit of enquiry in man was not the intellectual enigma, and not every death, but the *conflict of feeling* [my emphasis] at the death of loved yet alien and hated persons. Of this conflict of feeling psychology was the first offspring. Man could no longer keep death at a distance, for he had tasted it in his pain about the dead.
>
> (*SE XIV*: 293)

Rousseau's narrative of Pleince displays exactly the same kind of ambivalence: Pleince's emotions surrounding the catastrophic event are completely conflicted. The aggressor is far from triumphal – he cries in pity. According to Freud's model, then, a certain "erotism" will have had to enter the picture, since only "love" could modify the satisfied triumph of self over other, the denial of one's own mortality at the expense of another's death. Indeed, we find this to be the case in Rousseau: the exchange of tight embraces is described by Rousseau as arousing "une émotion confuse qui n'étoit pas sans quelque douceur." How much closer to a "triumph" is the staged "pity" proffered by Fazy: no confusion of emotion and no love-dimension either. His aggression goes unpunished except for Rousseau's impotent narration of it, but more than that, because it is based primarily on the form of opposition of self to other, it does not afford Fazy the "experience" as it were of his own death. What is at stake for him – despite his melodramatic cries – is a ritual spanking at most. No threat of death or loss here.

At this point Freud's text predicts the invention of a spirit both to mitigate the pain of loss, and, more importantly perhaps, what this loss would mean for himself, whom he also loves: for the loved other has become a part of oneself, and its death means some of it is gone. The idea of an immortal spirit is invented to recompense the loss of the loved/hated other, whose death is now as deeply regretted as desired. Self-love, interested in denying the ego's own death, finds primeval man raising the dead, compensating the death of the loved one by creating a ghost. He denies the finality of death, unwilling

> to acknowledge it, for he could not conceive of himself as dead . . . he devised a compromise: he conceded the fact of his own death as well, but denied it the significance of annihilation – significance which he had no motive for denying where the death of his enemy was concerned. It was beside the dead body of someone he loved that he invented spirits, and his sense of guilt at the satisfaction mingled with his sorrow turned these new-born spirits into evil demons that had to be dreaded.
>
> (*SE XIV*: 293–4)

This is the birth of conscience, and, also, the origin of the cult of the ancestor, to whom we are indebted, and whose ghost, Tönnies writes, must ever be propitiated with ritual offerings.

Rousseau's text invents no spirits or ghosts, but does invent a fiction – the fiction of a relationship ("longtems je la regardai comme ma mère et son fils comme mon frère"[40]). He marks the non-presence of an economy of loss, or infinite or pure debt: he insists that he forgets them, little by little.[41]

Metaphor, the imaginary yields human cultural life: it opens a wide range of mental, conceptual, and emotional possibilities otherwise foreclosed (Freud's "spirit of enquiry" and what Rousseau called *la perfectibilité*), partly because it permits us the possibility of coming face to face with our own death and with the other without having to acknowledge fully their reality. The task Rousseau's fiction, his art, takes for itself, is to re-mark the faltering of the essential action of this initial metaphor (spirit, for example). A partial lie, which covered over the way in which the ego tended to consider everything other than it to be remainders and remains whose death or life remains unavailable to consciousness, it nevertheless had both a self-protective and a commemorative function. He reveals both the arrogation of the powers of metaphor (to obscure or hide) in the interests of the ego alone, the narcissistic ego, and its moral bankruptcy in the case of Fazy.

While the "paternal" metaphor fails, is it possible for the "maternal" metonym to supplement what it lacks – the relation to the other? In the second tale, rather than suppressing the facts before the threat of encountering a judging father, Pleince brings the injury he has done, along with the victim, immediately to the attention of a sympathetic, healing and nurturing mother, who salves the wounds with natural herbs and maternal care.

> The good lady nearly fainted when she saw the state I was in. But she managed to retain enough self-control to look after me and after washing my wound thoroughly, she treated it with lily flowers steeped in alcohol, and excellent vulnerary which is widely used in Geneva. Her tears and those of her son so affected me that for a long time afterwards I regarded her as a mother and her son as a brother, until eventually I lost sight of them both and gradually forgot them."
>
> (*Fourth Reverie*, 79)

Swathed in an intensely fictive atmosphere (the pastoral garden of the mother), unimaginable in a society commanded by the moral rule of fathers, this silent tableau (no *style indirect libre*, even) exists for one purpose in Rousseau's work: it performs the role of pure counterpart, sheer otherness to the received ideas of how interpersonal relations must be formed within an economy of profit and loss.

No relation of natural sympathy framed exclusively by the critical issues of love and death has ever existed for "man-in-society": his pity is mirror-staged. Our common moral existence is practiced in the ways of the stage (Goffman's "We are all merchants of morality") and consists of representing what cannot be seen, heard, or experienced without threat. The grand sublimations and evasive ambiguities of the moral economy (truth is a form of lie; reward is a form of punishment) are the sum total of our ego-bound experience. More than this, by explicitly invoking the Pleince episode as one that comes after the Fazy episode, Rousseau challenges the nostalgic, "paradise lost" version of human contact. It is a fiction that, together with Fazy, shows us both how things are and how they could be otherwise.

The kind of social linkage the mother has fostered in this passage is that of brotherly love in a primary form which recognizes rivalry openly and overcomes it in her bosom. It is played off against the purely theatrical form of brotherly solidarity exhibited by the Fazy passage. But it does not really offer us a relation to the other beyond that of fraternal union.

The "mother" offers no alternative to patriarchy, whose *moeurs* and whose arts have masked for so long aggression against the maternal (natural) body.[42] The primacy of "second" nature precludes any effort to reproduce the mother/son relation, at least by Rousseau's account, in artificial form. One has only to see Mme de Warens – "Maman" – and her various *ménages à trois*, filled with bitterness, rivalry, destruction (Anet's suicide) and thoroughly legislated by substitutive metaphors: when Anet dies, Rousseau gets his suit and his job; when he returns from Lyon, Wintzenreid/de Courtilles has taken Rousseau's place. In the "real world" the mother too pits brother against brother: they are not permitted to stand together in the same relation to the mother at the same time – really brothers – though that is the ideal form of the maternal relation. It reproduces, that is, the "primogeniture" which Locke argued so vigorously against Filmer.

The mother has not got us to the point of real community. It appears that the metaphoric order, the order now of the brother who invokes the name but not the conscience-provoking power of the father has triumphed in life as in art. Yet Rousseau has more to give us than the departure of the parents and the rise of fraternity. In what follows, I will trace the itinerary of Rousseau's presentations of a *hommosexuel* imaginary (brotherly "love"), a heteroerotic symbolic (both in his *Confessions*), through to his repositioning – radically – the situation of art as a means of renewing the essence of "conscience." It requires powers of imagination and the staging of relationships not possible under the current regime, including the root relation of the self to itself. It is the *Letter to D'Alembert on the Theatre* that will become the key text, but only because it is read in relation to the book of the ego (*The Confessions*), the book of the political ego (*The Social Contract*), and the fiction (*Julie*), the depiction of a relation to the other that permits both these egos to acknowledge their relations.

Narcissism and the social psyche: *The Social Contract*

As far as I can determine Rousseau is the first to have understood the structure of the polity as indeed a *psyche*, i.e. a relation among ego-id-superego, rather than as a "rational state." Rousseau gives a picture of a social bond that is neither legislative nor customary in character:

identification. In IV,i he tells an "origin" myth of peasants gathered under an oak tree without formal contract but who nevertheless freely "consider" themselves a "single body" with one will for common security and well-being. It is what he calls the "social bond" and it is the primary model for all subsequent versions of the group.

Yet it is only so in theory, not in empirical reality. For one thing, the general will is always "right" but it is not always enlightened. It always wants what is good, but it can not always "see" it (IV,i:38). The partiality of its judgment, its vision, is another way of stating that it is an "unconscious." The Law[43] as we know it bespeaks a need to repress or to forget what it has supplanted as much as custom does: the significance of custom, Tönnies says, "consists in replacing an earlier, more natural (because cruder) practice and in restraining it."[44] Rousseau even tells us that the social whole can at times suffer from a collective "insanity" (II,viii:42) – Freud might have called it civilization's neurosis – because it, like ritual and custom, originates in a relation to a past that cannot be assimilated by conscious memory. What distinguishes the two, however, is that in the formation of a people under "Law," forgetting is no simple guilt and obligation to the past, but takes the form of a trauma. The past is a "horror" that cannot be either forgotten or made a part of consciousness.

> Just as certain maladies unhinge men's minds and remove from them the memory of the past, one . . . sometimes finds in the period during which states have existed violent epochs when revolutions do to people what certain crises do to individuals. When the horror of the past takes the place of forgetfulness and when the state, set afire by civil wars, is reborn as it were, and takes on again the vigor of youth as it escapes death's embrace.
>
> (II,viii:42)

"The people" is an effect of the Law, a "creature" of the modern (unexpressed) superego (the deleted he) in all its frightening connotations. This Law is a law which Rousseau tells us is the relation of the whole to the whole. According to Rousseau, to undertake the establishment of a people is to change human nature (II,viii:39), to form a social rather than an individual body. "The people" is the embodied form of the democratic "ideal," or more precisely of its Law, one which obviates distinctions (class, sex, ethnicity) and amalgamates individual persons into a "whole" being.[45] To fashion such a body also implies the construction of a "mind" or *"esprit."* Whether that *esprit* is prior to or an effect of the Law is what is in doubt: "The social spirit [or mind] which ought to be the work of that institution [the Law] would have to preside over the institution itself.

And men would be, prior to the advent of laws what they ought to become by means of laws" (II,viii:40). This is similar to Lacan's Polish joke in "Kant avec Sade," "Long live Poland, otherwise there would be no more Poles."[46]

The problematic of the democratic collective "self" then, is summed up in this quotation: the socializing of the self is the kind of impossible act that violates all rational formulations of conception, birth, and reproduction of a body and mind: it disrupts the parental relation. We may attempt to adhere to the customary paternal/maternal imagery that has served as model for our life in common, but in the modern case, we cannot really do so. The democratic self may be technically psychotic when it forecloses the name of the father. (Or it can invoke that name in vain . . . as persona of/for the brother.)

The legislative act of creating a "people" for the "people" transcends, Rousseau indicates, human will, human strengths, human virtues – everything that can be extrapolated from the notion of any "human force": the human has no authority to execute the Law (II,viii:40). This is partly because good laws impose "continual privations," and the human being is commanded to pleasure, not privation, so that the Legislator needs recourse to an authority which can "compel without violence." But such authority and such laws are themselves improbable structures if we start from any of the classical versions of the rational political self.

For, Rousseau tells us, those best suited for legislation are those already "bound" without "the yoke of the law," without customs or deep-rooted legislation that might block the advent of what is essentially a new, people-forming drive.[47] His "Law" therefore must be considered as something entirely different in character from what could be understood as the law of tradition (custom), which regulates paternal power but cannot *legislate* it. New laws are needed if the Law – which is a law of identity, relating the whole to the whole, the people to itself in the absence of the dead father, the presence of forgetting – becomes an executive power.

The great Legislator is the one who "solidifies" the institution precisely by ensuring that "natural" forces are "dead and obliterated" (II,viii:39). The perfect law is seen as what achieves its force by making the whole greater than the sum of its parts (natural forces) and which renders its participants "nothing." In short, repressive Law taken to its extreme becomes the final suppression of difference, the forging of the perfect whole on the basis of a refusal to recognize difference – including, I am arguing, sexual difference.

Rousseau divides "new" Laws into "political" and "civil" ones.[48] "Political laws" cut the members' bodies off from relation to each other in order to tie them instead to the whole, to constitute the relation of *the whole of a social body to itself*. They construct, essentially, the relation to the other. "Civil laws" relate the members of a society *to each other* (II,xii:48ff.). The drive of the political laws is to make the influence of the civil laws as minimal as possible, and to maximize the relation the members have to the whole. If we compare the Lacanian concept of Oedipus (and/or its translation as the castration complex) as the cut in the field of the social, then Rousseau's definition fits the decisionist frame.

Now Rousseau declares that only the political laws, which specify the relation of the members to the whole, are open to willed revision (II,xii:48): they are, or represent the power of *self-governance*.[49] Apparently, they, like all paternal forces, can be overthrown. This is because they are the site of generative power: having sublimated both mother and father, the political is "born again," without parents, through a secondary forgetting: "When the horror of the past takes the place of forgetfulness and when the state, set afire by civil wars, is reborn as it were, and takes on again the vigor of youth as it escapes death's embrace" (II,viii:42). The actual "origin" of a "whole" people is thus traumatic. Now unconsciously split, its "rebirth" is a secondary idealization of its self-image. (The process is not essentially different from that which is at the root of "ritual" or custom, as in Tönnies' paradigm, but its entire accent is different – the orientation toward "youth" rather than elders, the anxiety toward death, the negation of past differences, the fear of abjection.)[50]

Once the political dominates the civil relation – the social tie – to the other is recognized as the primary power, the people still stand at a crossroads. The privative laws of the "political" are, Rousseau tells us, to be non-violent in character, like the pleasure principle which commands and cannot be disobeyed. But they make of those subject to them not rational creatures but so many psyches: subjected not by their mind or their will, but by their desire. Desire is thus what is politically (in Rousseau's terms) or symbolically (in Lacanian terms) structured.

Reborn of itself, however, the people as a whole no longer assigns the parental role, setting the agenda of desire, to the superego, which should at this point take on the aspect of fraternity, equality, and liberty. But the "people as a whole" has been forged in the mirror-stage which denies (with horror) its own division by the other. A dramatic act of forgetting – powerful repression of a trauma in the Freudian sense – lies at the root of this "re-birth," and requires constant energizing. The dialectic of the "Law" thus results in the emergence of an unconscious, misrecognized superego, one which risks again becoming the tyrannical, despotic pre-Oedipal Father of *Totem and Taboo* (or the all-consuming Sovereign of Rousseau's *Second*

Discourse). The motive of the "people," the "democratic" drive is thus seen by Rousseau as a dialectic of desire, of a competition between eros and thanatos.

If the modern social psyche is driven to re-form itself beyond the traditional, paternal model, and its social identity is conceived ("reborn") as an escape from "death's embrace," it still misrecognizes the existence of the superego, the other. It is, in Lacan's terms in "Kant avec Sade," a sadistic superego, the endpoint of the imperative to pleasure, the self-binding of the law (of desire) one gives oneself. Because Rousseau, consciously or not, employed a vocabulary of desire and eros ("death's embrace") just at the point where the democratic body emerges, we are free to use his texts in a psychoanalytic way, that is, to think communal conscience – the Desire of the Other – outside the frame, at least provisionally, of Oedipus. For in order for a people to "escape death's embrace" it cannot be simply narcissistic: after all, the most notable mythic figure who "embraced" death by denying division within himself was Narcissus, drowning in his pool. The general critique to be read in Rousseau here must now be linked to the question of art, the other domain in which Narcissus exercises power. I turn now to the narcissistic modeling of the collective or general self and the role of the arts in defining its consciousness, unconscious, and its own birth of conscience.

Which brings us back to the theater. If, ever since Aristotle, the theater has been credited with major powers of forming the moral being of a group, the problem of so defining it, however, has to arise in the modern case, where the individual is the presumed telos and origin of the social ground.[51] An act of interiorization – the sense of one's own heart – is necessary to constitute the modern consciousness equally as a self and to link it to other like selves. Yet every act of the imaginary is a sacrifice of the other: it both conjures him/her up and conjures him/her away. Theatrical representation would have to reduplicate this narcissistic structure as public act for the modern individual-based "group" to be granted a society-shaping role, and even then it would not therefore form a group as a "moral" being in Durkheim's sense (that of a supplement created by apprehending a relation between and among its members, beyond the relation between individuals and the whole).

Rousseau tells us that in the theater, just as in Benjamin's urban landscape, we forget our relations with friends, neighbors, family (those passion-pits): the individual is most isolated when he is in a theater seat (II,viii:16). He emphasizes: no "true relations of things" appear on stage (II,viii:26). In effect, the theater does not stage relationship at all. It therefore follows that the theater is doing political work, the labor of the desire of the Other, in the strongest sense, i.e. minimizing the relation a social body's members have to each other, and maximizing their relation to the "whole." While such remarks on Rousseau's part seem to be his standard cant against artificiality, urbanity, and a *Gesellschaft* society which vitiates simple face-to-face interaction, and promotes social inauthenticity, etc., we can also discern right here the propagandist use of spectacle made by totalitarian regimes in the twentieth century, mass transference to the one.

What is most distressing, however, is that neither of these positions can possibly be distinguished from a neo-Kantian reading that would also conclude that isolating the individual from his "interestedness" is the highest ethos a society constructed on an ego base can hope to achieve: self-interest overcome in the interests of human kind. Since one's "relations" with the other are always ultimately self-interested, envious, and hostile, then for the theater to sublimate and transfer them to its stage is a miracle of transformation, from an interested to a disinterested, transcendental, general self.

In all three cases – a "good" modern theater fostering a disinterested "transcendental" self identified with all "mankind"; a "bad" modern theatre of fascism that intensifies narcissism, or *amour-propre*; and a superfluous modern theatre that can never quite recapture the purity of the primitive self – it is impossible to argue that the theatre has any necessary, systematic relevance to the formation of the identification of the political whole to itself in a democracy. The democratic is self-governed, self-identifying.

The *Letter to D'Alembert on the Theatre* is, however, in its bringing forward the uniqueness of the modern "theater of love," a systematic effort to analyze this theater as necessary to democracy in its modern form. This accounts for the strength of his attacks on the two antique classical genres, tragedy and comedy, which, according to Rousseau, are as unsuited to the modern democratic state as they were appropriate to the classical and contemporary patriarchal republics. Both as a major critique of Aristotle's principles of identification and purification via the theater and a critique of the Horatian imperatives – Enlightenment favorites – of pleasure and utility, Rousseau's *Letter* implies that no classical theory can define a theater adequate to the process of identification in a modern society, whose subjects are "re-born" in a misrecognition of themselves as well as of their role. Theater, that is, as we know it (in which a real actor underneath plays a role with a mask or persona) is inadequate to the problematic of social identification under conditions of modern democratic forms, those Rousseau sees being born where, as Diderot told us in his *Eloge de Richardson*, modern society is "le lieu de la scène"[52] –

its very substance theatrical. Rousseau's *Letter* explicates both why modernity is dramatistic in character, and it lays out, systematically, how the social theater relates to drama as an "art" or aesthetic form.[53]

Politics and the arts: modeling the collective self

In the *Social Contract*, the *Discours*, the *Essai*, "sovereignty" is a term for the form or way in which a people identifies itself to itself. There are innumerable models for such identification, amongst the oldest are the scapegoat, hero, king, and the father: authorized figures, figures that authorize our relations to each other. For modernized peoples, the possibility of self-governance entails the need for a revision in the mechanism of identification. In the modern as distinct from the traditional world, where dead elders rule, there exists a unique risk: self-governance without adequate models for otherness-and-togetherness can, even as a "popular" sovereignty, become one which enacts the Sovereign-as-despot.[54]

The specific mechanism of group-identification for Europeans – for Rousseau as for Kant – is the "maxim." Maxims popularly provide the "wisdom" of the elders, tradition. When maxims proceed from "authorized" figures in the modern state, however, they function as imperatives or ethical commands; while we give them to ourselves they still work as if they came from the "Other." In the *Social Contract* it is the *popular maxim*, not the pronouncements of the Government, that most accurately express the "general" will. This is because the Government's maximization has increasingly become the expression of one individual sovereign's will. As Rousseau puts it in the *Essay on the Origin of Language*, the sovereign-as-king in contemporary life has no need of language: since all he has to say is "tel est mon plaisir," he can do so with "soldiers on the street corner" and "posters on city walls." In this situation, then, popular maxims provide a counterpoint (indeed, after a certain point in the elaboration of governance, the only one) to *official maxims* – the dicta of state government. Expressions by the "people" become a remedy needed as often as there is intensive aggression by the state (the Government) against the "sovereignty" of "the people" who know themselves as "the people" through their counter-statements.

But the popular norm is not, for Rousseau unequivocally benign. In the *Letter to D'Alembert*,[55] he tells us (67 ff.) that the *moeurs* of a people is represented commonly as and by public opinion, which predominates over law, reason, and virtue. The best of "laws" has no effect on opinion, for laws cannot change the nature of things but are forced to follow it: only such laws are ever actually obeyed. There is a potential for another sort of tyranny, since such laws have no effect on the unexpressed but real desires public opinion harbors. In the situation of modern democracy, the "popular norm" dialectically reverses to become the locus of repression of desire: where the maxim resisted the edicts of government, public opinion now legislates. The popular maxim not only can but does become the locus of authority, official identifications, the "officer of morality," to continue the oral metaphor. Folk wisdom, folk sayings, opinions, are thus the "poison" – what the mouth of the Sovereign would not swallow – under circumstances where self-governance (modern democracy) really takes effect. They produce what Lacan would later call the "unconscious." Where is the Other (or the other) who could offer this modernized society any form of counter-reflection – it is its own Other, and more often the source of aggression and crime than of conscientious acts. For Rousseau, the absolutely different Other to modern society is less "nature" than a more strongly conceived art: the theater. This art has to be characterized entirely by and as difference, not a mirroring of the same. It is perhaps less the shift from passive reflection to active expression, mirror to lamp that takes place in his "romantic" art, than a shift from a thoroughly narcissistic tendency in art (intensified under the neo-patriarchy) to an art that legitimates and recognizes the relation of otherness. Rousseau's express desire to be "à la fois soi et un autre"[56] has to be read strongly in both ways, as the statement of the narcissistic artist's unlimited power to replace all others through art – and as the only place where recognition of the other's difference is seen in relation to the self: the narcissistic double bind made conscious, heightened – and partially overcome.

It is at the theater that *the* political question, the recognition or misrecognition of the other and the superego in the democratic state – is answered. For narcissism, Freud taught us, produced the "object" of desire as an imaginary object, but it cannot give us desire on a social scale, that is, symbolically. The imaginary does not give us access to *das Ding*, the satisfied desire, the "end" of a drive satisfied by the sublimation of a natural aim. Narcissism is an idealization by means of identifying the self with an imaginary object intervening in the identification process. There is no ethical sublimation performed by the arts on behalf of the "brother."

The role of the theater in social identification

To use the theater as a means of identification under circumstances where the popular sovereign is an ego on a group scale is to reinforce a "moral" order which verges on tyranny. The narcissistic theatrical imaginary supports (Rousseau calls it "flatters") the ruling passions of the group, and these just happen to be, he tells us, aggressive and arbitrary in character. But has not the modern theater liberated itself from being the site of official morality, of commandments? Modernity defines the theater, he tells us, as the antithesis of the church, which instills moral maxims and a sense of duty. Theater is a form of *divertissement*, not a ritual or re-enactment of customary codes. Rousseau challenges strongly Aristotelian assumptions of moral force in the theatrical performance: "Why should the *image* of suffering born of the passions efface that of the transports of pleasure and joy also born of them?" (21). These lines can be read in such a way that the "transports of pleasure" are the pleasure taken in cruelty, in seeing the alien other suffer, while we are secure in our theater seats. Egoistic passions are "flattered" by their rehearsal on stage, they are not corrected by them.

Rousseau, however, finds that the theater is not really the space of an aesthetic of pleasure, either: it is bound by established feelings and norms:[57] "Let no one attribute to the theater the power to change sentiments or mores, which it can only follow and embellish" (19).[58] The general effect of the theater, that is, is not legislative (articulating the Law), but is itself regulated by customs and traditions which are understood only unconsciously, experienced only as feelings.

Now, everyone knows, of course, that Rousseau banned the theater from the ideal republic, Geneva, just as Plato excluded the poets from his. Readers of his *Letter to D'Alembert* seem forced to conclude that Rousseau repeats Plato's gesture with respect to his own homeland, the Republic of Geneva: a corporate civil society based on the Calvinist individual and his internal relation to God. Indeed, in this text, Rousseau's Geneva actually appears as an ideal, classical republic – not Athens but Sparta. Like Sparta, Geneva bans the theater, excludes women from public life, and sustains its economy independently of other states.

This "ideal" republic is not technically, a democracy, however, but a theocracy with a highly patriarchal stamp. When as a boy Rousseau left this city, he left, he tells us at the close of Book I of the *Confessions*, his destined patriarchal place in it as a good son, husband, father, citizen, workman, and man. Geneva is one society, even without a king, that is capable of achieving clear social identification as a patriarchy.[59] That it has done so without using the theater as a site of identity-formation is what fascinates Rousseau: from Greek antiquity on, the theater has been supposed to be the fulcrum of social identification, the very place where a society comes to self-consciousness and forges its own image of itself. Geneva seems serenely, supremely unified without the use of the theater, whereas in modernized, post-theocratic societies group identity has constantly to be remade ("reborn") out of a patchwork of differences (often so severe that the polity is torn in two), its wholeness – the "people" – constantly re-formed.

Geneva, like Sparta, is a unified totality: it lacks nothing. It needs to negotiate no "differences" among its people. In fact, as we read Rousseau's depiction of Geneva we discover that its central norm is that of the segregation of the sexes. Genevan men socialize with each other in clubs just for them; Genevan women have sewing circles and associate only with each other. Even married, the two sexes meet only rarely, and have sexual relations solely for the sake of propagation. So separate are the sexes that Rousseau begins almost literally to see the city as Sparta, where, he explains, if a woman even appeared at the communal festival of the Olympic games she was killed! (It is significant that no reader of Rousseau I am aware of has ever taken this description as bitingly ironic: it shows how deeply imbricated we are in the misogyny of the ideal polis/republic fantasy.)[60]

One central aim of this patriarchal order, then, is the complete sublimation of the woman as a player in the construction of culture and group life: she is excluded from public life whether in terms of politics or amusements in which group identity is formed. Lacedemonian girls, Rousseau reminds us, could dance naked in the streets without there being the least concern that anyone might cross the line and accost them – or even notice them. Their negation is absolute, through murder or simple denial of their presence. Obviously, then, the advent of the theater – at least the classical theater – could never threaten this kind of patriarchy, or even be inimical to it.

But once we set aside Geneva/Sparta as democracies (technically they are not), we get down to business, and can look at what the theater does in respect to group psychology under conditions of modernity. Thus Rousseau declares: "Everything is still problematic concerning the real effects of the theater" (15). In modernity there are no heroes, and thus, no tragedy: there is comedy even less. Without heroes, the hinge-point, the mechanism of (Aristotelian) identification, consolidating the norms of the polis – Rousseau's "political laws" or relation of the whole to itself – falters. (The same frustration holds in reverse for comedy, where distance and even irony – disidentification – are thought to reign.) For the domain of the comic is revolutionary: it makes itself at home in a world without ancestors, overturning, Rousseau tells us, all sacred relations. It "shakes," he says, "the whole order of society" (35). Yet here in the *Letter* is just where Rousseau places his critique of *Le Misanthrope*.[61]

The modern problematic is this: having violated the ancestral norm, in a social world where authorizing "figures" can only act "as if" they were "fathers," "kings," "gods," or "heroes," the role that the theater plays for our modern world cannot be understood along classical aesthetic lines. Rousseau's *Letter* none the less does formulate a new theater which, in its special way, can and does respond to popular sovereignty, self-governance and modernity, and is an art for its time.

The *Letter* fully intends, I am suggesting, the theater as destruction of Genevan patriarchy, the land of segregated sexes, the polity made ideal in that relations between its members remain as close to zero as possible. It is only because Rousseau seems so much the "Swiss pastor" denouncing cultural proliferation that we do not see his primary target is less the theater of love than the conventional theater of his day. This is the theater which reinforces group identity as it already exists. We might wonder why Rousseau does not take the homosexual fraternity, apparently so functional in antique Greek models, as appropriate for modern democratic order, but he does not. This problem has already been raised: homosexuality as an infantile regression is necessarily linked to the imaginary, and opens yet another path to the narcissism he sees as the greatest temptation of the democratic, self-governed body.

The contemporary theater, when it indulges narcissism, is indeed the target of Rousseau, precisely because the narcissistic erotic option is all too easily chosen by the democratized, modernized self. Contemporary (not "modern") theater, he tells us, permits the audience to imagine itself *as a group that possesses a clear identity*. But this is an illusion, since, like the mirror that over-organizes and idealizes the child's self, the theatrical mirror creates and sustains group-level illusions of being an ideal, whole body, entirely and only on the basis of opposing it to some other group: in London, he tells us, plays achieve popularity when they depict the traditional English hatred of the French; in Goa, they succeed when they show Jews being burned on stage. The theater in these instances is following group norms, marking it as fundamentally "traditional" and not "modern" in character, and in the most unattractive way. It has not even begun to address the modern group as a psychic structure. It is this theater which is indeed superfluous in the case of Geneva, a theocracy, but not necessarily in the case of democracy as a new, modern form.

There is, however, another theater that is at work in the modern case, and it would not be superfluous in Geneva: it would destroy the ideal republic. To bring out this other theater, which is to be found in the *Letter to D'Alembert*, we must take our lead not from those who think they already know and understand the shape of democratic institutions, but from Rousseau himself.

Rousseau went to great lengths to define and distinguish the *modern* stage, especially the French one, absolutely from classical drama and from the contemporary popular stage. The modern theater is one of which the Greeks, he tells us, knew nothing: it is the theater of love. In contrast to the sociopolitical impotence of both tragedy and comedy today, the modern theater has both a legislative and a regulatory power. But it is most to be distinguished from the antique form because it is the domain of women, not of men or of heroes. "Love is the realm of women: It is they who necessarily give the law in it."[62]

The "love" *Letter to D'Alembert*

In Book IX of the *Confessions* Rousseau tells us that the *Letter on Spectacles* is actually a love letter, an allegory of his relations to Sophie d'Houdetot, Mme d'Epinay, Grimm, and St Lambert: "unconsciously I described my situation of the moment: I portrayed Grimm, Mme d'Epinay, Mme d'Houdetot, St-Lambert, and myself . . . . Alas, there are proofs enough in that letter that love, that fatal love . . . still remained in my heart."[63]

Because it is difficult to reconcile this odd statement with the egoistic, narcissistic Rousseau we all know and hate, no critic of whom I am aware has ever made much of it. I would like to take Rousseau entirely seriously, and to read the *Letter* as a meditation on sexual politics. Since drama is the very art form in which (for Aristotle) social and political identification is achieved, and since Rousseau has discovered the problematics of the modern social psyche, it is crucial to understand the way this tangle of amorous relations is reflected in or repressed by the *Letter*,[64] especially since the *Letter* disturbs the classical separation of the sexes in very much the way the eighteenth-century novel disturbed the separation of styles and classes of personages in the drama.[65]

When Rousseau gives the woman-on-stage the "same power over the audience as she has over her lover," (*Letter to D'Alembert*, 47) he is, of course, not giving her much in the current system of relations: the only real power she has with her lover is the power to yield – to his force or to his seduction, prefaced, to be sure, by a certain "resistance." She satisfies her lover's desire, or more precisely his passion, the brother's passion, the desire not to desire. When Rousseau separates moral amelioration (identifying with the noble, higher men on stage) from the society-creating force found in staging "eros," he is relying on models in the courtly love poetic tradition. This tradition Lacan has analyzed as one where the aim of becoming a "poet" is eminently served by sublimating the erotic relation in artistic form, and more importantly, where the feminine object is elevated to the status of *das Ding*, i.e. where she becomes the focal point of all libidinal aims and displaces these aims (*Sém. VII*, 134).[66]

Lacan showed the motive of sublimation in art is the repeated reconstruction of "paternal power," otherwise known as the sublimation of the knowledge of engenderment as produced by the mother's body.[67] Every deferral, every staging of the *Domnei's* body as an allegory of the construction of moral values in the courtly tradition is one more step away from the actual exercise of feminine power in real life and one more affirmation that the lover, like the artist, desires not to desire. The corollary to Lacan's insight that courtly poetry upholds the morality of *das Ding* (the lover's desire not to desire) is that staging the woman covers up the actual exercise of male power – his capacity to *resist* (overcome) her resistance. But why should such a theater ever "threaten" any masculine utopia, both Geneva, modeled on Sparta, and the homosexual democracy of Athens, site of the classical theater?

Rousseau grants this feminine theater another kind of power besides that of attractive resistance: the power to rewrite the law. The staging of eros has the critical power to destroy, he tells us, all claims the official, moral maxim has on us: "The depictions of love always make a greater impression than maxims of wisdom . . . . However love is depicted, it seduces or it is not love" (54). This is a radical claim, one which makes the theater the site of a "feminine" politics, a reverse "political" or "symbolic" in which the relations among the society's members are potentially increased rather than diminished by installing feminine eros in the symbolic position, *the position of lack, that is, of desire*.

Rousseau thus puts the question to the "new" republic, the "modern, democratic" state, the question of its own identity and the means of constructing – and "revising" – it. If, indeed, the modern collective self is modeled by and as the actor – the brother-as-if-he-were-father, then in the actress there seem to be residual revisionary powers, a new possibility of forgetting and renewing. Let us follow Rousseau for a while as he works at "forgetting" Geneva, the republic without women.

After the patriarchy: reconstructing sexual difference

After Rousseau leaves Geneva in the *Confessions*, he stages an endless succession of women who serve as metaphoric substitutes for one or another aspect of the feminine (nature, the mother) who are supposed, like Pleince's mother, to found a fraternal community –

but who do not. When, and if, they do, like the actresses in modern theater, they are denied legal recognition in it. As Rousseau moves through the first six books, he is specifically looking for what Geneva could never afford him, an illicit, but sustaining relationship with a woman. He indeed shapes his autobiography as a series of sexually oriented encounters: but they are encounters principally with men, including himself – not with women.

Rousseau jauntily and ironically shows himself setting out to seek a romance damsel in a castle, one who will, à la Quixote, sustain and foster him. He notes, of course, that it is peasants who are supplying him with the means of subsistence; yet he continues to believe in the potential societal and political power of the woman. He, in fact, declines all positions and employment in which he can not see "a woman's hand in it."

Although the romance he seeks, in Quixote's wake, seems to originate with literature, Rousseau lets us know that it has a real origin as well – in *discipline*. As a young child he had received certain spankings from Mlle de Lambercier, spankings which raised erotic feelings in him. Mlle de Lambercier detects these aroused feelings and abruptly ceases the punishment. "Discipline" is another way of saying culture or civilization – restraints placed on a subject's relation to another, but also a painful joy in such limitations. The spankings have placed power and dominance in feminine hands: what better emblem of the ideology of *Kultur* can be found? Lambercier (and later Goton) are the personal equivalent of what Rousseau, in the *First Discourse*, calls the power and function of the arts and sciences. They are flowery garlands that enchain and enslave us by appeal to our aesthetic senses.

Henceforth all the upper-class women Rousseau encounters figure as authorizing his desires – from the little Mlle de Goton who forces him to submit; Mlle de Vulson who requires obedience; Mlles de Graffenried and Galley, who capture him as "prisoner of war;" Mlle de Breil; Mme Basile pointing to the space at her feet, and so on. They all rehearse, in one form or another, scenes of domination by a culturally and socially superior woman, the traditional figure of courtly love.

Re-enacting the posture of the spankings permits him to act out gallant submission before a courtly dame. Rousseau's trajectory is a clever parody, one that instructs us about the ideology of the courtly dominatrix as well: for only in the act of spanking a small male child (who is not even her real son) is a woman given any power at all in this world. The ideology of courtly romance covers up the real power relations in society. For what the first six books of the *Confessions* narrate is that, empirically, sexuality itself, sexual acts are the province of men alone. More specifically acts of desire and lust are directed by men *at* Rousseau: the list of incidents is as long or longer than that of the damsels he has adored. There is the Croatian who pretends to be an Arab or Jewish convert in order to obtain support from the Church and who molests Rousseau in the chapel; there are the priests who condone the false convert's homosexuality as a much lesser evil than fornication (one mentions that he had himself once been honored by such an advance when he was young); there is the priest who attempts to seduce him in Lyons; and finally the worker who wants to masturbate in tandem with him.

What the repetition of the homosexual situation does for or to Rousseau – his protests of continued innocence after these repeated encounters notwithstanding – is less to initiate him into a homosexual world of ever-expanding dimensions, than to place him *in the position of the woman* – the one who is sought after, seduced, while all the time needing to be, to remain, "innocent." He describes it thus when he narrates his encounter with the false convert. Remembering the brutality in the look of sexual pleasure written on the man's face, Rousseau realizes how "we" (men) must look "terrible" to women in this particular encounter.

These incidents (of unknown success; we only have Rousseau's word) have readily played into the hands of those who want to read Rousseau as a paranoid-homosexual. Literally symptomatic of his "illness" or not, they none the less encode Rousseau's evident and utter inability to engage in heterosexual relations in the text as something more than an idiosyncratic or personal problem.

What is peculiar – symptomatic about us, perhaps – is that, despite their dramatic foregrounding in his narrative, little attention has been paid to the rampant homosexuality in the narrative: it is we, rather than Rousseau, who fully accept it as a norm. It is intriguing that so few readers of Rousseau have read him within the homosexual frame, even though material there would lend itself to a reading of Rousseau's pursuit of women as a "case" of hysterical homophobia. The fact that this aspect of his autobiography is generally overlooked is symptomatic of our resistance to recognition of homosexual roots in our eroticism.[68]

At another level however, we are correct *not* to read Rousseau as a "case." For he seems to me to be patently bringing forward his heterosexual failures both as effects of his own ego (the Marion episode) and also as effects of the ideological order that has equally been shaped in the mirror. Rousseau is actually working out something that is almost in the nature of a scientific treatise on the absence of relation in modern social life.

Rousseau systematically states, stages, and overstates this rampant homosexuality for a purpose: exposition of the defects in the "symbolic" order as it stands. Symbols are supposed to be relational; not only does Rousseau lack, as a naïf, the common coin that would permit sexual interlocution, he is dramatizing that only one sex has control of the means of symbolizing relation – the masculine. The sexual symbol (the phallus) is never held in common. The symbolic form in which we "know" desire and through which we enter a sexual relation is marked with a male sign: the one that was supposed to signify "lack" but which has been produced in the imagination as plenitude, fullness, and therefore, satiety, already enjoyment.

In his letters to the censor, Malesherbe, Rousseau insisted that he was never satisfied, that even if all his fantasies had become realities he would have imagined, dreamed, desired still, that he was the site of an internal void. When he discusses the imaginary "J.-J.", his imaginary self, however, in the *Dialogues*, he tells us that for him "to desire and to enjoy are for him one and the same thing." For the "desiring" Rousseau, the Rousseau of autobiographical lack, there is thus only one option: he must take the feminine position, the one which opposes (imaginary) phallic fullness.

At this point, the reader is justified in wondering how this can be a correct reading, since Rousseau is masculine, he loves women, even if he is a bit ambivalent, and he certainly has no control over the symbols (really images at this point) of desire. Moreover, the women, as I have said, are for him in the "superior" male position. Indeed the women in the *Confessions* are, in general, much more sexually sophisticated than he. But that is part of the point. The women's apparent consciousness of their explicitly sexual desires, and their obvious ability to communicate them plainly, is the very hallmark of the female characters in the *Confessions* (from Goton to Larnage). Rousseau makes it clear that he is not free to choose, but only to be chosen, by them.

Rousseau's *Confessions* permit us, in the first place, to ask an unaskable question: whether Rousseau is not, in this book, after all a "woman"? Like later Victorian heroines, Rousseau describes himself as subject to attacks of hypochondria and the vapors, in the grip of what will later become the "feminine" disease of hysteria – until he begins to have sexual relations. He certainly fits the later nineteenth-century feminine stereotype better than the masculine heroic one when it comes to his sexual "knowledge," which reads like a Lacanian catalogue of the *méconnaissances* of desire. As a *woman*, Rousseau is perfectly comprehensible: he simply suffers from an alienation of desire as acute as any female patient Freud put on the couch. Rousseau could be called "Mademoiselle."

But we must beware of assuming that a simple reversal of gender roles will explain Rousseau's trajectory. It is true that the panoply of girls, mothers, young wives, fellow servants, aristocratic ladies, etc., appear to "know" sexual eros in a way that no female characters since the eighteenth century have, and while they fuel the many myths about the feminine power to desire "before the revolution" ("lost" with the bourgeoisie), it is nevertheless important not to look at this "feminine" desire, feminine love as the simple answer: it simply perpetuates the asymmetrical, mimetically reversible model for the "subject who is presumed to know," a structure which always permits one ego to press his/her appetites on a subject who is ignorant and powerless.[69]

Rousseau's women, up to a point in the *Confessions*, that is, desire on the model of men; they have not framed or symbolized their own modalities of desire. Desire and knowledge are still not divided equally, without remainder, still not being shared by two: they are not symbolic. Instead, they are the property of one (or the One) and therefore technically *phallic* in constitution. In this light, the fact that Rousseau becomes a "woman" in the *Confessions* can be read as propaedeutic to his "becoming-a-man" if "man" is defined as "he who is a man because he loves a woman." That situation – a man desiring and loving a woman – is entirely absent from his experience: the world he meets in France is, after all, not unlike Geneva, in terms of its equal absence of sexual difference.

Interestingly, it is sexual difference that, Rousseau tells us, was the necessary soil for his fiction to grow in, and he struggled to conceive afresh the notion of a "natural" sexual difference – fictionally. Unfortunately, he could do no more than invent a simulacrum for it: that simulacrum is Saint Preux's affair with Julie.[70] At the same time he felt compelled to invent something also outside the order he experienced – love between women:[71]

> I imagined love, friendship, the two idols of my heart, in the most ravishing of forms, and took delight in adorning them with all the charms of the sex I had always adored. I imagined two women friends, rather than two of my own sex, since, although examples of such friendships are rarer they are also more beautiful.
>
> (*Confessions*, 400)

Now the most (really the only) promising opportunity he had, as a youth, for a simple sexual liaison with a girl of his approximate age and station (although he is younger and poorer than she is) is a failure – not for emotional but for clear, structural reasons. Moreover, it took root in the rivalry, not the co-operation, between two girls. It is the journey with la Merceret. He has been given the opportunity to undertake a trip with her unchaperoned (*Confessions*, Book IV). She is one of the two young girls who have had their eye on Rousseau; the other is Mlle Giraud, whom Rousseau rejects outright because she, a mere upholsteress, dared to think herself as "being of the same sex" as the aristocratic ladies she worked for. "Sex" is revealed as an imaginary social position, and social "class" is both a fantasy and a power-position which counts more than biology in the creating and alienating "desire." But though he accompanies Merceret, he is equally unable to entertain romantic thoughts regarding her.

> Such was my simplicity that although Merceret was not disagreeable to me, not only did the slightest temptation to gallantry not enter my head, but I did not so much as think of anything of the kind; and even if the idea had come to me I should have been too stupid to know how to take advantage of it. I could not imagine how a girl and a boy could ever manage to sleep together. I believed that such a frightening familiarity would require ages of preparation. If the poor Merceret expected some compensation for the money she was paying out for me, she was deceived. We arrived at Fribourg exactly as we had left Annecy.[p]
>
> (*Confessions*, 141)

The situation should promise, in Fielding-like fashion, to produce a *gauloiserie*, an uncomplicated sexual encounter, it does not for reasons that transcend the consciousness of the two parties:

> Merceret, being younger and less brazen than Mlle Giraud, never made me such lively advances. But she imitated my accent and my intonations, repeated my expressions, and paid me all the attention that I should have paid her. She always took care, since she was very timid, that we should sleep in the same room, an arrangement that rarely stops at that point in the case of a lad of twenty and a girl of twenty-five on a journey.
>
> (ibid.)[q]

There is only a semblance of otherness here: what masquerades as sexual difference is legislated by one sex, and it is the masculine one: *despite Rousseau's conscious intention, which has no male designs on the girl, it is a male libido that acts as a model* – boy meets girl, and boy ventriloquates girl. There is only an imaginary belief in an equal division between masculine and feminine sexes. Boy meets girl and he is more of a girl than she; and she is more of a "man" than he. But also, tragically, absolutely less of one than he is. It is not merely a matter of gender role confusion (she is the older and richer, the one who "knows"). This formal dissymmetry in no way precludes an ego-logic of equality, reciprocity, *return*: it is expected, pretended too.

But this exchange never takes place. The most important and effective barrier is that, while there is *distinction* (age and money), there is no *difference* between them. For Rousseau sexual difference and reciprocity are mutually exclusive. The "even" exchange prefigures, but cannot ultimately be, the only model for the symbolic. If we have no communal property, no *noa*, we have only *tabu*: Rousseau's inability to touch la Merceret. The pattern of "boy meets girl" simply does not exist; narcissism fulfilled obeys the imperative of pseudo-heterosexuality ("choose him or her") founded on an equal but unstated imperative *not* to choose the mother, the sister, the father, or the brother. The only alternative appears to be: the self. Narcissus. Of course, the ideological twist Narcissus would take is "brotherly love."

If Rousseau used the *Confessions* to make the devastating analysis of the absence of sexual difference and a relation to the other, and to lay out the homosexuality which is covered by this absence, he resorted to two different art forms to depict the missing difference. The first was his fiction. But in the theater he saw a way to locate a certain alternative.

Sophie in love: re-modeling the relation to the other

In Book IX of the *Confessions* Rousseau traces the genesis of *Julie, ou la Nouvelle Héloïse*. He had wanted, he said, to depict – and I am interpreting him as wanting to depict – a missing sexual difference, in his portrait of love between two young persons of the same age. Not surprisingly, he found that he had no models – in life or in art – for his project. Though Julie's love for Saint Preux ultimately fails it has a certain success for Rousseau's own life. He tells us his power to love Mme Sophie d'Houdetot derives directly from his fiction: "I saw my Julie in Mme d'Houdetot, and soon I saw only Mme d'Houdetot, but endowed with all the perfections with which I had just embellished the idol of my heart"[r] (*Confessions*, 410).[72] He loves in her, we might say, something less than her – reversing the murderous "tu es" of Lacan, subtracting from her the idealized object – Julie – with which he had (narcissistically) identified both himself and her. But she is still the site of a "sublimation": she is elevated in value and thus encodes a social desire. She is like Julie and unlike the courtly love *Domnei* for two reasons: she does not "resist" as her way of becoming "the moral thing;" and she speaks about – we might say, symbolizes – her desire. What I mean by this very specifically, as I have tried to explain in the introduction, is that she is meeting her lack in such a way as to confirm her own identity rather than negate it through an ever-alienated desire. This woman

knows what she wants, and in making everyone aware of her knowledge she becomes a distinctive, unforgettable woman, in sad contrast
to la Merceret, who will always be remembered as Echo to Rousseau's
Narcissus. For even though we get no direct report of Sophie's
speech, we can gather from Rousseau's description that it is not, as
la Merceret is, ruled or coded by a male Other.

Ironically, Sophie's desire is not for Rousseau (or more precisely not
only for Rousseau) but for St Lambert. What Rousseau is about to do
with Sophie is *to have her stage her desire for his benefit*. As she – who
is so different from him – occupies the subject position of the one-
who-desires – who wants, really and not just metaphorically wants.
As she desires both him and St Lambert, she becomes the relay that
permits Rousseau also to "desire" St Lambert. Or more precisely to
become his "brother."

> To finish me off, she spoke as an impassioned lover to me about
> St Lambert. Contagious power of love! As I listened, as I felt myself
> beside her, I was seized with a delicious trembling that I had never
> experienced beside any other person. As she spoke, I felt myself
> moved; I imagined that I was only sympathizing with her feelings,
> when really I was beginning to feel as she did. I swallowed the
> poisoned cup in long draughts, and at first only tasted its
> sweetness. In the end, unbeknown to us both, she inspired me
> with all the emotion for herself that she expressed for her lover.[5]
>
> (*Confessions*, 410, modified)

Is Sophie the classic woman of exchange, the one Lévi-Strauss and
Lacan discovered, the instrument and medium for solidarizing relations among men? Yes. But she is so only up to a point. For here the
truly patriarchal "Oedipal" system of exchanging women is breaking
down, and for a very brief moment here, we are getting a glimpse of
something else that might have been – before the Regime of the
Brother quickly covers over that possibility. By the time the rule of
fraternal love is established, the rapid, manic coupling and uncoupling we now experience – the collage couple – of romantic fiction
already becomes the dominant image of a "relationship."

But Sophie is not the female member of a binary, imaginary pair.
She is also, as no woman at least from the courtly love frame on
down, permitted to express her *own* desire at the same time: and it
is "odd" not even. Sophie wants both men to remain attached to her,
nuancing the relation to each differently. She is shared, that is, and
neither handed from one to the other nor "divided" between
them.[73] Rousseau tells us their love was not reciprocal: Sophie does
not "return" Rousseau's love: it is, he tells us, "non partagé" (443).
But having made this description, he reconsiders it: "But I am wrong

to say a love not shared; mine was in some way; it was *equal on both sides*, although it was *not reciprocal*"[174] (emphasis mine).

The response of Sophie is, like Julie's, generous. Rousseau is not young and loveable; she is not weak. She does not "break" with Rousseau: is it because that would cause scandal, and what would she care about that? She is not just "letting him down easy," either: she does not break with Rousseau at all. "She was glad to keep *for herself and for her lover* a friend she valued: she spoke of nothing with more pleasure than of the intimate and sweet society we would be able to form among the three of us, when I had once again become rational'"[u] (*Confessions*, 411, modified extensively; my emphasis). (Note that she is the rational one and he the over-emotional, hystericized one.)

In the theory of the "other" superego (the other of the Other) the feminine one required for there to be symbolic and not simply imaginary *fraternal eros* that I have been developing here this is one of the most significant remarks in the *Confessions*. For the relation of Sophie to Jean-Jacques and to St Lambert is an after-effect of *Julie*, and what *Julie* has produced, or even reproduced is a model for desire which allows the participation of everyone.[75] What permits this triplicity is the realization of the reduced or empty role of the mother and the father as symbolic or imaginary mediators of desire. For just as, in turn, Claire, Wolmar, Bomston, everyone – the maids, the readers – share in Julie's erotic model, Sophie's staging of her desire for St Lambert for Rousseau (and the convertibility of the grammaticality of the "for" here is indicative of the structure) permits a strong re-formulation of desire-in-common, a sort of social-homosexual eros entirely dependent upon the existence of the feminine, sexually different, desiring subject, who is one who affirms her identity by and through the nature of her desire.

Because such a desire could never be identified with any form of "will," unified or totalitarian, it displaces the "*père jouissant*" of the repressed democratic superego with a highly modified or restructured "Oedipal" programme. Julie's/Sophie's "power" lies in her ability to teach us how to desire differently than on the appetitive model of cutting someone out, splitting.[76] Rousseau achieves the depiction here of what his chimeras failed to find in patriarchal or matriarchal frames: a "democratic" social body which is openly formed by desire. Mme d'Houdetot is not a substitute mother – she does not repeat Mme de Warens. And St Lambert does not have clothes or shoes or a name to fill, a place to take – he is no Claude Anet. There is no father at all. The brothers and sisters seem to "enjoy" (or not enjoy in the satisfied sense) together.

Such is Rousseau's most positive vision of how conscience can be "born" under the Regime of the Brother – by recourse to the model of a "feminine" desire which both specifically differs from male desire *and* makes evident to consciousness the object of male libido: his brother.

What I have argued in this chapter is that this "other" Rousseau, Rousseau the lover, has alternatives to binary pairing and narcissism for modeling relation in the democratic state. But more importantly, he decodes why a "theater of love" where women reign threatens the "new" republic, founded on "fraternity": insufficiently democratic, hiding its murder of the mother (Nature) and the father (Lordship) both by "remembering" them as principles, it misrecognizes its desire and represses the sexual other ("the sister"). Rousseau offers us his portrait of Sophie as a counterpoint: as neither an "Oedipal" woman who covers her lack modestly (she frankly desires, she has her demands) nor as the woman cancelled by the Regime of the Brother, a cardboard image designed only to complement the man's narcissistic self-image. As she stages her lack, which is to say, her desire, she forms her identity on a model rather different from either of these. For Rousseau, Sophie is the "other" of the brothers. What is tragic is that she has no "daughters": her "desire" anticipates a liberation of "feminine desire" that fails to take place. Instead, we have a more predictable revenge of the sister (as in Duras's *The Lover*), and a revenge of the woman writer in *Lol V. Stein*. But even their story is not the dominant narrative of our era, our political life, and can be read only with an eye to woman's real negation by the imaginary of our time.

Nevertheless, even at its most narcissistic, its most hommo-sexuel, *staging desire* refounds group life. In a famous footnote at the end of the *Letter* Rousseau recalls a festive moment that occurred once in his Genevan childhood. An ideal artificial group, the Swiss army, returns from its exercises one evening high on itself. So exuberant are the men that they begin to dance and embrace each other with such abandon that, Rousseau tells us, the segregated women and children, arise from their sleep, and, seated in their windows as if in a theater, begin to watch the increasingly passionate men. At that moment, a division in the social body is overcome: for the women leave their bedrooms and go out into the streets to fraternize, as it were, with the men, and the children, only half-clothed, mingle freely with their loving parents. Joyful incest? The other side of authoritarian desire, the joyful fusion into oneness, predicting descriptions heard of pre-war fascist rallies?[77] It is hard to say. I would not, however, separate this "fête" from its formal relation to the repressive Republic of Geneva, i.e., it seems that only such a carnival could, momentarily, overturn established (non)relations. It is not necessarily the theater for a democratic society.

Let us continue to remember that Rousseau granted the political laws – and only the political laws – susceptibility to being revised. While politics have, as our history has amply shown, almost unlimited powers of alienation over art, exploiting it as the executive of the brother's desire, they have no fundamental powers of transformation of their own laws. That power, for Rousseau, is located neither in the king's men nor the police, but in the arts. Political laws can be rewritten – in art: even though they may be retrenched in daily life. That is the positive and liberating possibility that modernity has brought, though our experience of it has been all too resistant to this particular freedom.

Chapter 4

Feminine Eros: from the bourgeois state to the nuclear state

THE BOURGEOIS STATE: FROM ROUSSEAU TO STENDHAL

Kant's philosophy has long stood in for Rousseau's, making the latter's "feminist" side almost impossible to see. My reading of an "other" Rousseau, however, has been enabled and empowered not by a philosopher, but by a more astute psychological and political reader of Jean-Jacques than Kant: Stendhal, perhaps the best reader Rousseau ever had. His depictions of women, moreover, are almost universally approved by leading world feminists, like Simone de Beauvoir, who claimed his were the only "true" women a man had ever written.[1] Little attention has been paid to the specific social and political reforms Stendhal proposed in his De L'Amour[2] and still less to the ways in which his understanding of Rousseau inspired them: in the book he makes a plea for the education of women, recommends curtailing the excessive pampering of male children, and intends his writing to value women as they really are and not as fantasies or as purveyors of "feminine mysteries." It is, moreover, as a "lover" of Julie that he does so: but he specifies – Julie in her youth, not in her married state.

Kant defined marriage (rather abjectly Benjamin thought, as did Goethe) as an even exchange of sexual parts between husband and wife. Hegel defined it as that sexual relation where each is one with the other in the being of the consciousness of each, i.e. an ideal relation. Their conceptions seem absolutely opposed,[3] yet the arrangement between the sexes remains, for both Kant and Hegel, a variant of the perennial battle of the sexes. A war underlies both their dreams of marriage – either as a communion (exchange) or as union (substitution; two become one).

In marriage, as conceived by these two philosophers at the opening of modernity under the regime of the bourgeoisie, the man pairs with the woman as a gender opponent (Kant) so that each vies for political control; or, the man and woman reduce the pair to the *impair*, understood not as the "odd" but as the "one." In either system – Kant's or Hegel's – it is the status of the concept and place of man that determines the concept of the woman, and therefore limits the couple. What determines the couple as couple is not the relation and difference between two sexes so much as it is the degree to which one sex dominates the arrangement.[4] Although Kant appears to alternate the political power in marriage between husband and wife, assigning them separate domains to rule, Derrida demonstrates that in terms of the context – the totality or community – Kant's apparent attention to gender difference remains within an ultimately masculine form. There is no *woman*, either "in herself" or "in relation to a *man*."

We cannot fully appreciate Stendhal's "feminist" undertaking, I think, without a comprehensive look at his rejection of the marriage of Julie. To understand it we need to make a dialectical critique of this crucial novel, showing how Rousseau portrays in Julie a woman like Sophie, rational and affirmative, the subject of her own identity – and who is, at the same time, tragically, also the object of the most intense commodification. In her adolescent affair with Saint Preux she is entirely her own woman: it is not he who seduces her, but she who takes pity on his suffering. In her marriage to the elderly Wolmar (to whom she has literally been given by her father in a purely patriarchal exchange), however, she is much less than "her own woman." Her particularity and identity are completely negated in the married condition: as Mme Wolmar she becomes nothing more and nothing less than the absolute image of "domestic woman" – woman in the bourgeois state. Not surprisingly, she is ultimately – and this is critical – divested even of her traditional maternal place. For it is Wolmar who shapes her "legacy" to her "daughter" after her death. What the novel confirms is the ersatz quality of the patriarchal household under the bourgeoisie – and the increased devaluation of the woman in it, covered by a rhetoric and a myth of her infinite value. It is this heightened artificiality in the pseudo-patriarchy (the new brotherly regime) which Stendhal will exploit as a resource.

The loss of familial (especially maternal) models for love and desire mark all bourgeois institutions (from marriage to democracy) in Stendhal's texts.[5] What makes him, however, exceptional is that he harbors no sentimentality, no nostalgia for the models lost to bourgeois culture as so many romantics did. He presses us forward into facing the possibilities that the momentary absence of familial fundamental fantasies opens up, and it is these possibilities I wish to lay out here. The way takes us on a tour through *Julie*, and also through one version of love Stendhal found inspirational: courtly love. Like Stendhal, Lacan too looked to the courtly alternative, though not the institutions and history of courtly love in reality but "in anamorphosis."[6] Showing, more radically than Derrida in *Glas*, the incompatibility of marriage with sexual pleasure Lacan finds an alternative history, one in which sexual difference operated, briefly, under the sign of the feminine subject, not of the phallus. In this he followed Stendhal, but not by much, as we shall see below.

Julie and Clarens: fantasizing the *ménage à trois*

The most extensive utopian treatment of an artificial society formed after the death of the father is Rousseau's image of Clarens in *La Nouvelle Héloïse*. Julie, in the context of Clarens, is painted in very attractive terms – she is a doting mother, dutiful wife, a generous friend. Clarens seems a model of harmony and order, a patriarchal estate perfected by art and incorporating "touches" of the feminine and the mother. Many of Rousseau's readers assume it is a genuine ideal to him.[7] Yet I think Rousseau intended his depiction to be a critique of a fundamental fantasy of the Regime of the Brother: concocting a conscious and artificial re-enactment of the "best" of patriarchy while acknowledging it is only a fantasy, a pure product of imagination and will.

The estate of Clarens is self-sustaining, the very model of the patriarchal ideal, and it appears to reconcile and harmonize everything and everybody in a new "whole," a total order, with Julie at the center: Julie can have her Saint Preux (on Wolmar's terms), she can have nature within culture (her garden), she can live with her "father" as husband (Wolmar is of her father's generation), she can be a mother, mistress of the estate, its architect, designer, and decorator. Purely artificial (everyone is pseudo here), the Clarens "patriarchal" estate nevertheless is lived and liveable – life within the limits and joys of art. Clarens thus is a collective that has been specifically designed to absorb and attenuate, rather than expel, the passions and ravages of sexual difference.

And it is dreadful. It perverts everything, being all the more deceptive in its covering up the return of the *père jouissant* in the form of the non-desiring (because satisfied) figure of Julie's older husband, Wolmar (wohl – mehr?). This figure, who would have voluntarily become "un oeil vivant," commands Julie to "enjoy" Saint Preux under his surveillance (Wolmar gives his wife an ersatz *cavaliere servente* by inviting Saint Preux to come act as tutor to the children, as he once tutored their mother). He places Julie in a position of near worship. But what is really being enacted is a sexless *ménage à trois* in which the woman's own desire is denied while her husband's fantasy of her desires is brought magically "to life." (Lovers in their youth, Julie and Saint Preux are chastely and peacefully reunited under the fraternal-paternal gaze of Wolmar.)

The sign that Julie is caught in the Regime of the Brother, not the father, and that we are no longer in the traditional patriarchy is this purely "formal" fulfillment of her "desires." For Julie has already, in her famous letter on her marriage (in which she simultaneously gives up her lover for her husband, her self-awareness to God's all-seeing eye, and her name for his), "ethically" forsaken her desires. She obeys the imperatives of her father and the father-like Wolmar (like him or not, Wolmar is supposed to be in the position of ethical superiority). But if Julie must sacrifice same-generation "sexual" love to a higher duty – that of being a wife (and what could be more patriarchal, classically Oedipal?) why is she "given" the fantasy of satisfaction in return? After all, Wolmar grants her a limited but prestigious social role within the family as its radiant figural center in exchange for her identity, for silencing her real needs and desires. If she is offered the opportunity to occupy the site of "superiority" courtly romance gave the woman, it is only as a "model wife," not as a real woman. Wolmar's concessions to Julie, that is, satisfy Wolmar's and not her own desire: he acts as the Other, here, but this role, ersatz, denies in the mode of the gift.[8]

Wolmar's every move, from his permission for her to decide how to decorate each room to his invitation to Saint Preux, has to be read as exercising a total negation of her real powers, replacing them with merely figurative powers architected ultimately by himself, and at whose root is a concern to repress Julie's relation to the other – to himself, first of all (he confesses how cold he is), but more cruelly still, to her former lover, Saint Preux.

Saint Preux is genuinely opposed to Wolmar by Rousseau in terms of his positioning of Julie. In herself she exceeds all merely social "titles" to his love: she is his life, his being, and his soul. In her relation to him (a sexual relation) before her marriage to Wolmar, Saint Preux naturally uses the terms "mistress, spouse, sister, friend" (I, lv: 124) to describe her. In contrast, Julie is primarily, even exclusively, a wife and mother for Wolmar. Her value is distinctive for Saint Preux as well. Their "inconceivable night" of love-making (by her choice at her invitation) has a value that is not relative, but relational: Julie is "incomparable Julie" ("chef-d'oeuvre unique de la Nature" I, lv: 123[9]), meaning she cannot be either replaced or exchanged, that she has not exhausted her "value" even after the consummation of their mutual desire.

Why, then, does Rousseau force Julie, who had resisted the seduction of Saint Preux's words, to submit to the terms of the marriage contract? Saint Preux's Julie is literally given away to Wolmar by

Rousseau and, simultaneously, given an "ethical" aura. But it is an aura that is very deeply ironized by Rousseau. For example, she dies saving her son for his father, giving her utmost to the patronym embodied by her son. Yet that patronym is, in fact, a pseudonym: the "name" Wolmar is an alias, chosen by Julie's father for his old friend, in trouble and in need of hiding his proper name.[10] Thus her death is sacrificial, yes, but to what a tawdry version of the collective – a fantasmatic, even farcical repetition of the dream of patriarchy, figured as the utopia of Clarens – the place where desire is never admitted.

Julie dies still "worthy of being [Wolmar's] wife" (VI, xi, 708), having been a paragon of moral resistance and having passed every test of her womanly virtue. But why, then, is she sacrificed? She did everything according to code: the perfect model for the domestic woman, the true transition between the woman of the old and the woman of the new regime, she lives up to Wolmar's programme meticulously, becoming the perfect woman for the new order. But this is not "perfection" to Rousseau-the-lover. For him, Julie's death dramatizes the critical failure – once again the woman's failure to be able to live her own desire, her own identity as anything other than a male fantasy.

More significantly, Wolmar's treatment of her death dramatizes the lengths to which the modern regime will go to prevent the woman's reproduction of her own identity, her own kind of desire in her "daughter." By her marriage to Wolmar Julie lost her power and right to desire, she was imprisoned by his gaze, held forever in the household of her father's renaming, and barred from being valued for her participation in a relation. By making her an empty "prestigious" center she becomes very easy to replace, as we shall see.

Julie and the reduction of mothering

Enlightenment women who are portrayed as essentially bourgeoise have a distinctive moral code and tone: they are to be modest and retiring behind a veil of modesty (pudeur). There is a definite class distinction that is morally coded in Montesquieu's De l'esprit des lois: aristocratic women, Montesquieu tells us, are free to choose, voice, and act on their desires; bourgeois women must not.[11] When fictional bourgeois women in eighteenth-century novels attempt to be active, to affirm their own choices (like Clarissa), the patriarchy/fraternity demands the last word: Clarissa sleeps alone in her enigmatic coffin, and, defeated, returns to her "father's house." The new woman is to be limited in her field of play to two roles: wife and mother, but especially the latter.

Eighteenth-century women – mothers and daughters, mothers with daughters – do not get very far in speaking, writing, symbolizing, or experiencing their own desire, even to each other. This is true of Rousseau's Julie, whose mother fails her and whose "nurse," instructing her and her friend Claire in coquetry and the ways of the world, neglects the ways of the heart. It is the absence of this component of mothering that Julie makes one last effort to supply: she wishes to pass on to her adopted daughter what she knows of human passion. She writes a posthumous letter to Saint Preux, asking him to tell her son, Marcellin, that it cost her nothing to die for him. He is also to tell her other son that she lived (and loved to live) only for him (*VI*, xii, 730). Her contribution to the collective is bracketed by these two terms, elder and younger son. But she has already supplemented her sons with a daughter to whom she communicates directly: as she lies dying Julie asks to speak to her "daughter" *à part*. Henriette, the "daughter"[12] in question, is not her biological child, but her friend Claire's little Henriette. Julie's deathbed *entretien à part* with the girl is extensive, but its content goes unreported (*VI*, xi, 699): she neither tells us what she has said to the girl nor writes it to her beloved Saint Preux. We might wonder if the subject of her conversation with Henriette is what she can, married, no longer voice: her desire.

Her failure to reproduce her desire in her daughter is made the more poignant by Julie's effort to circumvent the causes of this absence. As a girl, Julie had once known her own heart – in her relation to Saint Preux. Having known her desire, it should have been possible for her, as it would not have been for Freud's "mother"[13] in the "'Civilized' sexual morality and modern nervous illness" to transmit it, reproduce it in her children. She does not do so, even though, apparently, she tries. But she is already countered by Wolmar: he makes it his "fatherly function" to keep a mother's passions repressed from the daughter's awareness: that is what the "father's Metaphor" is supposed to do. In true Lacanian fashion, Wolmar employs a specific substitution to perform the "foreclusion" of the desire of the mother.[14]

Henriette's real mother, Claire, we are told, mourns Julie with extreme vehemence ("passions violentes" [*VI*, xi: 726]). Wolmar feels it his duty to hide these strong feelings from the children. To do so he provides a stand-in for Julie (thereby also demonstrating that Julie can be replaced, by a daughter, who can assume all her important functions). He has Henriette, who resembles her "petite maman" (that is, her substitute mother, Julie) dress up as Julie.

Henriette is asked by Wolmar to imitate the domestic Julie. This substitutive (metaphoric) identification with an artificial mother, shows the process of overcoming the mother in its simplest form: it prevents Henriette from identifying with the strong passions of her mother (Claire), and it marks Julie as being remembered only in and through her relation to domesticity, not to her love relations: Henriette will not "identify" with the passionate adolescent Julie d'Etanges, the sexualized adolescent girl.

> Henriette, proud of representing her "little mama", played her role perfectly, so perfectly that I saw the domestics cry. All the while she gave her own mother the name of "mama", and spoke to her with the proper respect; but emboldened by success, and by my approval, which she noticed very markedly, she took it into her head to take up a spoon, and to say with a sally, "Claire, do you want some?" The gesture and the tone of voice were imitated to the point that her mother shivered at it. A moment later, she erupts with a great burst of laughter, holds out her plate saying, "Yes, my child, give; you are charming." And then, she began to eat with an avidity that surprised me.[a]

The *representation* of Julie by her adoptive daughter "cures" Claire of her excessive love for her female friend by finally destroying the other within Claire, freeing her, in some sense from Julie: she falls to eating with such "égarement" (wildness) that Wolmar orders an end to the games. But it succeeds in turning Henriette into "Daddy's" little girl ("my approval, which she noticed very markedly").

Such stagings are the only reproductive power granted to Julie, who as wife and mother was already only an extension and fantasm of the husband's household. The "father's" empty place has been filled by the brother; the "mother's" place is in the grave, and not in her daughter's desire. That desire is henceforward "licensed" only by the paternal function, shaped by metaphor, and aimed exclusively at Papa. The fundamental fantasies shrivel and fade the more they appear to be fulfilled. Despite the glorification of her marital fidelity, Julie's marriage pact is worthless from the point of view of reformulating the passions. What *Julie* permits us to see is that the key absence, the missing relation, is that of mother to daughter. As long as the mother cannot occupy the position of the-one-who-desires, her daughter cannot come into her own: she can only mother sons.

De l'amour: Stendhal on love[15]

Between Rousseau's paradoxical assertion (1752)[16] that the passions of love arise from the very laws that restrict them, and Freud's pronouncement (1908)[17] that the restriction of sexuality to the aim of legitimate reproduction is the source of modern neurosis, stands

Stendhal's favorite book on the laws that govern love – his own *De l'Amour*. It is a text that has seldom been read with rigor, and most critics take it for a lightweight text, at best a source of amusing comments on national character, wittily framed in the context of varieties of love-making. We find the stolid German housewife, now dutifully producing a baby a year, yet who was, before marriage, the most romantic of all feminine souls. There is the Swiss father giving his daughter for the night to any passing traveler; the English wife hypocritically tarrying after her husband who leaves company to retire to bed, lest they be suspected of interest in sexual intercourse. There are national stereotypes: the Spanish are portrayed as overly proud in love; and the Americans have no conception of it, as every intimate relation, including that of parent to child, is legislated by economics.[18] All these "national" forms are subsumed under the two polar types: "Italian passion" and "French vanity." In Italy one loves and hates the other with equal vigor; in France the primary passion is to maintain one's self-image before the other, real or imaginary.

It was Stendhal's genius, however, to be able to imagine love – and woman – beyond the bourgeois nation-state – outside it: for him, "one must seek the model and the true country of love under the darkling tent of the Bedouin Arab."[b] For Stendhal this love is technically utopian, literally "nowhere": for it lives only "in the camp" ("dans le camp" [200]). Though Stendhal concludes that sexual love is not a western phenomenon (it is "Bedouin" or pastoral in origin) his is a structurally political rather than a historical deduction.[19] Erotic love has remained largely extraneous to the development of sexual arrangements within the Eurocultures: at least consciously. The love we in the west experience is half-love, or love only of the self in its personal or general form: narcissism. It excludes the civil and political recognition (subjective, legal, and representational) of the other. Stendhal has read his Rousseau, and has applied him.

Stendhal first reverses the terms barbarian/civilized: whereas we associate "civilization" – religion, nobility, the city, orderliness, behavioral norms,[20] even social conventions – with the moderation of aggressiveness, Stendhal finds it actually promotes aggression. Surprisingly, for him it is the vagabond, rootless "nomad" (who appears as the symptom of disorder in our civilization) who provides him with the exemplary counter-case. In the fluidity of the portable homeland, the tent and the pitched camp, generosity and equality between the sexes flourishes; it is here that aggressiveness is transformed into eros. Stendhal writes:

For love to assume its full stature in the heart of man, it was necessary that the greatest possible equality should be established between the mistress and her lover. In our miserable West there is none of this equality; a jilted woman is either wretched or dishonored. In an Arab's tent a pledge once given can *never* be broken. Contempt and death are the immediate reward of such a crime. Generosity is so sacred among these people that they are allowed to *steal* in order to give. . . . Even in their gatherings the Arabs speak but little. (*Love*, 174)[21]

Stendhal not only values the sexual relation to the real other in *De l'amour*, he tries very hard to imagine the woman as equal partner in it. He is thus compelled to devalue to a large extent the word, marriage, and the west. Almost as if predicting Denis de Rougemont (who insisted that loveless marriage was the "cornerstone" of western civilization), Stendhal concludes that the completeness of sexual love in nomadism, rooted in equality *within* sexual difference (as distinct, say from the "equality" found in the mass of which Freud and Benjamin speak), is the direct consequence of the Bedouin "convention for divorce" (*Love*, 177). "Love" between a man and a woman is out of the question without the "greatest possible equality" for the human heart attains happiness only "by inspiring it as ardently as it feels it" (ibid., 174). *L'amour*, that is, is that unique entity that is shared as it is divided and distributed.

Stendhal's "Bedouin" example of successful love confirms his support for the Rousseauesque equation as I have determined it: that one of the democratic goals – equality – must first be rooted in sexual equality, i.e., in the accession of the feminine subject to desire. In promoting the status of the woman from non-entity to equal partner (making equality the result of recognizing sexual difference) he gives us his concrete illustration of a democratic social model.

What, then, of the political, in Rousseau's idiom, the way differences are determined? I have already hinted that what licenses sexual difference in Stendhal has to do with the sign. Explaining the direct connection between the possibility of difference as the basis for relation, Stendhal roots it in the possibilities created by the sign:

I see in their convention for divorce a touching proof of the Arabs' respect for the weaker sex. During the absence of the husband from whom she wished to separate, a wife would strike the tent and then put it up again, taking care that the opening should be on the side opposite where it was before. The simple ceremony separated husband from wife forever. (*Love*, 177)

Stendhal's "divorce" here – the foundation of the possibility of mutuality in love – assaults both the primacy of speech and of act as ways of symbolizing community: this woman is not *saying* "no," in part because, oppositional, words can always be taken "rhetorically" i.e., to mean the opposite of what they say. (Recall Stendhal's apocryphal citation from *The Red and the Black* that "Speech was given to men to hide their thoughts.") Rotating the tent is not a physical but a *symbolic* act: it signifies a desire ("from whom she *wished* to separate" [my emphasis]).

But here we need to stop at the term, "Bedouin": it, too, is only a concept, and does not refer to an actual ethnic identity. It stands for "nomadic love," a mobile site, as sole locus of sexual success. It is conceptually opposed not only to the institutions of western civilization, such as marriage, but to any "civilization" that is only a code word for "the city state" in its phantasmatic imaginary form. When "civilization" is just a cover for turning other beings into aliens, then "civilized" love is structurally equivalent to the "barbarism" Freud (and later Engels and Benjamin) discerned in it, the brutal reduction of the other to the one (the expulsion of a remainder). Stendhal undermines even the tentative "cultural contrast" of the occident to the orient by comparing his "nomadic Bedouin" to "citified" Arab love, making clear that it is the *ideology* of civilization (whose deepest roots are in the city-as-fortress model) that is at issue. "Nomadic love" opposes not only western, but *all* forms of civilization which overvalue a particular spatial form (being-there, in place – household, temple or monument, city, nation), as forms of permanence and resistance to the potential for change. (His is not a debate of time over space, but of the continual need to rewrite the law, including the law of form, in which time and space are co-dependent.) The *polis* under the new totemic substitutes a fantasy of peasant rootedness for the nomadic as its base, and asserts the reign of art and artifice by denying the mobility and motivations of the signifier. The intercourse of diversities, the cosmopolis, the fully political and not the imaginary city, is a model unwelcome in the regime of brotherly love, where the desire not to desire deflects consciousness away from the passions that ground institutions – and potentially transform them.

Modern marriage

In France all our ideas about women come from the penny catechism . . . . There must be no divorce, because marriage is a *mystery*, and what mystery? – the symbol of Christ's union with his handmaiden the Church. And what sort of a mystery would it be if the *Church* had happened to be personified in a more masculine way?

(Stendhal, *Love*)[22]

For Stendhal, every social and political institution is rooted in a psychic "passion," including the ego's passion for itself. Thus it is that his inquiry into the one institution in the west whose ostensible purpose is to represent a permanent liaison, a link or social tie between two sex-opposed beings – marriage – does not rest until it arrives there, at the narcissistic passion. Marriage hides the fact that there is "pas de rapport sexuel" behind the very image itself of sexual union.

Stendhal arrives, that is, at the unconscious of marriage. Stendhal tells a little tale of "Love in Provence" at the time of the troubadours, the story of Marguerite, in chapter 52.[23] She is the wife of a fiercely jealous husband, Raymond de Roussillon.[24] Marguerite has fallen for a troubadour, Guillaume, a poet who has earned her love by pleasing her with his love songs (and, more importantly, by reading her signs of passion, her "semblants" of love perspicaciously [De l'amour, 192]). Guillaume has been hired by Raymond de Roussillon as a concession to vanity: his great poetic reputation is to add to the prestige of the household, much as Julien's famed Latin abilities in Le rouge et le noir cause M. de Rênal to hire him.

When Raymond confirms his suspicions that his wife is Guillaume's lover, he kills the troubadour, cutting off his head and cutting out his heart. He then roasts the heart and serves it to his wife. Showing her its source – the severed head of Guillaume – Raymond cruelly asks his wife if she found it good to eat. Marguerite's response is unexpectedly concrete: the lover's organ, she tells Raymond, was so good and savory that no other food or drink would ever be able to remove the taste of Guillaume from her mouth. With that, menaced by Raymond's sword, she throws herself from a balcony.

"Legitimate" married love is thus seen as a particularly narrow assertion of the rights of *man*, in the gender and not generic sense of the term. A fundamental brutality and possessiveness on the part of the male lies at its base, making the aggressiveness of a male ego the underside of legitimate "marriage." What is striking in this story is, for me, less the love affair and the excessive rage it evokes in the husband than the legal and moral response it calls forth. For if we read this episode in a "western" legal sense, Raymond's revenge is deplorable, but . . . the crime is justifiable homicide. But in Stendhal's chronicle, the king and his vassals (the legitimate powers, highest representatives of the law) are "pained" and "saddened" at the death of Guillaume and Marguerite, whom Raymond had put to death with such "ugliness" and as a result, they wage war on Raymond for his offense. They capture and imprison him, whereupon he dies. On his death, the king returns his property to Guillaume's parents and the parents of the lady who died "for him." A monument to the dead lovers is then built in front of the church doors.

Without hesitation the entire juridical order is mobilized on behalf of the lovers, and not as ours would be toward the end of preserving the "married" state. Provençal law is not, in Stendhal's reading, out to protect at any cost a patriarchal household's sanctity, to keep its woman faithful and pure. Like Rousseau, that is, Stendhal sees how "political laws" are subject to change, and alterations in their way of "cutting" the patterns alters the ("civil") relations between self and other.

What Stendhal has thus done with his tale is to take it to court – to the courts of love. Stendhal appeals to catharism for an alternative to western marital hypocrisy. What makes these courts of love appeal to him is that they offer a system for "discipline," "education" (the essential components of any "civilization"), but without the many drawbacks – where the love relation is concerned – that result from the egocentric, narcissistic version of Oedipal civilization we have now. Thus he fully intends the tale to contrast the Provençal/catharist condemnation of the husband's brutality with our "contemporary" marital laws (no divorce), norms (decency, modesty, and domestic fidelity), and financial arrangements which favor the male's domination, his physical and mental cruelty toward the wife. The Provençal marriage contract licenses male brutality, but the *moeurs* of the day rule against it. Yet the modern marriage contract is no different, for Stendhal. Those legal reforms which might actually improve rather than degrade the condition of women and other "others" remain as yet unwritten because they and their desires have been deemed "illegitimate."[25]

So Stendhal "expels" the sexual relation to the edges of the western world, to orientalism, and to ideology to serve a strategic and not a fantasmatic function: by insisting on the fundamental absence of relation in the very heart of the only institution that is supposed to support and sustain all others by being the "bedrock" home and hearth, the domestic scene, of civilization, he opens out an analysis of the ideological-political functions of all fantasies of relation elaborated by the nation-state. To attempt domestic reform without restructuring the subject relations involved is futile. Stendhal begins by advising that women should first be educated properly, to permit them the exercise of judgment and criticism, and he also suggests they write. The woman should be free to read Shakespeare while her husband earns a living, even free to discuss the bard with him on an equal footing, when he gets home.

Still, having begun with these somewhat abject and cynical remarks about the way marriage works in everyday life, Stendhal ultimately despairs of any alternative within the context of the current class-structure of the contemporary political state. Even his "enlightened woman" remains a quasi-prisoner in a domestic jail, the wife who may rightly demand and be granted certain liberties – to read, think, discuss – but only within very narrow limits. At best, the "liberated" housewife in an "enlightened" patriarchal household has a mental, moral and emotional life which remains, he tells us, a mixture of "chance" and of "foolish pride" (*Love*, 181 ff.).

He then tells women that they should not waste their unique opportunity: as they are in charge of their son's education, they should take care not to rear their sons as little despots:

> As mothers they provide their male children, the young tyrants of the future, with the initial education which forms their characters and gives them a bent to seek happiness in one way rather than another, a matter which is always decided by the age of four or five.
>
> (*Love*, 182)

What is missing, and has to be, from the bourgeois marriage as it is originally conceived, recall, is the education of and to the heart. Julie's "instruction" of a Saint Preux (who foolishly thought he was *her* teacher) has yielded entirely to the kind of paternal instruction Wolmar gives little Henriette: the reproduction of domestic mother-hood which is designed only to raise "future tyrants." There are no longer even any Mme de Warens around who think that an *ars erotica* can be taught. But with what means, using what models can a "happiness" be taught which is not the gratification of an ego-passion?

Courtly love in anamorphosis

It is, I think, in the spirit of a Rousseau, the Rousseau of *Julie*, that Stendhal urges a cultural remembrance of courtly love: to recapture its minority position (feminist, catharist, Provençal, "arab") rather than its majority form (the emphasis on the male-knightly quest, the ideologies of languishing love). He gets "back" to catharism by deconstructing Petrarchan love. His is a critical romantic mode. The "medieval" nostalgia beginning to take root in his time and destined to provide social-corporate anti-capitalist models for romantic reaction later in the century is the target of his critique: it is a ruse of aristocracy.[26] Stendhal opposes the abuse of the ideology of medieval romance in contemporary life, the imagery of courtliness, *politesse*, *gentillesse*, to excuse the growing hegemony of a male or "phallic" empire. But the modern laws of love, despite their "romantic" gloss, are political laws, laws of state, and if they respond exclusively to a masculine imaginary and to fundamentally egotistic fantasies, they are subject to change.

"Romantic medievalism" is a political ideology, open to a certain group psychology analytic. Stendhal's La Chartreuse de Parme, for example, implicitly asks us: who, after all, in modern life plays the role of the fair lady of a romance quest? Fabrice's passion is for the Emperor Napoleon. The erotic character of Fabrice's fascination for Napoleon (he is drawn like a magnet to this leader) should be noted. Though it could be shaped politically (by his belief that Napoleon represents the democratic ideals his aunt has taught him), Stendhal makes it abundantly clear that Fabrice's love for the Emperor has been framed by the modern modishness of a degenerate romance code, "love in Milan." The opening pages of the novel recount how daily life there repeats courtly love forms – but as farce. Cavalieres serventes are routinely written into the marriage contract (shades of Wolmar!); love sonnets are de rigueur embroidered on rose-colored taffeta handkerchiefs, and so on. But the whole is brooded over by ennui, by a code too much a code (an ideology): an absence of passion.

Stendhal nevertheless imagines reviving the courtly form from the feminist-subject angle. For him, the only historical success of hetero-eroticism in Europe is in medieval romance of the minoritarian sort – catharism and Provençal love. There is no alternative model. The feminine contribution to the formation of love relations has been supplanted by heroic love – Greek, military, male, aggressive in character. Lovelace, Valmont, and Don Juan promote a positive ideology of male fraternity (the brotherhood of rakes), but nowhere (with the possible exception of Rousseau) has anyone drawn a positive portrait of a feminine model.

But is not Stendhal himself a "Don Juan"? Critics have understood him this way, and have hardly bothered to puzzle over his appending Capellanus's laws of Courtly Love to De l'amour.[27] The man who made endless lists of his lovers' initials in Henry Brulard seems himself to fit a traditional heroic male "lover" mold. And yet, in Love he has given us his analysis of the egotistic Don Juan, an analysis that finds Don Juan playing out the deadly narcissism of the modern ego. Anticipating Freud's later insights into the (il)logic of the pleasure principle, Stendhal depicts Don Juan, the arch-antagonist of sexual equality, as a figure of satiety:

> Don Juan disclaims all the obligations which link him to the rest of humanity. In the great marketplace of life he is a dishonest merchant who takes all and pays nothing. The idea of equality is

as maddening to him as water to a rabid dog; this is why pride of birthright becomes Don Juan's character so well. . . . He must be forgiven; he is so obsessed with self-love that he fails to perceive the harm he causes. . . . The dismal drama draws to a close. We see an ageing Don Juan who blames his satiety upon the world outside him, never upon himself.

(Love, 207)

While he might appear to enjoy unlimited satisfaction, he has sated only one desire: his desire for power over his sexually different equal.

In the end he himself admits the fatal truth; and from that moment his opportunities for enjoyment become restricted to the exercise of his power and the overt practice of evil for evil's sake, this is indeed the last extreme of chronic unhappiness.

(ibid., 207)

Don Juan's is a fantasy of independent self-determination. It is also a fantasy of desire fulfilled. Like the brother/son of *Totem and Taboo* who acts as the sovereign, Don Juan is given satisfaction – of his desire for fulfillment, his desire not to want, not to need, not to desire. Of course, at the deeper level, he is left entirely wanting – happiness escapes him, a happiness that exceeds the pleasure principle, the imperative to "Enjoy!" the supposed self-governance he has.

If Don Juan is the typical phallic male, the "lover" who needs woman-as-other only to reinforce his own hard, male gender identity – and his own isolation – Werther is the belated version of the courtly "lover." He seems the subject of passion; he is also curiously "feminine" in the modern negative sense: dependent, mastered by an ideology of love. Werther, who literally makes his life dependent on another, in complete contrast to Don Juan, is less at risk for his masculine identity than Don Juan, but then he, of course, is at risk for his very existence.[28] It is the recognition of a tie to the other that defeats the ever-present imperialism of narcissistic love, in which, as Freud put it, the "satisfaction of the instincts is partially or totally withdrawn from the influence of other people."[29]

Don Juan's satiety is the simple reverse of Werther's unsatisfied longing: desire for Werther triumphs completely over his will. Werther is all unreconstructed desire. The contrast is one of the most widely cited of the classifications in *De l'amour*; Barthes must have had it in mind in *The Lover's Discourse*. So it is that critics also identify him with Werther. But Werther – he actually means Saint Preux[30] – who is the modern representative of the *cavaliere servente*, unfulfilled, is still not exactly the paradigm of desire for our time that Stendhal (like Rousseau) seeks to define: a desire in which satisfaction is neither eliminated entirely (Werther) nor its only definition (Don Juan). Like Rousseau, Stendhal found its only incipient prototype in woman who is a subject rather than an object of desire. This woman is missing from the modern historical stage.[31] She can only be glimpsed through the new way a man relates to her: Stendhal looks to Saint Preux.

Werther-Saint Preux exists neither in-himself (Don Juan's ego) nor for-himself (Werther's alienation) but *only* because Julie, the new Héloïse, existed. Both Don Juan and Werther are completely "memorable" quite apart from their erotic others (the yellow waistcoat); but Saint Preux without Julie is inconceivable. What both Don Juan and Werther do not have and Saint Preux does, is an identity formed on the basis of a vivid *relation* to a real, yet different, other.

Stendhal specifically links the satisfaction of Rousseau–Saint Preux's model of an attenuated narcissistic desire – can we not call it "love"? – to the absence of the male voice: "those truly in love lose the power of speech" (*Love*, 106), Stendhal writes, and a "man who is really in love says the most delightful things, and speaks in a language unknown to him" (ibid., 105). Citing, as he so often does, Rousseau's *Confessions* for an inverted model, Stendhal catalogues moments he considers exemplary of this other definition of "satisfaction" (neither satiety nor Narcissus's embrace):

> Try as [men] might J.-J. Rousseau and the Duc de Richelieu could not have exchanged their amatory careers with each other. I am inclined to believe that the Duke never experienced moments like those of Rousseau in company with Madame d'Houdetot in the park of la Chevrette, or listening to the music of the *Scuole* in Venice, or at the feet of Madame Bazile in Turin. But neither can he have had occasion to blush for the kind of foolishness which Rousseau perpetrated with Madame de Larnage, and for which he reproached himself to the end of this days.
>
> (*Love*, 206)

To have cited the relation to Mme de Larnage as "foolishness" – the one relation Rousseau claims granted him sensual gratification – and to cite the silent, even static moments with Mme d'Houdetot and Mme Basile as examples of a lessening of narcissism in love (in Stendhal's words, "satisfied desire")[32] should strike us as somewhat odd. These are all incidents in which the relation to the other does not result in simple physical love – but they are not marked, either by Stendhal or by Rousseau, as moments of *unsatisfied longing*. They are not, that is, "courtly passion-as-suffering" that we associate with the romantic. What they show is Rousseau marking an erotic relation to the other independent of verbal expression.

Stendhal offers another example, in the person of the Duc delle Pignatelle, someone who "showed us at Munich the true way to achieve happiness through satisfied desire, even without passionate love." It is again accomplished by silencing the masculine voice:

'I realize that a woman attracts me,' he told me one evening, 'when I find myself tongue-tied in her presence and don't know what to say.' Far from making his self-love blush and cry for revenge because of this awkward moment, he cherished it as the source of his happiness.

(Love, 205)

But this condition – "really in love" – is rare indeed, and is often only an imitation. For Stendhal, Petrarchan love is an imitation of the essence of the courtly romance. The latter returns in a new ideological form – crystallization – that takes full cognizance of the ego and the imagination. As such he is able to make use of modern fictional productions as fantasies linked to desires long ago abandoned by the ego, relegated to the unconscious.

Undoing Petrarchan love

In order to redirect courtly romance away from its abject bourgeois resolution, Stendhal makes a strong effort to undermine its historical "perversion" in Petrarchism, whose conventions still flourish in his day. Petrarchan love is seen as a form of dissimulation of the phallic modality in Stendhal's eyes. The Petrarchan lover of *De l'amour*, Salviati, appears to abandon himself to a "metonymic" mode of desire. He does not seem – at first – to need have any metaphoric programme for his passion. He and his lover "understand each other at a glance" (*Love*, 98–9). Their encounter, like Petrarch's with Laura, Dante's with Beatrice, seems a matter of lucky chance, random, stray desire unorganized by the logocentric order. It seems to be the "metonymic" mode full of associative richness without the hegemony of metaphor and the copula. But, in fact, Salviati speaks constantly of love, "He never tired of sounding love's praises" (ibid., 101); what he keeps quiet is the expression of his specifically sexual desire to his beloved: we never find him speaking *to or with* her about this love that he is so eager to speak about in general: "Everything seemed to have taken on a mysterious and sacred glow; my heart pounded as I spoke to an elderly scholar" (ibid., 102) – not to Léonore. "Understanding each other at a glance" is equally ironized by Stendhal. The tale of the two souls outside the common run who "understand" each other at a glance, the story of Jenny and Mortimer, demystifies this form of "understanding" by the eye.

Jenny has left Mortimer's letters unanswered; returning from the Continent, he rides to her house unannounced to find her:

> When he arrived she was out walking in the grounds. He ran to her, his heart pounding. They met, and she gave him her hand and greeted him in some confusion; he saw that she loved him. As they strolled along the paths, Jenny's dress caught upon a prickly acacia bush. Later Mortimer gained his heart's desire, but Jenny was unfaithful to him. I maintain that she never loved him, but he says that the way she received him on his return from the Continent is proof enough of her love. Yet he cannot recall a single detail of their meeting. He is, however, visibly shaken by the sight of an acacia, and this is really the only distinct memory he has preserved of the happiest moment of his life.
>
> (*Love*, 104–5)

That the acacia which catches the dress, a tear in what clothes her, is the "only distinct memory he has preserved of the happiest moment of his life" is a symptom, not a sign of love. Seeing the lover, like *entendement* (hearing) through the ear, is egomimetic, echolalic. We speculate on the other's love for us, imputing to the other our own narcissism in reverse (I love myself, therefore s/he must love me also). This is a willed ignorance of the reality of our own (and therefore the other's) secondary desire – to do away with each other. "Love" such as this, mirrored in the eye of the other, is just as reversible as Schreber's euphemistic vocabulary:[33] Salviati, in fact, like Schreber, tries to make words say their opposites: "The very harshness of the beloved is infinite grace" (*Love*, 102).

The appearance that the Petrarchan lover operates in the metonymic mode is thus swiftly ironized by Stendhal: the "chance" that draws Salviati to his beloved is one which implies a significance, a destiny, a fate, and a design. Salviati believes himself guided by no specific aim when he happens to be led past the window of his beloved; but he also knows it is not quite by chance:

> I strode through the streets under a cold rain; chance, if you can call it chance, led me past her windows. Night was falling, and as I walked by, my tear-filled eyes fixed upon the window of her room. Suddenly the curtain lifted for a moment, as if for a glimpse of the square outside, and then it quickly fell back into place. I felt a spasm at my heart. I could no longer hold myself up, and took refuge in a neighbouring portico. My feelings were running riot; it might of course have been a chance movement of the curtain; but suppose it had been her hand that lifted it!
>
> (*Love*, 99)

As a "sign" the window is unreadable: it tells of no particular relation between Salviati and his lover. But it carries portents, omens, significance, and as such, it functions as the phallic signifier does, promising and never fulfilling a meaning. Moreover, the elements loosely associated with the beloved are rapidly fetishized and they displace the beloved altogether: relayed from one (empty) center (the beloved) to another (substitutes for her), all of Salviati's affection, his passion is poured into the substitute: "If anyone mentioned the city gate near the house where Léonore's friend lives, I blushed scarlet" (ibid., 102). Here again, the "madness" of love is a perversion in the consumption rather than production of imaginary attachments: after the other's subjectivity is lost to the first objectification, object after object can stand in for her and definitively defer the male subject's having to arrive at his destination – the aim. A true "brother" then, his poetic and erotic associations permit him not to desire.

For Stendhal Salviati's verbal love is noble, knightly: an archetypal unsatisfied lover, Salviati exclaims that, "It is only since I fell in love that I learned how to be noble" (*Love*, 101). Léonore and Salviati are said to be "two souls outside the common run" (ibid., 100), superior. A purely imaginary *noblesse* in the post-revolutionary setting of Stendhal's writing, the "heroic" side of aristocratic love (the right to the woman of lower station) is absent, or strangely effeminate – Salviati is a "wimp," an imitation "Petrarchan" male lover who is equivocally "male." But he is not nice either: neither gentle nor generous. His "nobility" reveals that his rather vapid love to which he sacrifices himself so publicly has an essentially military and aggressive character: Salviati reports that "although I behaved myself, I was a mere child at Napoleon's court, and in Moscow. I did my duty, but I was unaware of the heroic simplicity which comes from entire and whole hearted self-sacrifice" (ibid., 101). Salviati's "suicidal" passion follows the masochistic-sadistic pattern delineated by Freud.

Stendhal's rapid dispatch of the Petrarchan lover claims our attention. Petrarch hovers over other Stendhalian texts as a foil for the alternative mode of romance; in *La chartreuse de Parme*, for example, in the first meeting of Fabrice and Clélia. She is twelve; although this age distorts the chronology of the text it seems to have been done purposely to enforce a comparison with Beatrice and Dante or Laura and Petrarch. But so different! For we have the incident from her point of view, too: it is the girl of twelve who reads the passions of her elders and Fabrice. Additionally, Fabrice later communicates from his prison tower with Clélia by writing his messages in his book of Petrarch's sonnets. (But, *in the margins*.) The courtly paradigm means something else to him. Lacan can help us here.

From Ford Madox Ford to feminism,[34] we find the claim that the poetry of the troubadours, one of the expressions of the courtly love tradition, is little more than an ideology destructive to the woman which places her on high so that her empirical subjection to man goes unperceived. Lacan, too, notes in *Séminaire VII* that the figure of the *Domna* ("she who, occasionally, dominates,"[c] 188) has to be read alongside the "deeply narcissistic character"[d] extant in the *ideology* of "l'amour courtois" (*Sém. VII*, 181). It also has to be read alongside the "true story" of women like the Countess of Comminges, daughter of Guillaume de Montpellier, who was repudiated and mistreated by two husbands and subjected to the "the wills of the most powerful lord"[e] (ibid., 176).

But Lacan, like Stendhal and Rousseau before him, is intrigued less by the ideological inversion of the courtly paradigm, than by what he calls its "anamorphosis," which entails a function of the mirror that differs from the ideal projection of the subject, and which, as he puts it, "fills another role – that of a limit"[f] (*Sém. VII*, 181). The inaccessible "dame" is she who functions as the mirror-border which cannot be crossed: the inaccessible object. The object is also separated from the languishing, jealous, and ill-speaking lover. It is also misapprehended, hidden from sight, never "given" except through an intermediary. The structural intervention of mediation is such that *la dame*, Lacan tells us, becomes the *bon vezi* or "good neighbor" in the poems of Guillaume de Poitiers. As such, the object becomes, *à la* Freud on Christianity, the apotheosis of the "thing."

Courtly love, in this mode, is the "ethical modality" of the obstacle, the deferral of desire. The erotic form at the root of deferred pleasure is actually a "pre-Oedipal" sort: foreplay or pre-genital pleasure. The pleasure of desiring becomes a pleasure in unpleasure, deferral. Yet it subsists or persists in the act of courtly love, it does not merely precede it. The union of the *merci* is preceded by the "services": drink, speech, touch, and *le baiser* ("l'osculum"): for Lacan the erotic discipline of the "highest degrees of catharist initiation"[g] (*Sém VII*, 182) is enigmatic to the point of having its analogue only, he tells us, in Tibetan Hinduism, an ascetic discipline of pleasure.

Thus, although the courtly poetry had a hand in the idealization of the woman as "feminine object," Lacan (very much like Stendhal) is intrigued and somewhat stunned by the paradox of how erotic, physical pleasures generate the morality of *das Ding*. Just as Stendhal's *De l'amour* takes its source in Ovid's *Art of Love*, so too, Lacan finds that the most ascetic texts used in courtly love borrow their substance from the same book: the treatise for libertines. Ovid's formulae, sprinkled throughout the text, inspired the later troubadours, among them *arte regendus amor* (love ought to be ruled by art) as well as *militae species amor est*: love is a kind of military service. Thus does Ovid's little book return from the grave.[35]

What counts in the "discipline" of erotic pleasure, for Lacan, is that the woman sets out under the courtly Symbolic to occupy both the *position of the Other and that of the object* (193; "Critique de Bernfeld"): she is the site of Desire, she sets its agenda (in Freud's terms, "aim") and is its instrument (the "object" for Freud). What happens, however, in what Lacan calls the alternative rule of "des signifiants raffinés" (193) (refined or civilized – phallic? – signifiers) is that the Lady is "idealized"[36] and thus

> suddenly, brutally, in the place cleverly constructed by refined signifiers, finds herself displaced in all its rudeness by the vacuity of a thing, affirming itself in its nakedness to be *the* thing, *her* thing, the one found deep within her bosom in her cruelest emptiness. . . . this Thing is unveiled with an insistent and cruel power.[h] (193)

From subject of the Symbolic to becoming the "truth" of castration is a short but decisive step, and a real step down, for the Lady. She has been "forgotten" in the cruelest mode of "remembrance": in the ocular mode of the fascinated male gaze, she is reduced to being the head of the Medusa; from being the educator of the heart in relation to the body, she becomes the bearer of the bad news about castration, sublimated as the glad news about the power and strength of the phallus. . . . The woman in the bourgeois novel is thus prefigured.

The novel became, from the point of view of the woman, the locus of the failed encounter with the other. Just as it seemed about to open the way to her becoming the "subject" of desire it immured her in the bourgeois household. When we reach our own nuclear age, the patriarchal household no longer needs literally to confine the woman: in its fraternal variant, it has expanded to the proportions of the city, the state – it passes, especially under colonialism – for being civilization itself. As we move into this nuclear age, father-free, we live within the ideology of brotherhood without having realized it as a structural and political set of institutions and laws. It produces a new perversion: "lovers" entirely destructive in their function. The neo-romantic couple we find everywhere in modern literature and film is one that is programmed and orchestrated by the desire of the brother.

THE NUCLEAR STATE: FROM STENDHAL TO DURAS

"It was within the city walls that I became his woman/wife."[i]

(*Hir.*, 88, modified translation)[37]

"Nevers, where I was born in my memory is indistinct from myself. It's a city a child can walk around."[j]

(*Hir.*, 89)

Marguerite Duras is Stendhal's woman. Is not "Lola Valérie Stein" a play on the interlingual stone valley that Stendhal took for his authorial name? and who else has been her peer in writing about women who love? Stendhal, after all, was the only man ever to have written women who were "vraies" – true.[38] In making this connection I have, however, more in mind than the fact that both Duras and Stendhal can accurately depict "women in love." They also see clearly where and how the "woman" and her "love" have been programmed by the real conditions of their existence – most specifically in the case of Duras, by war. But the degrees of recognition of these conditions are infinitely varied and they range from the most unconscious to the most perspicacious in both authors.

It would be legitimate to compare the two if only on the grounds that, in order for them to *write woman*, both Duras and Stendhal apparently found it necessary to situate that woman very materially, in space, in a particular domestic and class arrangement, and in a definite political – and technological – context. (Myths of feminine "nature" or the categorization of woman by her biological role – mother/daughter, for example – are almost entirely absent from their texts, which none the less show where the mythic "woman" unconsciously shapes certain collective forms – destructively.) Whether it is the domestic home and hearth, the nomad's tent, or ground zero at Hiroshima, space is a political battleground that specifies the arrangement between the sexes.

In philosophies of romanticism, implicated in the elaboration of the national state, there is no paradigm for feminine eros that is not deadly – the uterine enclosure precedes and postdates "life." The social role of the domestic woman, apparent both in Kantian criticism and Hegelian romanticism, is reduced to this: she awaits the death of a man. She gives her son, her husband, her brother up to the state. But the whole needs to be framed by a larger issue: "why war?" Why is the male essentially defined by his readiness to go off to war? Why do women stay home, in a uterine space that is also the measure of death? Perhaps the nation-state can only make such radical claims to both male and female bodies in the name of its need to make war, even in times of peace.[39]

For Freud, in "Group psychology," "lovers" participate in "group feeling" rather than resist it, and thus sustain the violent side of the bourgeois order: nationalism, narcissism, aggression. The bourgeois state (or the city, or civilization) freely supports the relation usually called "love" – while it excludes sexual difference.[40] Why do lovers work for the state rather than against it? Writers like Stendhal and Duras provide unusual answers: but only if read as *not* continuing the post-Rousseauesque romantic tradition of star-crossed lovers who battle society.[41] This is a false lead, since theirs is a specific and fundamental critique of the way ideals of love work to strengthen the aggressive state, while damaging absolutely the relation to the other. Duras, who plays with a fuller deck than either Freud or Stendhal because of the historical event known as "Hiroshima," is able to provide the most complete revision of an alternative to brotherly "love" for modeling the relation to the other. Her state is, technically, no longer simply bourgeois, it is a nuclear one.

We find ourselves, indeed, confronted in Duras's *Hiroshima, mon amour*[42] both with an unprecedented situation and a story as old as can be. On the one hand, there is a post-romantic, post-nuclear couple so apparently "free" from old Oedipal and patriarchal restrictions and obligations that they need mount no rebellions – husbands and wives, children and former lovers, the state and the law present no obstacles to their "love": Riva, a married French movie star, meets an also-married Japanese engineer while acting in a film at Hiroshima, and they spend a voluptuous, strictly casual, night together at a hotel. The "art" depicted here seems to be "new," too: "serious," moral, the film they are marketing is for peace. Fraternity has blossomed here, in Hiroshima, to become the general form of human love: Riva works on behalf of brotherly love as she acts her part in the protest film. There is a freedom, too, in a new emotional casualness: love affairs are no longer tragic, but ridiculously easy to fall into and out of – Riva is "predisposed to chance encounters."

But there are signs, from the beginning, of something amiss: Riva's occasionally tortured face; the ambiguity of their bodies (in parts?) as the film opens, the strange marking of racial stereotyping between the two ("Are you completely Japanese, or aren't you completely Japanese?" (*Hir.*, 25)). And there is Riva's complaint: that the bourgeois romance has assigned them mundane roles: she calls her affair in Hiroshima "une histoire de quatre sous," a dime novel, a trite "love story." As usual in melodrama and soap opera, the lovers signify nothing to each other, but act as substitutes for same-generation "others" whose relation to them they conveniently forget, sublimate for the occasion (he takes her German lover's place, she occupies his wife's bed, etc.).

It is telling, in this respect, that Duras depicts her Riva as a narcissist – her real *alter ego* is a cat ("the stare of the cat-Riva" [*Hir.*, 98]) – placing her as one who "enjoys" in the modern condition. Yet she is not, evidently, a brother. She is supposed to be the "new woman," after all. But if we specify the conditions of her "enjoyment" – her pleasure – we find that hers is a sadistic pleasure, from start to finish. She enjoys her sexual encounter with a Japanese man by conjuring up images of the victims of the atomic bomb, while claiming that she has personally witnessed their mutilation and destruction. And she drinks her German lover's blood. But Riva is only one side of the woman in her relation to war, to the dead hero . . .

Love and the bomb

Duras's *Hiroshima, mon amour* is exceedingly harsh on the question of the destructive programme of what we now call "love." In this text she openly codes what passes for an erotic relation as violent aggression. When the heroine of *Hiroshima, mon amour* takes an enemy (a German soldier) for a lover (or does he take her? There is violence in their initial encounter – she says, "someone seized me by the shoulders, it was the enemy" [*Hir.*, 106]), she mentions that "his hands quickly gave me the desire to punish them . . . . I bite his hands after lovemaking"[k] – even though it is she who has bound up his wounded hands in her father's pharmacy. Her illicit "love" for the enemy, which seems romantically to violate the state's political position of declared war against the Germans, is clearly being structured by the hostilities.

Yet we do not see this aspect of *Hiroshima, mon amour*, at least not at first. We begin to read the text with rather post-romantic feelings, already half-sympathetic in a sentimental mode to the poor French girl whose love for the enemy soldier is thwarted by arbitrary national differences, who suffers, as Duras puts it, "the ultimate of horror and stupidity": having her head shaved for being a collaborator. She was merely in love with an anonymous boy who was killed and whose dying body she tried to merge with, "I was not able to find the least difference between this body and mine . . . . I could not find between this body and mine any but shrieking resemblances, you understand, he was my first love"[l] (*Hir.*, 106).

But, beware. A closer look reveals that we are dealing less with a romantic commonplace (star-crossed lovers opposed to and by society) than its uncommonly critical treatment, allied with the Freudian and Stendhalian critiques.

Feminine eros (as "death") becomes radically clear in the nuclear state, where mutual destruction is assured across national boundaries. In the nuclear state, soldiers die not on the battlefield but in the home, and so do their mothers, sisters, daughters and wives. Riva's Japanese lover explains his personal survival of the nuclear holocaust: "My family, it was in Hiroshima. I was off fighting the war'"ᵐ (*Hir.*, 28, modified translation). Let us take an initial look at *Hiroshima* as we trace the path of feminine eros from the national to the nuclear state.

In *Hiroshima, mon amour* the heroine seems to be a "new woman." She boasts numerous extramarital liaisons; her politics and her art are unified, committed: she is acting in a film which stages a demonstration against the bomb. Apparently free from old, moralistic forms, seemingly devoid of racial prejudice, she claims to be unbound by domestic fidelity, transcending narrow nationalist views. She works for peace. Liberated, educated, artistic, anti-ethnocentric, the nameless woman whom Duras begins to call by the name of the actress who plays her, Emmanuelle Riva, engages onscreen in the most glamorous forms of cosmopolitan work and sexual tourism.

Riva appears consummately unconstrained by traditional women's roles, leaving the borders of her native France, the limits of her hometown of Nevers, as she left her cellar at the end of the Second World War. That cellar, part madhouse, part jail, part grave (her parents tell everyone she is dead while her hair grows back) – housed her during her melancholy madness after the death of her young lover.

She seems, moreover, to be "ethical" in a larger sense: she compulsively recalls the fact of Hiroshima, the Hiroshima we otherwise repress, even while she is enjoying herself. That she remembers Hiroshima especially while making love to a Japanese man who is not her husband is an odd note, like her shaved head, as extreme a sign or advertisement of her moral position as can be imagined: she marks and remarks her guilt. Sexually amoral (she is, she tells the Japanese, "predisposed to chance encounters") and perfectly, Oedipally guilty at the same time – what more could we ask of the new woman? A lot, is Duras's answer.

Why does Duras demand that we question Riva's allure so harshly? Or rather, why does Duras have *Hiroshima* pose this question? A close analysis of the text, its *avant-propos*, the *appendices*, Duras' *directions*, reveals that what is at stake for Duras in this work is precisely a chance for the new woman, offered by the bomb: she can break the link between the older version of love, narcissism, the domestic woman, and war-death: "Une chance, quoi? – Oui. – Pour moi aussi" (*Hir.*, 37). Riva does not take it. For Riva clings, tenaciously, almost frantically, to territoriality, domesticity, and narcissistic aggression, even though the event Hiroshima has given her a choice to really leave "Nevers."

For Duras, Hiroshima has a specific meaning for the woman – and I do not mean the Mom-and-the-Bomb of the *Enola Gay* (the plane that dropped the bomb was named for the pilot's mother). Hiroshima does something to "the woman." It frees her to tell the story of her lost love: it is the news of Hiroshima that permits Riva to leave her madhouse cellar and go into the streets. It does not change the terms of that love, but it relieves her secret, brings it up. Before Hiroshima, the first, the only lover "Riva" could have was a soldier – a dead soldier, an enemy. This is the form of the couple framed by conventional war, the wars of the nation-state: absent, dead, enemy male, female allied with, married to his death and loss: "I see my life. Your death" (*Hir.*, 63) and "You might say she's helping him die,"° as she covers the dying German soldier with her body (*Hir.*, 87, modified translation).

Conventional war empowers the real man to enter the sexual relation only as a memory, as one who is *lost*. It is not her German soldier lover that is Riva's secret. What has been kept secret is the tragic form of the love relation for the woman in the context of the war-drive inherent in the nation-state. Within the nation, the woman is asked to play on only one stage, in one scene, the domestic: it is there she prepares her men to go off to war in defense of the state, and to return – whether dead or alive matters little. Her womb is, from the point of view of the state, merely a pre-figuration of the tomb.

Duras leaves no doubt that this form excludes all other possibilities even outside the war zone, that it hovers over men and women even in times of so-called peace: until Hiroshima.

Hiroshima means men do not have to go off to war any more. Or even, we might add, off to work. There need be no distinction between soldier and civilian, French and Japanese, man and woman: "My family, it was in Hiroshima. I was off fighting the war" (*Hir.*, 28, modified translation). (Interestingly, this makes the war in Vietnam technically a "nuclear" war in so far as its effects were not confined to the war theater but spread to the streets of our cities: one should recall the slogan, "Let's bring the war back home.") This was perhaps the unconscious and necessary response to our understanding that war is no longer able to be strictly limited to a circumscribed region under nuclear and other technologies. What once allowed the traditional soldier to return from war (either alive or as a dead hero), triumphant and guilt-free, was a home, hearth, and culture untouched by the death he had suffered (himself or in others) – his assurance that the domestic sphere is just that – a closed sphere. Hiroshima (but also the two world wars already) reveals that the fragmentation and/or mutation of the home and the "I" (the wife) who is "at home," is not only imminent, but certain. The entire structure of the family and its domestic arrangements would under these conditions have to be revised, since it is no longer the woman alone who passively awaits the death of others.

What becomes of investments in domestic bonds in the atomic world, when the state is Hiroshima? What is the property value of a home built on ground zero? Without an uncontaminated "home" (or funeral monument) to return to, the soldier who is about to kill and be killed would have to encounter death as an incalculable chance and as an absolute fate; and, as in Vietnam, so would the civilian. The domestic arrangement, especially the arrangement between the sexes, is open to revision; the nuclear situation is a critical turning point for consciousness of this need; but the conditions of that revision were already created out of the world wars: Duras's *La Douleur* demonstrates it in the Second World War, but Freud shows it to us as extant in the First World War.

The War: A Memoir

Duras regards the "emotional life" of the woman as basically formed around and by three elements – space, domestic arrangements, and class. Take, for example, the opening pages of *La douleur* (in English *The War: A Memoir*)[43] in which Duras places the domestic woman between a telephone and a grave. The narrator, Madame L., is awaiting a phone call, hoping for news of her husband as the Second World War draws to a close. He had been deported to Germany by Vichy France for his political activities and is interned in Buchenwald. She sits in front of a fireplace, waiting for the phone to ring, or for her husband to walk through the front door – like any husband coming in at the end of a working day – and say "I'm home." A domestic woman, a "wife," her capacity to imagine him as alive is specified by her material situation, her sitting at home.

But she also imagines him as already dead, lying in a ditch with his mouth half open. The telephone will never ring, but he will have made his last call – his mouth is open, she thinks, not because he had cried out in pain or in need, but because he had called her name. "Just before he died he must have spoken my name" (*War*, 7) . . . "He died speaking my name" (*War*, 8). As the narrator puts words in the imaginary dead man's mouth, Duras reveals – harshly – the structural egocentricity, melodramatically romanticized, which is built into domestic love: woman at home, man facing dangers in the outside world exclusively for *her*. And she lives and relives this imagined moment of her husband's "death."

The narrator goes on to "boil potatoes" in the "kitchen" for the man, D, who has already taken her husband's place in the home. But now she suddenly imagines that she has already been a widow for a fortnight, that the romantic "moment" of death has come and gone, and is already a condition, not a one-shot scene. Her place at the table suddenly sickens her, and she feels she must vomit up her own cooking. "The bread is bread he hasn't eaten, the bread for lack of which he died. I want D. to go. I need room again to suffer. The apartment creaks under my step" (*War*, 10). The domestic stage is creaking, cracking. Death as a condition, not a moment, changes things for her.

And so the scene shifts. The narrator describes her work outside the home and hearth: at the Gare d'Orsay deportees – not French soldiers, but deportees, liberated concentration camp internees – are being repatriated. She works in an undefined space doing tasks without a job description, keeping her eye on the goal – to do what the phone cannot – get the word through to their families that they are alive. But she is also really trying to redefine them as husbands, sons, and lovers, not as prisoners, detainees – something which the officious Gaullists and former Resistance members who "take charge, who make them wait in long lines and insist they salute" them because of their uniforms never attempt. No fire, no phone, no table – the officials take her table away.

The romantic housewife whose heroic husband dies with her name on his lips is a mystification, appropriate perhaps to nineteenth-century war – but it is not the reality of the woman left at home during *this* war. The husband did not go "off" to war – he was taken; and he will not come back either alive or as dead hero – he comes back literally a living skeleton. Something new has taken place on the world stage, and the domestic arrangement is forever altered.

Freud: "Thoughts on war and death"

Freud maintained in "Thoughts on war and death" that we show an unmistakable tendency to "put death on one side," to see it as opposed to life; and yet, the opposition itself devalues living:

> Life is impoverished, it loses in interest, when the highest stake in the game of living, life itself, may not be risked. It becomes as shallow and empty as, let us say, an American flirtation, in which it is understood from the first that nothing is to happen, as contrasted with a Continental love-affair in which both partners must constantly bear its serious consequences in mind. . . . Thus the tendency to exclude death from our calculations in life brings in its train many other renunciations and exclusions.
>
> (*SE XIV*, 289)

The risk of real death ought to renew eros through guilt:

> The first and most important prohibition made by the awakening conscience was: "Thou shalt not kill." It was acquired in relation to dead people who were loved, and as a reaction against the satisfaction of the hatred hidden behind the grief for them; and it was gradually extended to strangers who were not loved, and finally even to enemies.
>
> (ibid., 295)

At this point, for Freud eros combats death not by denying it but by accepting its existence. It does not so much exorcise or forbid hatred as struggle actively against an equally powerful desire to kill the alien other. Venus and Mars are traditionally twinned not because (as in romantic tradition in general) love leads to death, but because love is summoned up at the point where death is recognized as real *for oneself as well as for others*. Freud writes that the "final extension of the commandment [of 'Thou shalt not kill' to strangers and enemies] is no longer experienced by civilized man." In *The War: a Memoir*, Madame L. fights indomitably to bring Robert L. back to life ("The struggle with death began") and she does so for reasons devoid of sentimental love (she is planning to divorce him). But she has decided for life over death, making her struggle a far more real love than its romantic framing could ever express or be. (Interestingly, Robert L, left to die by the American soldiers who see how ill he is, escapes their well-meaning but inept hands through the help of friends, one of whom is D., his wife's lover. They rename him "D. Masse" to smuggle him back to Paris. This name is surely an allegory of the fate that *die Masse* – the masses, "the people," *le peuple* – has suffered at the hands of the Germans with their myth of *das Volk*, and at the hands of the Americans, who cannot fit the collective together with the individual in their ethos, and who stand by, helpless, as the form nearly disappears.)

War, then, should restore a sense of the value of life – life and eros when it is defined as whatever opposes death, and this should be even more so in the case of nuclear, total war. Freud found unbelievable our capacity to delude ourselves about the imminence of our own death under the conditions of the Great War: it is, he writes, "evident that war is bound to sweep away [the] conventional treatment of death. Death will no longer be denied; we are forced to believe in it," since in this war,

> People really die; and no longer one by one, but many, often tens of thousands, in a single day. And death is no longer a chance event. To be sure, it still seems a matter of chance whether a bullet

hits this man or that; but a second bullet may well hit the survivor; and the accumulation of deaths put an end to the impression of chance. Life has, indeed, become interesting again; it has recovered its full content.

(SE XIV, 291)

The bomb should also make this painfully clear: its victims will not be "symbolic" others; they will be *us*. Survival is no longer even promised. The denials and exclusions which have supported our ego/other arrangements along strictly oppositional lines must be restructured; there is no way to distribute atomic death and post-nuclear life along socially organized lines of choice.[44] If in the nuclear world, everyone dies at home then domestic love reaches its culmination as both source and telos of death. Is another erotic model possible?

But just as Freud found with the general expansion of death's domain in the Great War, *Hiroshima*'s Riva, in the face of the bomb, identifies her love with the nuclear bomb's effects. She prefers her old role as ally of destruction to the absolute reality of death – and of sexual equality – made crystal clear by the bomb. Riva's waiting, her purely passive form of reception, confirms her passive catharsis in relation to the image of war, even so powerful an image as the bomb, that keeps its death at a distance: in the opening scene she is making love, evidently maintaining her excitement by holding in her mind graphic images of the Hiroshima horror. Her lower belly melts and contracts as she thinks of burnt flesh, eye extraction, genetic deformations.

By placing the bomb at the beginning, then, Duras has revealed the secret of traditional heterosexual love as already a fusion and fission device; the language of the script – which flows from this insight – is in advance a critique of it. When the Japanese lover wants to be set on fire by their love, consumed by it, when Riva exclaims that he destroys her, the call is for an exquisite death of the subject, melting into the other, becoming one: "You destroy me, you are so good for me. Take me. . . . Deform me to your likeness so that no one, after you, can understand the reason for so much desire"[p] (*Hir.*, 35). That this love is never mutual but always one-sided is made clear by such a statement, which could never be simultaneously uttered by both lovers: only "I" – a single I – can ever be "in love."[45]

The form of pre-nuclear love – alienated desire in the later Lacanian sense – is preserved. Riva reduces her German lover's body to her own: "I could not find the least difference between his body and mine."[q] The great ruse of the ego is pre-nuclear "love," which masks the self's victory over the other as a dream of unity, union –

and thus, oneness. Riva's melancholia in Nevers is a sign of her jubilant triumph at having survived/outlived her German lover – like any soldier's wife. The telos of pre-nuclear love is to incorporate the other, eat it: "I liked blood ever since I tasted yours" (*Hir.*, 55); "your body had become mine"[r] (*Hir.*, 106).

The rhetoric of love–death is just that: mere rhetoric, whose sole aim is to preserve the "I" from accepting the reality of death. Riva's seemingly conscientious "remembrance" of Hiroshima is really then only aesthetic: she is a spectator, safe on the sidelines, enjoying the show: "J'ai tout vu" she insists. She does not, that is, identify herself in the reality of the death the bomb delivers: for the "I" in love, ultimately only the *other* will die: "Je vois ma vie. Ta mort" (*Hir.*, 98). She has not read Hiroshima's lesson. Riva does not face her own death, nor does the Japanese face his: "Tu n'as rien vu" ["You saw nothing"] is their reciprocal litany as the film opens with their two partial bodies covered with carnal sweat or nuclear rain. And she clearly redomesticates her sexuality: instead of the tourist hotel room she moves in to the Japanese lover's established home, his wife being away. And it is here that they pronounce their "love" for each other. Let us turn from the home, the domestic, to the city.

The city of love

Hiroshima's love litany is also crossed with another repetition besides that of seeing the bomb's aftermath: that of *place names*: "Hi-ro-shi-ma," "Ne-vers." Pre-nuclear love has, it seems, a certain city center. Riva tells us of her German lover, "C'est dans les murs de la ville que je suis devenue sa femme" (*Hir.*, 127).[46] At the height of lovemaking, Riva cries that Hiroshima is a city "made to the measure of love"[s] just as the body of the Japanese man is also "exactly to her measure" (*Hir.*, 35). She makes Hiroshima the same as Nevers, the city ("indistinct de moi-même" (*Hir.*, 128)) which as a child she could walk entirely around, Nevers, where she undergoes adolescence: "A l'âge d'une jeune fille" – the age she takes her German lover – Nevers became a closed circle: "At that time Nevers was a circle that closed on itself. It grew as one grew"[t] (*Hir.*, 89, modified translation). Yet it is precisely at that point Riva tells us love cannot take place, can never have taken place within the city walls: "C'est dans les murs de la ville que je suis devenue sa femme," but it was not a happy marriage: in Nevers, felicity in love is "impardonnable." "Happiness is the crime in Nevers. Boredom is a tolerated virtue there. Madmen, vagabonds, dogs, love circulate in the suburbs"[u] (*Hir.*, 90, modified translation).

Riva is telling us that her love affair with the German, within the city walls is neither free, nor happy, nor ultimately love at all. The bomb, which makes city walls entirely outmoded, should change this set of equations: closed circle, expulsion of the relation to the other. Riva should be able to love in a post-nuclear mode. Instead she chooses repetition of the form: when, at the end, she is considering remaining in Hiroshima, a reconstructed city, "I will stay in Hiroshima"; He: "Stay in Hiroshima,"[v] Duras explicitly frames this exchange by telling us "their absence from each other has begun"[w] (*Hir.*, 75).

The *polis* should be a cosmopolis – a place where peoples meet. Riva misses her chance: in *The War* Madame L. says: "It had suddenly struck me that there might be a future, that a foreign land was going to emerge out of this chaos where no one would have to wait anymore" (*War*, 48). Riva almost says (this did not appear in the film, it was not spoken): "I want no longer to have a country. To my children I will teach wickedness and indifference and love unto death for the country of others."[x][47] Instead she replaces, renames, and rebuilds the city, the pre-atomic city, centered around an empty but intact nucleus, modeled on the ego, the I alone. Duras writes of the film's end: "They will call each other still. What. Nevers. Hiroshima. They are not in fact yet anyone in their respective eyes. They have place names, names which are not."[y]

Riva appears to choose otherness, but she has instead only chosen "elsewhere" as an alibi in the etymological sense, an alibi for *not* thinking love nomadically (in Stendhal's sense), post-domestically, and without the violent negation of the other. For if, in the nation-state, the ultimate *telos* of being a wife is to be a widow; of being a son's mother is to outlive him, to lose one's men to the polis, sacrificing each to the ethical good of the state, the bomb throws the definition of the state as a territory into question, and, along with it, the place of the woman.

For what has a "state" ever really been? No more than a dream of being-there, spatially located, in a territory created by borderlines around a necessarily empty center. It is only a place name ("Hi-ro-shi-ma" "Ne-vers"), to which the women sacrifice their men. A name that hides and excuses the egoistic nucleus.

If Riva were really a new woman she would long for no place: there would be no ground, no common ground but ground zero: the "center" which has destroyed the myth of its plenitude and revealed its absolute emptiness:

> Between these two beings geographically, philosophically, historically, economically, racially at the farthest from each other it is possible to be, HIROSHIMA will be the common ground (the only one in the world perhaps?) where the universal givens of

eroticism, love, and unhappiness will appear under an implacable light.[z]

(*Hir.*, 9–10)

Riva compulsively drags herself "à travers la ville" (*Hir.*, 16) the Japanese man follows hypnotically in her wake as their *histoire de quatre sous* reaches its destiny not in post-nuclear eros but in the war between their cities. They refuse to read, as Duras has, in the implacable light of the man-made sun. *Their* sun is a rising sun, ever-renewable, a phoenix; love is essentially repetition. Did the flowers not bloom more brightly after the bomb? John Hershey, in *Hiroshima*, wrote "Weeds already hid the ashes, and wild flowers were in bloom among the city's bones" (New York, Bantam Books, 1959, 89). Grounded, rooted, the alibi of flowers indicates how territorial this love is, how little it has read itself in a nuclear light.

The city as polis, as civilization, police, politeness, polish – none of these guarantee the survival of eros, any more than home and hearth. Is eros to remain formless, invisible, u-topia rather than eu-topic?

But perhaps it is only a matter of class struggle: the bourgeoisie, urban, and domestic. Let's turn once again to the analyst of bourgeois love, Stendhal.

The city and the nomad: homeless love

Here it is instructive, perhaps, to contrast "citified love" with the radical (im)possibility of nomadic love – by which I do not mean the rapid uncoupling that term conjures up under the Regime of the Brother, but the one Stendhal imagines in *De l'amour*.[48] There, nomadism is a root form of the cosmopolis, a place to meet the other – whereas Stendhal describes *l'amour actuel arabe* as shaped by the *holy* or closed city – Mecca. While not exactly the same as the public Forum or the Acropolis – crucial spaces for western man which are always "phallically" marked with monuments – the most sacred Arab city has an apparently empty center, marking it as a site of desire: the "hollow Caaba" (*Love*, 176; *De l'amour*, 199). It becomes increasingly clear, however, that this center – perhaps because of its very centrality, is site of the phallic legislation of the desire of others. Though it hides its fullness as an emptiness, a *crypt*, it is where the other is "buried," a marriage/burial ground for lovers, for the libido: The "hollow Caaba" looms up in his text to displace the metonymic space of the mobile camp.[49]

Masquerading as a blank nucleus, the synthetic ego at the heart of the group, the Caaba functions like the leader, ordering and arranging its subjects' libidinal ties:

> In one of the far ends of the city, one discovers an immense edifice, roughly square; this building surrounds the Caaba; it is composed of a long series of porticos necessary under the Arabian sun for making the holy promenade. This portico is very important in the history of mores of arab poetry: it was apparently for centuries the sole site where men and women found themselves together. They made the rounds, pell mell, with slow steps and while chanting sacred poems to the Caaba; the walk takes three quarters of an hour: these turns were several times repeated in the course of the same day; that was the holy ritual for which men and women flocked from all parts of the desert. It is under the portico of the Caaba that arab mores were polished.
>
> (*Love*, 176)

Poetry grows from this segregation of the sexes: under the porticoes surrounding the Caaba, families circumnavigate, endlessly walking around this central void for ritual and religious purposes of pilgrimage, but also for their "boys" and "girls" to fall in love. That these couples are, of course, also being kept apart and under the surveillance of brothers and fathers, is the mechanism and the trickery in the device: the "love" it fosters has two concrete results – poetry and conflict, not the sexual relation. Father–owners and would-be lover–owners fight over the women; and the lovers must invent poetic sublimations to "communicate" (and satisfy) their desires.

> Soon there was established a conflict between fathers and lovers; soon it was through love odes that the Arab unveiled [*dévoila*] his passion for the young girl strictly under the surveillance of her brothers or her father, beside whom he walked the sacred promenade.
>
> (*Love*, 176)

Like Duras, then, Stendhal specifically correlates destructive love with the built environment, the meaningless name-of-the-place. Civil order takes spatial form; its "loving" couples arrange themselves symbolically and physically around a civic center, which is an unconscious representation of the ego. But is this to say we cannot be civilized, that we accept the brutality of modernity, the failure of culture and its productions to be anything other than repositories of narcissism, in which the real relation of self to other has to be deposited, hidden, and set aside from the great cultural constructions: Baltimore in the early morning?

It is a question of how the city of love is constructed. If, as I have shown, the household has already been touched by total war so that it has become the source of renewed brutality, then it is less the familial relation *per se* than the false consciousness of its persistence and permanence that is at fault. For the high point of domestic civilization has been revealed as an excuse for a brutal egotism: the perpetuation of one's own private, particular and separate life, the domestic (and ego) sphere as "home," "nation-state," "linguistic and cultural homeland" alibis, through emplacement, of the brutal negation of the alien, the other, although this is not necessarily true in every case, of course. Freud's analysis reveals that once the household becomes a representation – a nostalgia for *Heimat* – it also becomes the technical means for unleashing the unconscious, both repressing the inevitable death of the ego and desiring the elimination of the other. He points specifically to the representation of the soldier's "coming home":

> When the furious struggle of the present war has been decided, each one of the victorious fighters will return home joyfully to his wife and children, unchecked and undisturbed by thoughts of the enemies he has killed whether at close quarters or at long range.
>
> (*SE XIV*, 295)

This is a lethal irony: we perceive the nuclear and domestic family, like the ego, as the very "source" of civilized and symbolically ordered life, yet it is this faith in a mere image that is returning us to barbarism, to the indulgence of hatred for the other. But it is a failure of representation that is at fault only in so far as the "home and hearth" are purely imaginary – the room, as Duras put it – to suffer, our own "space." When the other's suffering becomes merely imaginary, the "stuff" of spectacle, it heightens rather than belies the illusion of a clear-cut separation of "life" from "death," the very illusion which intensifies rather than moderates – civilizes – our brutality toward the other.

Duras's *The War: A Memoir* provides an example: Madame L. sees how the suffering of others becomes a spectacle as she describes the anxious waiting of wives of "prisoners of war," sleeping all night at the station, who are closely watched by

> lots of people who are not waiting for anyone [and who] come to the Gare d'Orsay just to see the show, the arrival of the prisoners of war and how the women wait for them, and all the rest, to see what it's like; perhaps it will never happen again.
>
> (*War*, 16)

Would that not be a shame? Riva's "j'ai tout vu" seems to me to participate in precisely this form of spectator sport, entirely consistent with her affirmed narcissism (remember all the cats!): her love for the bomb is a narcissist's suicidal dream, that with his/her death will also come the "end of the world." When I go, everyone goes too.

It is clear that the nuclear condition *per se*, where the bomb could fall at any time, mitigates, but does not of itself alter our collective narcissism. We cannot represent it for ourselves except along Aristotelian lines that moderate, cathartically, its pity and its terror. Even if – perhaps especially if – we exchange ourselves imaginarily with the victims, we remain – imaginarily – the sole real survivor. We can watch the "morning after" or dress up as mutated victims, or look at chalk marks on the sidewalk outlining those instantly incinerated. But our consciousness cannot dream of not surviving.

In order to read Riva's tie to the German soldier correctly, and to see where, even in her alienated version of desire, the nuclear state is wearing away at the underpinnings of the Regime of the Brother, we need to look at the way she relates to her former lover. He is not exactly a ghost – no spirit for whose death she must atone – but he is not entirely swept away as the triumphing primeval man in Freud's "Thoughts" sweeps away his dead enemy. This soldier, lover and enemy both, has never really died for Riva, because, as narcissist, she would never permit a part of her to die. She has ingested him, incorporated him, eaten him – and as in Freud's "Mourning and melancholia," he remains "alive" within. Duras has fully exploited the resources of cinema for capturing this process (the simultaneous triumph over the other and refusal to recognize any loss of what had been a part of one's whole, complete, narcissistic self), the process begun by the sons' ingestion of the father's signifiers in *Totem and Taboo*. When Riva at last begins to introject the German – to "tell" her love to the Japanese, her face is shown to grow lined and haggard – she has lost part of what was "satisfying" her.

Hers is not, it must be made clear, a melancholia rooted in Oedipal, but in post-Oedipal guilt, the guilty enjoyment characteristic of the Regime of the Brother. Riva has made her choice, rejecting both her mother and her father (at one point, she explains that when the German overhears her playing the piano she has played for her father each evening, that it is the first time a "man" ever listened to her play). No forgotten sister or daughter she, but a woman who has fully identified herself with her murderous, enemy "brother."

It is thus that Guattari's anti-Oedipal analysis of cinematic melancholy as an ideological production in "Like the echo of a collective melancholy,"[50] which might seem to apply to a work like *Hiroshima, mon amour*, finally does not (though it might seem to) apply to a work like *Hiroshima, mon amour*. Guattari expands Freud's concepts of (Oedipal) melancholy (guilt) beyond individual psychic to more general analyses of politics, art, and technology. The media takes

events which are emotionally charged (he speaks of terrorist kidnap-
pings and murders, but he could equally well be referring to events
like Hiroshima), and places them entirely at the disposal of social
control and repression. In them, death functions not as real, but as
"an outlet or exorcism in two acts, a double sacrifice meant to inter-
nalize a collective guilt" but not to prevent the repetition of the
murderous act: the Oedipal cycle goes on endlessly rebuilding the
"'infernal machine' of guilt inducement"[51] In other words, "the
most reactionary media, the game of collective guilt" is mistaken in
its "target," in its "methods," in its "strategy," in its "theory," in
its "dreams" in so far as filmic melancholia "today has become a
fundamental given of current political strategies."[52] We take guilty
pleasure in the death of the other.

Something Riva seems to do – but in fact does not, really. For the
German soldier has never really died: for her, in her. In this perspective, the peace film-makers she works for may be taking a guilty
pleasure in Hiroshima – but Riva never admits death at all. Duras's
own film is attempting something different: to have done with the
"pleasurable" depiction of horror by horror. She also means to show
how Riva's beauty, like the "beauty" she sees in the bomb is literally
being fed by living human beings. We must be willing to grant a
distinction between author and actress/character on this point. So
Riva's is not an Oedipal guilt: she is fully identified with the "post-
patriarchal" world, the Regime of the Brother.

We can read Riva's "eros" better if we turn to some recent refine-
ments in the definition of melancholy. The most elaborate psychoanalytic revision in modern semiotic terms of Freud's "Melancholia" is
found in the cryptonomic work of Maria Torok and Nicholas
Abraham.[53] They see the dead other as fantasmatically incorporated,
as actually kept alive within, and continuing to exert projective powers.
As Laurence Rickels explains, this is a new path for the narcissistic
trajectory, the intrusion of Narcissus into the process of mourning:

> The melancholic's self-reproach is . . . ultimately his way of reliv-
> ing, as openly as is possible for the crypt-carrier, that bond which
> was taken from him. Even the melancholic's grief is a detour taken
> to relive the bond with the unmourned dead. The melancholic's
> excessive mourning acts out the deceased's grief at losing him. In
> melancholia it is always ultimately the living dead or phantom who
> must thus perform the mourning rites. Only the phantom mourns
> – always to the point of not surviving the loss of the haunted
> melancholic. The melancholic never loses his dearly beloved. He
> only mourns in anticipation – of his own demise.[54]

In this perspective, Riva's filmic "projections" of Riva – her memories while making love as well as the film in which she acts – of the mutilated dead of Hiroshima – are displacements of the real other in whose death she participated: that of her German soldier lover. It is this other, fantasmatically incorporated, whom she has actually kept alive, immured inside her, and who may seem to be "guiding" her subsequent erotic and restlessly vagrant behavior.

Let us look at Hiroshima, then, but not in the way the heroine does. Duras tells us that she wants to look at Hiroshima, but also to be done with the description of horror by horror: "A peculiar aura crowns each gesture, each word with a sense supplementary to their literal meaning. And there that is one of the major designs of the film: to have done with the description of horror by horror"[aa] (*Hir.*, 9). Duras wants us to see Hiroshima through the horror of the "beauty" (the lovely actress), the private, intimate "love" that outlives it, the horror of the desire for an ever renascent atomism: the aureola, the supplement of romance of Hiroshima – "love" – is the alibi for destruction – an alibi because it (narcissistically) refuses to admit the reality of death. Duras wants, with her film, to "make this horror rise again from its ashes by incorporating it in a love that will necessarily be special and 'wonderful'"[bb] (*Hir.*, 9). So too, we cannot take seriously Duras's remark, so clearly miming the egotism of Riva, that her shaved head (communal shame for being a collaborator with German occupiers) is the "ultimate of horror and stupidity." What kind of ultimate horror is a shaved head compared to Hiroshima? Duras directs that images of Japanese women, victims of radiation, their hair coming out by the handful, be included in the film.[55]

It is Riva's kind of "love," vampiric, egotistic, entirely narcissistic that Duras condenses, showing how her own clear separation of the aims of love and death collapse, under Narcissus, into a romantic love–death "theme." But we must not let this self-indulgent equation – the most fundamental fantasy of the Regime of the Brother – go unchallenged with the advent of total war. Modernity is no longer just a general undifferentiated horror for all but our very own self: there is now a nuclear difference. To rethink the domestic, the mother, the woman, and give us another scene, we have to re-write "uterine space" (as Kristeva called Duras's world) differently. Despite the fact that "private," interior space has already become public, and the domestic sphere no longer a space apart, we seem to cling with intensity to forms of representation which demand that such spaces exist somewhere. This is precisely the forceful effort Marguerite Duras's scenario is making.

The woman as other, as partner, as sharing the same fate and taking the same chances, as erotic. The woman as "perfect," a gleaming, smooth "object" of desire, a curtain between us and destiny:

these are the choices. Can we continue to take women as *objects of desire*, machines for the pleasure of reproduction as well as sites of destruction? (Or, by cutting off their demands for a share of satisfaction, into energy saving devices?) The nuclear situation has empowered us – for the first time in a long while – to think of woman as the subject of desire. It offers us the chance – if we take it – to situate woman beyond the confines of her domestic prison, the total confinement into which the brother placed her at the opening of his regime – Julie's Clarens, Clarissa's coffin, Manon Lescaut's grave. What is a woman if no longer "she who awaits the death of a man"? What is a man if he also waits? The scene of representation is no longer an innocent staging of the other to purge him from the domestic sphere, but a staging of this Aristotelian mimesis itself.

Thus the fate of "love" under the pseudo-Oedipal regime. Narrative, theater and film have often served the Brother and his imaginary majesty well; it is thus up to narrative to mount a counter-offensive. I am suggesting here as throughout this book that we need not accept Narcissus as the sole occupant of our unconscious: loving murder may seem the inescapable, inevitable, and unique form of tie to the other. We have, indeed, collectively agreed to the modern programme of "forgetting the dead" for the sake of the single ego.[56] Interiority, urbanity, fictionality, and now film circulate around the loss of the other, an other who had been once the object of a desire: father, mother, the woman. But the unmarked other – the other who could have been the *subject* of their own passion: the anonymous masses, the colonized, women, those without the "phallus" – is the crucial piece missing. The absent heterology is whatever is left out of narcissism. If I am correct that a plurality of subjects is required to form symbolic relations, then we need to model such "other" subjects now, and though we must perforce use the reflective and aesthetic forms which aided and abetted the denial of relation to the other, we will have to use them differently. The special status of film in relation to the nuclear and post-colonial world becomes an open question. Like the early novel the movies are only beginning to play out their particular dialectic. Re-patriarchalized, they are a powerful reserve for the Regime of the Brother, and serve escapist fantasies, like Joseph's, in Duras's *The Seawall*, of the lady at the movies. But if not?[57]

Part III

The end(s) of love in the western world

Chapter 5

The end(s) of love in the western world

At this juncture of nature and culture, so persistently examined by modern anthropology, psychoanalysis alone recognizes this knot of imaginary servitude that love must always undo again, or sever. For such a task, we place no trust in altruistic feeling, we who lay bare the aggressivity that underlies the activity of the philanthropist, the idealist, the pedagogue, and even the reformer.

(Jacques Lacan, "The mirror stage," *Ecrits*, 7)

As in all Colonial cities, there were two towns within this one: the white town and the other.

(Marguerite Duras, *The Seawall*, 135)[1]

Edward Said remarks in *Orientalism*[2] that the relation of the white European male to colonized persons does not differ essentially from his relation to oppressed minorities within his home culture: "delinquents, women, the poor, and the insane." He does not, however, reverse the terms and inquire much into the relation such "delinquents, women, the poor, and the insane" might entertain with the "indigenous" or colonized people. Nor does he ask about the white European female. Yet in texts by Jean Rhys (*Wide Sargasso Sea*[3]), Ruth Prawer Jhabvala (*Out of India*, and *Heat and Dust*[4]), and Duras (*The Seawall*), the peculiar relation between "white women" and men (white or not, indigenous or not) in the colonial situation has increasingly featured in the literature of decolonization, neo-imperialism, and its discontents.

I am interested here in love at the "end(s) of the western world," that is, in the ties made in opposition to certain (imperialist) political cuts. Conversely, these ties make another kind of "cut" – into the aggressively "imaginary" relations noted by Lacan in the above citation. Interdictions against social ties between colonized peoples and a colonizing woman are customary, but, even in the case of the most reactionary of white women, those ties seem bound to be made. White women who, willfully or not, transgress the laws of a

fundamental apartheid, are, I think, responding to another kind of
"law," the symbolic in its best "western" sense: undoing the "knot
of imaginary servitude."[5] This is because of the essential symmetry in
status both they and the colonized have with respect to the white man
(now to be seen as one essential "truth" of the Regime of the Brother).
The white women's perspective on the colonized men and women
with whom they deal is shaped by their own non-position within their
"own" white culture, leaving them, not the men, susceptible to being
"defined" or redefined by the colonial other. We are brought up short
when Duras has her narrator describe herself in *The Lover* as that
"fifteen-and-a-half-year-old white whore from Sadec," or when Rhys's
Antoinette – whom Rochester rebaptizes "Bertha" – is called a "white
nigger" in *Wide Sargasso Sea*. Sexual outlaws they are, too, within the
imperialist version of western culture, sleeping with "the natives."
They are none the less also often "heroic" in our own terms.

It is, therefore, disappointing that Said's great book virtually leaves
the Euro-woman out.[6] He is very sensitive to the situation of the
indigenous woman who has been taken up and defined by the
ideology of "orientalism" and the financial order of capitalism (the
oriental woman is the epitome of exotic and luxuriant sexuality), but
he does not try to turn the same eye on the white woman. He takes
the side of the indigenous woman when she is reduced to an equation in a formula (a Lacanian "tu es") by the Euro-male (for example,
he complains eloquently when an Egyptian prostitute is turned by
Flaubert into the very "type" of oriental sexuality (*Orientalism*, 188ff.).
However, Said neither allows her, as Spivak[7] does, to "represent
herself," nor does he, reversing the "oriental" perspective, call the
sexuality of European culture to account as it opens the Euro-woman
to attack, as though his insight into the equivalence between
"women, the poor, and the insane" and the "native" does not need
to be read from the inside. (In this respect Frantz Fanon's *The Wretched of the Earth* presents a more complex format.[8])

That the woman – both indigenous and European – is the figure on
which the re-evaluation of colonialism must rest is, I think, made
abundantly clear in the recent work of Gayatri Chakravorty Spivak.
She takes her stance as a "representative" critic who defies traditional categories (as a feminist and one whose country of origin is a
former colonial possession), and also representing, through her
translations, what she calls "subaltern" women writers and the
western feminist critics who take pains to deal with the colonized
woman. (She has made available to us the work of Mahashwati Devi,
in two stories, "Draupadi," and "Breast-giver" each of which treats
subaltern women – not men – as shaped by and/or resistive to
symbolic domination by Euroculture.)

It is not only the subaltern who has been dominated in and by the western ideologization of the "symbolic": writers like Orwell indicate as much. (See his "Shooting an elephant" and his analysis of the disillusionment of Rudyard Kipling about the empire.[9]) Men went out in the service of empire to "civilize" heathens, natives, and to share our western technological and rational advantages: as Orwell put it, "You turn a Gatling gun on a mob of unarmed 'natives,' and then you establish 'the Law,' which includes roads, railways and a courthouse." That is not the first reason Euro-women go to the colonies: they go to maintain the marital integrity of the European men.[10] They are used as a first line of defense (shades of Rougemont) against "oriental desire."[11] They, too, share in the spread of "civilization" (and economic empire), but they have different means of dissemination from that of their men: it is not the gun that lies at the foundation of their take on "civilization," it is the pen – and, in the case of Blixen and Duras's "Ma," the plow.

Yet even when they do the work of civilization (spreading brotherly love and reaping profits for the empire), they are also, by definition, "outlaws": their "sexuality," "madness," "poverty" are so many emblems of their primary "crime": being away from a patriarchally defined "home." As much as Clarissa ever was, they are caught in the double bind. This is perhaps the hidden logic of their unfathomable condition: for in contrast to the image of the colonial male, exploiting and self-enriching (like Rochester in Rhys's novel) the women are uniformly (Blixen not excluded) impoverished by their implication in imperialism, directly as a result of their colonial situation: it is as if the riches extracted from the colonies by their European male exploiters depended on their stripping their women of wealth as well.[12]

If the women are often depicted as "mad" – Annette and her daughter Antoinette are "insane"; so is Duras's Mother in *The Lover* and *The Seawall* – we have to note that this is a relative categorization, and one thrown strongly into question by the authors. Their "madness" confirms, from another angle, the alignment of the interests of the Euro-woman with the coloniz*ed* rather than with the coloniz*er*. One reading of Frantz Fanon's chilling account of the psychiatric classification of the shrunken cerebrum and innate criminality of the Algerian ("a born criminal") is enough to make us see the connection.[13] That is, unlike "nature," the "landscape," and the "native women" which Fanon tells us form the "backdrop"[14] for the white man (*Wretched*, 250), the colonized male stands out for the colonial westerner, he is not reduced to being a part of the background by virtue of his "dangerousness." The white woman, too, implies a certain inability to merge, harmlessly, with the scenery:

even the whiteness of the white clothes she is supposed to wear when she is conforming perfectly to her country's norms for their colonists[15] precludes that.

So they are "alienated," "mad." Yet as Euro-women, white women, they had only been doing their "duty," responding to a call, to an appeal, to a "desire," the desire of the Other. I would like to characterize the nature of the "call" and to make some initial distinctions among the Euro-women in these novels. The calls are made on the basis of what I call "romantic colonialism" and "moral imperialism."

The European woman who goes to or lives in the colonies follows a pattern of initial romantic attraction followed by disappointment, when she realizes her romantic ideologies are the mask for an economic exploitation: not only of the "natives" but of herself. Some of the women characters never experience an initial romance nor suffer disillusionment and impoverishment: these are the moral "missionaries" (bureaucrats, army wives, medical workers, etc.) who are convinced they are "benefactors," bringing economic well-being, law and order to the "natives." This first attitude we might like to name "romantic colonial" and the second "moral imperial."

The romantic colonial is a universal economical failure. Nevertheless, she sometimes – like Ma's solidarity with the peasants on her plain – succeeds in founding an intersubjective relation with the "Other." This is the woman who dreams of faraway places, romance – all the mystifications that our western Brother has been able to conjure up, and yet it is this dream which prepares the way, so to speak, for the ties she makes to the colonized.

The moral/economic imperialists, on the other hand, are rarely financial failures, but it is seldom clear why they "profit." Especially since they are so often characterized as simple and ascetic in their habits, do-good types, who never try to create the lavish colonial lifestyle that appealed to their romantic doubles, and the thought of "exploitation" would be anathema to them. As I have already tried to make clear, however, the "Brother" who denies the women their identity, place, the means to satisfy their needs, is himself the one who is being *satisfied* narcissistically, to the full. Sometimes (as with Riva) this "Brother" is even a woman herself, but one fully identified with – or more precisely by – her brothers, one whose difference, that is, is disavowed.

These narratives of women and empire begin to explicate how and why to condemn both the viciousness of the Regime of the Brother and the illusory desires that do its work in the heart and soul of women. They often do something more than present their searing criticisms: for, from time to time, they provide glimpses, *aperçus*, on another womanly identity, another womanly desire, another form of relation to the Other.

Romantic colonials

> Mr Mason stopped swearing and began to pray in a loud pious voice. "May Almighty God defend us." And God who is indeed mysterious, who had made no sign when they burned Pierre as he slept – not a clap of thunder, not a flash of lightning – mysterious God heard Mr Mason at once and answered him. The yells stopped.[16]

Annette in Jean Rhys's *Wide Sargasso Sea*, a Creole widow in the West Indies impoverished both by her husband's death and the freeing of the slaves who had maintained her estate, remarries John Mason, an Englishman who has courted her in her financial distress. Her dilapidated home, Coulibri, is repaired, she has servants, fine "English" cooking, and new clothes. Her daughter, Antoinette (the future Bertha Rochester) is no longer ragged, but is offered all the comforts of white patriarchy: Antoinette calls him "white pappy" and identifies with the painting he has had hung on the wall of the dining room entitled "The Miller's Daughter." It depicts a typical little English girl. Identifying with her, and feeling, for once, "safe," warm, and well clothed, Antoinette counts herself lucky. (She does admit to herself that she prefers Christophine's local-style cooking to English food, and it is also clear that the "English" identity can not go too far, since as a Creole from Martinique it seems evident that her mother Annette is of French extraction.)

Mason's "curative" presence, however, results in utter disaster for her: the servants he hires are disloyal; he ignores all signs – and Annette's warnings – of a growing resentment in the indigenous population (as poor or poorer than before emancipation) toward the family (aggravated by his decision, based on his "benign" sense of them as "childlike, innocent, and lazy", to "import coolies" from India to work his plantation). The result is that the blacks burn Coulibri, Myra (the perfidious servant) leaves Annette's feeble-minded young son, Pierre, to burn to death, and Annette goes mad. Mason will eventually marry Antoinette off to Rochester, who will repeat the scenario at a higher pitch and turn her into the madwoman in the attic.

Why? He is a savior, not an exploiter – or is he? The locals scratch their heads trying to figure out what he's getting out of the deal ("Why should a very wealthy man . . . why should he marry a widow without a penny to her name and Coulibri a wreck of a place?'' [*Sargasso Sea*, 28]: it makes no evident economic sense. Yet Rhys's analytic prose is unsparing: Mason, for all his ''white pappy'' paternalism, is in the business, all right, only he is clever enough to obscure his exploitation of the women, the blacks – and the children – with romance, paternalism, and morality. He deals them death and madness as he courts and ''loves'' them. Antoinette observes her mother and stepfather as they dance on their return from their honeymoon:

> There was no need for music when she danced. They stopped and she leaned backwards over his arm, down till her black hair touched the flagstones – still down, down. Then up again in a flash, laughing. She made it look so easy – as if anyone could do it, and he kissed her – a long kiss. . . . I was remembering that woman saying ''Dance! He didn't come to the West Indies to dance – he came to make money as they all do. Some of the big estates are going cheap, and one unfortunate's loss is always a clever man's gain.''
>
> (*Sargasso Sea*, 29–30)

Rochester arrives to marry Antoinette, Annette's daughter, when she is seventeen; the ''deal'' is made with her step-brother Mason: ''Dear Father. Thirty thousand pounds have been paid to me without question or condition. No provision made for her'' (*Sargasso Sea*, 70). Annette, we must note, is literally *sold* by her brother, to get her off his hands and ''safely'' away from being able to touch his inheritance. In Rochester the advent of the phallic Regime of the Brothers is perfectly clear. He is the actor: describing his wedding he says

> It was all very brightly colored, very strange, but it meant nothing to me. Nor did she, the girl I was to marry. When at last I met her I bowed, smiled, kissed her hand, danced with her. I played the part I was expected to play. She never had anything to do with me at all. Every movement I made was an effort of will and sometimes I wondered that no one noticed this. But I must have given a faultless performance. If I saw an expression of doubt or curiosity it was on a black face, not a white one.
>
> (ibid., 77)

He is egocentric, androcentric (the ''girl I was to marry'' ''meant nothing to me'') and Eurocentric: he detests every moment he spends on the islands and with their people. Ogling Amélie, the black servant he will later have sex with within earshot of his wife, he calls her ''a lovely little creature but sly, spiteful, malignant perhaps, like much else in this place'' (ibid., 65). At one telling moment he spends his time drawing a schematic image of Thornfield Hall – English, three storeys high, the third storey inhabited by a woman stick figure with a dot for a head. And he loathes the home, the place Antoinette has made for herself, at Massacre, where she tells him happily "This is my place and everything is on our side" (ibid., 74). Small wonder that his patriarchal house is, for the madwoman in the attic, "cardboard England": it reflects the stereotypically "phallic" flatness and hardness of Rochester's ego, the one that the national "superego" – the House of Culture – has been modeled on.

Rochester's economic adventurism, his sadism and "virile" negation of Antoinette, the blacks, even the natural colors of the Islands ("Everything is too much . . . Too much blue, too much purple, too much green. The flowers are too red, the mountains too high, the hills too near" (*Sargasso Sea*, 70)), serves to set off the structure initiated and obfuscated by Mason, by repeating it – as Marx would have said – this time as farce. Antoinette, who is tortured much more directly and in a much less sublimated fashion than her mother, nevertheless represents a certain "gain," based as it is in absolute loss (of her money, her name, her dresses, and her mind). It is as if the "romantic" mode reveals its own dialectical negation through her: whereas her mother "understood" the blacks were "alive" but clung to the white man's solutions to her problems, clung till they killed her and her son, Antoinette sees the blacks as being quite like herself, persons with living identities (her mother had told Mason, the blacks are "more alive than you are" and Antoinette seems to live out her mother's perception of them). And, when she is in her own place, she expresses and enumerates a set of desires of her own, including a sexual appetite that Rochester finds repellent. (When he is in "her place" he finds only her empty clothes excite his lust for her.) For Antoinette, the indigenous populace, not the mother-country, provide her with a lover (Sandi,[17] her colored cousin, not Rochester), mother (Christophine, the "obeah woman," not Annette), friends (Tia, Louise de Plana). Even when they are enemies. When Tia steals her dress and leaves her own in its place, she is asserting equality, albeit in a negative mode, as when she calls Antoinette a "white nigger": in fact, as a poor black, she is "better" than Antoinette, because her identity is at least logically consistent.

What she achieves (in her love for this exotic place and peoples she has made herself a home, a place, amongst) is absolutely out of Rochester's reach. She accomplishes the "transvaluation" of her cultural heritage without rupture or revolution, without money or guns: admiring Hélène de Plana (her friend in the convent) for the way she does her hair, Antoinette complains, after being showed how it is done: "Yes, but Hélène, mine does not look like yours, whatever

I do" (*Sargasso Sea*, 54). Hélène is "too polite to say the obvious thing," looking away. What is marvelous about the incident, is that "the obvious thing" is that Hélène is black, and that this had made no difference to Antoinette. More than that, the reader hardly realizes the significance of the passage simply because Antoinette's praise for the de Plana girls' "beauty" and "deportment" has already encoded itself, for us, as "white beauty."

It is a minor victory to be dredged out of Rochester's triumph over her, but a real one. And ultimately, even before the razing of "cardboard England" it is clear that Rochester's policy of apartheid for himself affects him, despite his belief that he can escape being touched by his relations with the "other." Mrs Eff cannot fathom the "change" in him on his return from the Indies: when Grace Poole objects to the charge she is being given to care for the incarcerated "Bertha" (Rochester renames Antoinette), she says, "I don't serve the devil for no money" (ibid., 177). Mrs Eff responds sharply

> If you imagine when you serve this gentleman you are serving the devil you never made a greater mistake in your life. I knew him as a boy. I knew him as a young man. He was gentle, generous, brave. His stay in the West Indies has changed him out of all knowledge. He has grey in his hair and misery in his eyes. Don''t ask me to pity anyone who has had a hand in that.
>
> (ibid., 177–8)

Like the satiated sadist he is he finds the deadliness of the pleasure principle's fulfilment written in his own face. How much he reminds us of Stendhal's aging Don Juan . . .

Let us look now at *The Seawall*, the semi-autobiographical novel by Marguerite Duras. The center of the novel is "Ma," the perfect picture of the romantic dupe: a peasant from northern France, college-educated and a schoolteacher married to another schoolteacher. "Occasionally, on Sunday, she stopped to gaze at the Colonial propaganda posters in front of the town hall" (*Seawall*, 17). These posters are imperative and appealing, telling her both "Enlist in the Colonial Army!" and "Young People, a Fortune awaits you in the Colonies!" (ibid.). They also offer alluring romantic images: "The picture usually showed a Colonial couple, dressed in white, sitting in rocking-chairs under banana trees while smiling natives busied themselves around them" (ibid.). The "maunderings of Pierre Loti and his romantic descriptions of exotic lands" clinch it, and she and her husband apply to teach in Indochina.

The result is "Ma's" widowhood and impoverishment by a colonial administration which has figured out a wonderful scheme for exploiting not only the indigenous but also their own "peasants" who qualify as homesteaders on a land concession. Ma scrimps and saves, working as a pianist at the Eden cinema for years after her husband dies – she never gets to see even one film, by the way. The land turns out, of course, to be worthless. Worse yet, the colonial government requires her to regularly "invest" a certain amount in the land in order to retain her "share" – an impossible task given that she has no income or yield from it. At that point, the cadastral agents will swoop in, repossess the claim – and resell it to the next unsuspecting dupe.

The snooping, avaricious cadastral agents are "the elder brother" which is figured in *The Lover*: "rummagers in closets." In that book, which I discuss in the next chapter, there is a family in the same situation as the one in *The Seawall* – except there is an "older brother," one inexplicably aggressive, domineering, greedy. "Marguerite" even characterizes his effect on the family as a reign of terror that totalizes, dominates mother, younger brother, sister, and the indigenous – and regulates the relations among them: the embodiment of moral authority without a shred of what "morality" was supposed to mean under Oedipal civilization. It is "Marguerite" who states what we have witnessed since the death of Clarissa: it is the spreading Regime of the Brother: excessive, terrible, horrible consequences in its concession of "moral" power to the elder brother:

> I see wartime and the reign of my elder brother as one . . . I see the war as like him, spreading everywhere, breaking in everywhere, stealing, imprisoning, always there, merged and mingled with everything, present in the body, in the mind, awake and asleep, all the time, a prey to the intoxicating passion of occupying that delightful territory, a child's body, the bodies of those less strong, of conquered peoples.
>
> (*The Lover*, 63)

A wild over-identification of the personal and the political, a typical "female" thing to do? Yes, Duras even acknowledges how wrong it is to "mix" the two up. Yet, at the level of ideology it contains a truth. The "humanitarians" who accompanied colonial exploiters – was it not the white man's burden to help his more primitive brethren, those "behind" him? – wittingly or no contributed to that exploitation, by obscuring the fact that an empire was nothing more than a "money making machine" (as Orwell once put it), with the moral claims of universal brotherhood. The Brother's moral imperative is "Enjoy and profit at the same time!": "Jouis!"

Obvious prototypes of this fictitious elder brother, the cadastral agents, are reduced to no more than what they can extract everybody else: they eat everyone else up. And "Ma" does not defeat them, though she holds them at bay for the duration of her life. However, she exemplifies two actions which foretell the ultimate demise of the unearned privilege of these "brothers." On the one hand, she forms an alliance, a kind of international class identification, with the peasants on her plain: she assumes leadership and – in the "best" manner of the west makes the only visible effort they have ever seen to do what the west touts as its great achievement: dominate nature and have it serve human ends. Nature, of course, wins; yet Ma is in some sense its equal, not (as mothers are supposed to be) its agent. It is no accident that it is the sea (Freud's "oceanic feeling" is maternal) she fights, and the regular and inexorable rhythm of her rise from each defeat matches its inexorable ebb and flow.

Each year the sea rises to flood the plain and destroy the crops: this is why her land, and the bits the colonials have left the indigenous peasants, is worthless. She rouses the peasants from their accustomed lethargy, and sparks their imaginations with the idea of building "une barrage contre le Pacifique," a seawall. It fails. As does everything else. The peasants harbor not the least resentment toward her for her failure. Not only has she made the attempt where the western men have not, she is slowly evolving toward economic equality with them, just as her house, with its wormy roof, and her Citroën B-12 are no longer self-contained, western bits of technology but now requires local natural resources (banana leaves for inner tubes) and human labor to run (their deaf Malay servant, the Corporal, must ride with water buckets and lanterns to supplement the loss of radiator and headlights).

She also exploits the exploiter: Monsieur Jo is the son of a wealthy plantation owner who makes his money by building workers' plague-ridden shantytowns and charging exorbitant rents. He is clearly devoid of any admirable personal characteristics, and even when he professes his profound love and desire for Ma's teenage daughter, Suzanne, he gets that wrong. (Having begged the girl to let him see her naked as she steps out of the shower, she consents: the narrator tells us that it is in vain, for the fellow, "did not have the look in his eyes that he should have had" [Seawall, 58]). Strutting around with his money and gifts he assumes he can have the girl: Ma and brother Joseph insist on marriage. Not that they are prudes – they tell him she can sleep with anyone she likes except him. From him, they demand marriage. He "agrees," still assuming he can win her with gifts, first to herself (makeup, for example), then, noting her love for her brother, a phonograph for him (another flop: it has "His Master's Voice" as a legend), and finally a diamond ring, which the girl dares him into giving her without having to sleep with him – for her mother's sake. Thus co-operatively they exploit the would-be exploiter.

A small and local turnabout. There is something else that Ma does which is, ultimately, more to the point. Joseph, her son, has little direction or aim, other than the traditional "feminine" dream of being carried off someday by a handsome stranger (a beautiful woman) on a white horse (a new Delage car), a dream he's picked up at the movies his mother has never had a real chance to see despite "the ten years she had passed in complete abnegation at the piano of the Eden Cinema" (*Seawall*, 19). She sneaked in once, was caught by the manager and expelled. Even though he does manly things (he hunts and has a lot of guns), and dutifully "gets away from" his mother, there is not much likelihood that he will ever be much of a "man" in the sense of deserving and occupying a symbolic position. Not leadership material.

But then, no man – none of the Joes or Joe Blows (Joseph, Monsieur Jo, the English yarn salesman Joseph Burner) in the book – is: only Ma has that quality. The Joes have their phallic symbols – their cars: the dilapidated B-12, Monsieur Jo's luxury car "Maurice Léon Bollée," and Burner's modified no-brand car with the rumble seat he has turned into a set of salesman's drawers in which to keep his threads. Each car actually symbolizes their various and untenable positions as white men in the colonial world: increasingly dependent on local natural and human resources, like the B-12, emblem of the tendency for assimilation and equalization between colonist and colonized when they are both impoverished. Increasingly separate from a populace and its sensual resources that rejects his proffered lures, like the Bollée, designating a "turn-off" to the lure of western luxuries on the part of the locals. Or a ludicrous vain attempt to keep categories straight, and colors sorted, and stopping the lines from getting crossed and entangled with each other like Burner's rumble seat – the very figure of colonial bureaucracy.

Ma, however, writes a letter, one that is never delivered, but which reaches its destination. In it she demands the concession of the five best hectares of her land to her forthwith from the colonial bureaucrats. She bases her claim on this: the peasants' love for her. If they repossess these acres, she explains that every time they try to hoodwink another unsuspecting victim like herself, a hundred peasants will surround the agents and will tell the prospective buyer of the trick being played. It is a magnificent letter. And it works, to a degree: Joseph reads it, and decides not to send it. The next visit of the cadastral agent is a catastrophe for the bureaucrat, an "unexpected collapse of his authority" (*Seawall*, 246): Joseph pushes back, demands that the agent stick to the letter of the law and visually inspect the "seawall" improvement the family has "made" – a menacing demand since Joseph implies openly that he or the peasants will be likely to dump the official in the sea – and when the cowardly agent refuses, Joseph takes his guns and fires in the air to frighten him off – for another year, anyhow.

Ma dies. And the letter continues to work on Joseph. As he leaves with his rich blonde, he takes his guns, all of them, heaps them on the table with instructions for the peasants on how to kill any agents that come around, and on where to hide their bodies. This book is written in 1950: need we say more?

"Ma," who, from the depth of her failure, her victimization, turns the romantic mode around, and uses the resources of the image and the symbol, her leadership and her writing, to begin the overthrow of the empire.

That empire, as Orwell puts it, as a "money-making concern" has never been doubted by anyone since Kipling, to be sure. But who knew exactly where its secondary manifestations, its delayed and relayed effects would appear, until we could read them in these women's writing?

The empire of the phallus and the Regime of the Brother

As in all Colonial cities, there were two towns within this one: the white town – and the other. And in the white town there were still other differences. The periphery of the white town was known as the *Haut Quartier* – the upper district – comprising villas and apartment buildings. It was the largest and airiest part of the city and was where the secular and official powers had their palaces. The more basic power – the financial – had its palaces in the center of the white town, where, crowded in from all sides by the mass of the city, buildings sprang up, each year higher and higher, the financiers were the true priests of this Mecca.

(*Seawall*, 135)

Ruth Prawer Jhabvala is a screenwriter, novelist, and short story writer. Jewish, originally from Poland, she married an Indian, and has written in a serio-comic vein about Indian/western relations, including one of the most subtle and ironically dialectical essays on the Euro-woman in Asia, "Myself in India," in *Out of India*.[18] Her stories are filled with every possible posture the white woman (pre- and post-independence) took with respect to India: there is the "ghost with backbone" of *Heat and Dust*, resident in a Swiss hostel, and purveyor of the motto that there's "no living in India without Jesus Christ."

Or Olivia, in the same novel, who manages to conceive a much longed-for child but does not know if its father is the current "sahib" (her British Empire bureaucrat husband Douglas) or the indigenous "ruler," the Nawab, Muslim descendant of brigands and trafficker in ill-gotten funds needed to run his palace and support his Alfa Romeos and Rolls Royces. The stories are filled with English girls who sleep with everyone, indifferently, as well as those like the sharp-eyed Swami impresario, the "Countess," in "How I became a Holy Mother," who police the sexual activities of an ashram founded in order to promote happiness between the sexes. The portrayal of the Countess is of a European woman blind to the absolute contradiction between her duty-oriented, business-like approach and the Hinduism she wants to bring to the west. Prawer Jhabvala shows her unwittingly molding her young protegé into a figure of Christ (pure white robes instead of saffron, long curly hair instead of shaved head, sexual purity and rejection of the body of the female, etc.) as she works so hard to "make something" of the boy. She is only vaguely aware that to "make something of him" must be translated as to "make money for me." (Few of Jhabvala's characters ever alter the notion they have that Indian "spirituality" and "universal love" – themes of Swamis they have listened to in the west – are an asceticism of eroticism, and not a denial of sexuality. They end up hating India for duping them, luring them with the Jesus-ized Swamis people like the Countess have presented them as in the West.[19])

Moral imperialism

We might take a moment to read these lines from Husserl as prelude to the next analysis of a story. Commenting on the universality, the "family-like" relation we Europeans have with India once we "penetrate sympathetically" into her, he continues,

> On the other hand, Indians find us strangers and find only in each other their fellows. Still, this essential distinction between fellowship and strangeness, which is relativized on many levels and is a basic category of all historicity cannot suffice. . . . We get a hint of that right in our own Europe. Therein lies something unique, which all other human groups, too, feel with regard to us, something that, apart from all considerations of expediency, becomes a motivation for them, despite their determination to retain their spiritual autonomy, constantly to Europeanize themselves, whereas we, if we understand ourselves properly, will never, for example, Indianize ourselves.[20]

Now if we turn to Prawer Jhabvala's story of "Two more under the Indian sun" in *Out of India* (182–98), we can compare the "romantic" call of colonialism and its dialectic with that of the "moral" missionary call of imperialism. The story involves two Englishwomen in India; one, Margaret a widow known for her good works, is constantly harrying her friend, the mild-mannered Elizabeth, wife of an Indian named Raju, to undertake charitable projects and to lend Margaret a hand in her many schemes for improvement. Margaret is high-minded, perfectly ethical and has few if any desires or selfish motives. Elizabeth is not selfish either, but she is clearly found "wanting" in the eyes of Margaret, who feels the girl is not doing her duty, as an English woman in India. Even Margaret's old servant prefers the way Margaret is – a real Memsahib, which Elizabeth is not. Elizabeth and her husband, who is successfully employed, are none the less not making it financially, and Margaret, who has a huge mansion she has converted into apartments for those who assist her in her good works, rents out a bedroom to the pair.

Margaret wants Elizabeth to get involved and to spend less time and energy on her relation with husband Raju – less time in the room they share in Margaret's capacious house. Margaret responds to Elizabeth's proffered, "I love you just the way you are," with, "Yes . . . that's the trouble with you. You love everybody just the way they are" (*Out of India*, 189). There is something at least Kiplingesque about this woman ("You turn a Gatling gun . . . and establish 'the Law'"). She makes Elizabeth feel dreadfully, woefully guilty toward Margaret, toward India, toward everything. Yet it is Elizabeth who has "married India" and despite Margaret's imperatives, and even when she and her husband are out of sorts with each other, she cannot bring herself to the point of really sacrificing her time with him. The story has little drama to it, as Margaret, who has been demanding Elizabeth accompany her on an outing she plans for some Indian orphans, finally gives up, and asks her guest, a rather senile old poetic Indian, to make the trip instead.

Not a very complicated situation. And yet, in a way, it is relevant to the question of "moral empire" that I have introduced briefly in relation to "Marguerite's" elder brother in *The Lover*, the kind of sense of moral "duty" some imperialists have and which is in no way the same as the illusions that draw people like "Ma" to the colonies. Prawer Jhabvala is brilliant at depicting such persons, often men who seem the direct heirs of Kipling, but she is even better when she depicts the women who do their white brothers' work for them – out of duty. Margaret has planted her mansion on Indian soil – and there is every reason to see it figuring as the post-colonial commonwealth: the kind of foreign aid and the legacy British colonial bureaucracy have brought. Somewhat like Rochester, Margaret is a separatist. Elizabeth happens to be brought into Margaret's own apartment in the great house, and she is utterly amazed. The room Elizabeth shares with Raju, as one might expect, mixes Indian and British objects, activities, lifestyles (they practice cricket shots with a rubber ball and a hairbrush in it, [*Out of India*, 193]). This room, Margaret's bedroom, reproduces exactly an English bedroom back home: from the old wooden furniture to the lilac sachets and framed pictures of her relatives. Margaret missed out: in contrast to Rochester, say, she had once thrilled to the tones and seductive ways of a Swami, (her current visitor, Babaji, is a kind of repetition) in an ashram, but did not or could not follow him. So her apartheid here is based in a sexual failure (she fell for one of her Swamis, but it did not work out when it was clear that he loved several women at the same time).

It also belies the "connections" she keeps urging Elizabeth to make (out of your bedroom and into social work) as false or phantasmatic connections. Her decision to go "with the Indian man" then can be read as a tentative admission that in fact that is what she has desired all along. Or it can mark her western drive to put everyone "to work," exploit them as "natural resources." Either way, the structure explains why she – and not Elizabeth and Raju – is financially well off: she is working for (quite unconsciously, of course) the empire of the phallus, the "white city" – her white bedroom. Such work is "rewarding."

What conclusions can we draw about the contradictions inherent in romantic-colonialism and moral-imperialism, in terms of morality, economics, sexuality, and or ethnic and racial relationships?

When we compare the narcissistic male with female characters in these three texts, it is clear that the males, with the possible exception of Joseph, simply and quite literally cannot "stand" their existence in the colonial world. Their "self-image" and "ideal gender identification" – *preclude* their relation to natives, immigrants, and "colonial natives," often causing violent physical symptoms (Rochester takes fever on his wedding night; in Jhabvala's *Heat and Dust*, Chid and Harry's rejection of the foreign is manifested as an inability to eat; Orwell's policeman in "Shooting an elephant," morally sympathetic to the natives [he has decided empire is "bad"], desires nothing more than to run a knife into a native priest's guts – it is clear his "moral" decision about empire is firmly rooted in the fact that it has broken down as a money-making machine, it does not work economically any more.) These fellows cannot compare with those female characters, (like Annette or the mother in *The Lover* and *The Seawall*) who experience the harshest of conditions without thinking to reject the new world they inhabit. Except, perhaps, by escaping at the movies.

Here I want to return to *The Seawall*, to look at the sister, Suzanne. She loves her brother Joseph very much. Like him, she claims to want a rich stranger ("a hunter") to come with a shiny car and carry her off from her poverty on the plain, away from her mother's ill-health and incessant yelling. Yet when the opportunity presents itself – Monsieur Jo comes along – she declines it. Why? He has the Bollée, but he also has an even more luxurious limousine in which she takes a ride in to the city. Their relation ends with the ride: with her "dream" at hand, Suzanne has no thought of accepting the chance. It has, I think, to do with the movies.

What role can we see radio/film and other electronic technologies (the victrola Monsieur Jo gives Joseph, that pours out the boy's favorite romantic song, "Ramona," and bears the legend, "His Master's Voice" for example) playing in relation to the "romance" of colonialism? What "reversal" might it have in store for the "European–center"/"colonial–periphery" relation?

At the movies

Suzanne has tried to walk around in the Haut Quartier, all dressed up in a frock borrowed from Carmen, the appointments girl in the brothel she and her mother are staying in while they try to sell the diamond. As she walks through the streets, the girl becomes what seems to be increasingly paranoiac, but this is clearly programmed by the economic and class structure of the city: colonial girls, those born in the colonies, have no place in the empire of the phallus, the financial center. She ducks into a movie house: escape is on the screen, an imaginary that promises the fulfillment of exchange:

> She was young and beautiful. . . . The men were crazy about her. . . . Naturally she has a great deal of money. . . . She travels. . . . It is at the carnival in Venice that love awaits her. . . . Before the least thing has happened you know that this is it, that he is The Man. . . . He says I love you. She says I love you too. The dark sky of waiting becomes suddenly bright. From the lightning of that kiss. Gigantic communion of the audience with the screen. You would like to be in their place. Oh how you would like it.
>
> (*Seawall*, 152)

Except that for Suzanne it does not quite work. Where others see, in the movies, imaginary plenitude, whole bodies, bodies fulfilled that they can imaginarily change places with, Suzanne sees only "*corps morcelés*," detached body parts that never "gel" into the imagined wholeness required for the narcissistic exchange. The lure of the filmed (like any aesthetic) image fails to take hold:

Their bodies entwined, their lips approach with nightmare slowness. And when their two pairs of lips are close together, their bodies become cut off, and then you see their decapitated heads, what would be impossible to see in real life, you see their lips facing, half open, open still more, and their jaws falling apart as if in death, and then, suddenly, in a brusque and fatal release, their lips join and suck like octopuses in a crushing kiss, as if trying with the delirious hunger of starvation to devour, to absorb each other and bring about a total and reciprocal disappearance and absorption.

(ibid., 152–3)

Suzanne's reaction: "Impossible idea, absurd idea, to which quite evidently the physical organs are not adapted." The "spectators" "communing" with the screen (and not, therefore with each other) are caught up in the identifying process to such a degree that they neither notice the discrepancies nor that the lighting up of the screen at the end of the show takes on "the whiteness of a shroud" (ibid., 153).

While Suzanne has not "escaped" at the movies, they have provided her relief from the societal-level persecution she, a white girl, has experienced in the white city: a place "where she could hide" (ibid., 151). For her, the theater itself is "an oasis, this dark vast room in the afternoon, it was the night of lonely people, an artificial and democratic night, the great equalitarian night of the cinema, truer than the real night, more delightful, more consoling than any real night" (ibid., 151–2).

A new theater of "democracy" – as the old one of Rousseau finally was not – it is nevertheless, bound to fail by becoming the site of fantasmatic identifications. Mystification begins very quickly: and the humble democracy of the theater's space takes on an aura of the sacred and noble for the girl.

It was the chosen night, open to all, offered to all, more generous and charitable than all the charitable institutions, than all the churches, it was a night in which to console yourself of all the shames, in which to lose your despair, to wash youth clean of all the frightful filth of adolescence.

(Seawall, 152)

Suzanne exaggerates the theater's power. And yet even out of this mystification, which crashes on the shoals of those appetitive lips, a secondary appreciation for the natural or real night installs itself in Suzanne. After the movies, which have hidden her while daylight and whiteness waned, she emerges into the evening, and "it was as if it were the night in the theater which went on, the amorous night of the moving-picture. She felt calm and reassured" (ibid., 153). Though this continuation of the night of the theater fails to bring her the man, it is an "amorous" night in so far as it is no longer the scene of hate and contempt she has (imagined or experienced; projected or received) felt in the streets before. It has also, incidentally, permitted her to hang around in the streets long enough to encounter her brother, even though he will soon enough be "lost in the crowd, lost in the monstrous vulgarity of love." He believes in the movies. With reason.

Chapter 6

The reconstruction of mothering

If the sister is missing in modernity's family romance, it is because her mother has never occupied the symbolic subject position, has never herself been able to be a superego for her daughter: daughters are only supposed to have nature for a commanding mother. This is, I think, an assumption that needs to be rejected – at least provisionally. Now, we will try to imagine how a mother and her daughter might be reconstructed beyond the phallus. The texts I treat in this chapter hint that the Regime of the Brother has not entirely covered the woman with its distorting mythic veil, nor succeeded absolutely in quashing the mother and daughter relation. But they mark only a beginning in a struggle. The woman, the sister, and the daughter need a different kind of mother to achieve value and identity in the modern world.

Reconstructing the desire of the mother

For society must take as one of its important educative tasks to tame and restrict the sexual instinct when it breaks out as an urge to reproduction, to subject it to an individual will which is identical with the bidding of society.

(Freud, *Introductory Lectures* XX[1])

Only a mother – or some part of her maternal function – could model a daughter's desire, beyond the suppression, denial, and alienation that term stands for when her brother is in charge. But what does a "mother" want? In the Oedipal frame, for the child to respond to the desire of the mother rather than accepting the name of the father is technically "psychotic." To use Lacan's idiom, psychosis is determined by the ego's refusal of identification in the normalized mode, the foreclosure of the *nom-du-père*. The foreclosure is the result of identifying with the desire of the mother rather than accepting metaphoric identification (through the "name"), the exchanging structure which substitutes or replaces the mother with the father, her desire with his.[2] But, again, what is the "mother's" desire? The term is as vague as possible in modernity – an unexpressed, unnamed urge (does she desire our life, our death?). Thus for her daughter to follow its non-pattern, the results would be disastrously psychotic (the refusal of the name of the father), a kind of final absence of relation to the Other.

Must we be satisfied with this definition of the mother's desire? Marguerite Duras gives it to us much more tersely, and without vagueness. In the Regime of the Brother, and under the terms he has set, it is the son who is "the only object of her love" (*The Lover*, 7). Put this way we can begin to see how unlikely it is that the mother is the unique source of her own desire – it is far too congenial to the ego-needs of her son.

As I noted above, in a rare sociological aside Freud depicted bleakly (in "'Civilized' sexual morality and modern nervous illness" (*SE IX*)) the mother's desire: knowledge of sexuality withheld from her as a girl, an age and experiential disparity between her and a husband with many sexual options (other women, masturbation, other men), means the young mother begins to form sexual appetites just at the moment her aging mate finds his abating.[3] The result, Freud tells us, is a tremendous displacement by the mother onto the child not of her "own" sexual desire (of which she knows all too little), but of the fruits of its frustration. What she reproduces in her children is only a model of bitter lack of satisfaction:[4]

> To the uninitiated it is hardly credible how seldom normal potency is to be found in a husband, and how often a wife is frigid, among married couples living under the dominance of our civilized sexual morality. . . . The most obvious outcome is nervous illness; but I must further point out the way in which a marriage of this kind continues to exercise its influence on the few children, or the only child born of it. At first glance, it seems to be a case of transmission by inheritance; but closer inspection shows that it is the effect of powerful infantile impressions. A neurotic wife who is unsatisfied by her husband is, as a mother, over-tender and over-anxious towards her child, to whom she transfers her need for love, and thus she awakens it to sexual precocity. The bad relations between its parents, moreover, excites its emotional life, and causes it to feel love and hatred to an intense degree, while it is still at a very tender age. Its strict upbringing, which tolerates no activity of the sexual life that has been aroused so early, lends support to the suppressing forces and this conflict at such an age contains everything necessary for bringing about lifelong nervous illness.
>
> (*SE IX*, 201–2)

Freud treats the mother's neurosis, then, as a historical condition, no\ as a permanent cultural feature. More than that, he names what the mother is denied in and by her husband's neglect – "her need for love." What this passage makes plain (whether Freud "meant" it to be or not), is that the origin of her "desire" for her son has a source in her lived reality, her experience of being severed from relation to the man she has married – by that man and the social conditions of her sexual education and marriage.

Narrative support for this belief on Freud's part can be found. While the mother–son relation has dominated analytic thought (literary and psychological), later Victorian and contemporary literature has occasionally centered on the mother–daughter relation, reading it often just outside the confines of a fraternal-Oedipal dramatic frame. In the post-Oedipal symbolic, the nuclear, and the post-colonial situations, we can now read three texts that reconstruct the mother–daughter couple differently: *What Maisie Knew*,[5] *The Lover*,[6] and *The Ravishing of Lol V. Stein*.[7] The comparison is not altogether inapt from a comparative literary perspective: Duras adapted and translated two of James's short stories for the French stage ("The beast in the jungle," and "The Aspern Papers").[8] More importantly they each, divergently, focus on the relation of the young girl's desire to a maternal model – specifically to its absence – in the post-Oedipal Regime of the Brothers.

The modern daughter has no mother. Is she thus condemned to being seduced (and, as we later know, abandoned) by the patriarchy, annihilated by the brother, reduced to answering, like little Henriette for Julie, only the desire of the "Other" – the false father? Without a mother, can a daughter hope to form and formulate her own wishes, can she articulate her right to demand the love she, like any human being (but she in particular because she's been so long denied it) needs? The answer is both no and yes.

I turn first to two daughters from the post-Oedipal family who are the subject of my analysis in this book. The one is Maisie Farange, child of divorce, and stepchild of two people who become, in turn, lovers, in Henry James's *What Maisie Knew*. She comes to know "what (or perhaps *that*) she wants," and she does so in the absence of a mother. The other is the fifteen-and-a-half-year-old French colonial girl from Indochina who has an inter-racial affair in Marguerite Duras's *The Lover*. This girl also comes to know herself as desiring, though differently from Maisie: her mother plays a key role not by her absence, but by her exemplarity. She is a mother who does not desire as a subject – and who does. Her daughter reads her mother's desire dually, inside of, and outside the frame of her son, the girl's "elder brother."

What Maisie Knew and *The Lover:* of "amour"

> This self-betrayal of women always struck me as a mistake, an
> error. You didn't have to attract desire. Either it was in the woman
> who aroused it or it didn't exist. Either it was there at first glance
> or else it had never been. It was instant knowledge of sexual rela-
> tionship or it was nothing. That too I knew before I experienced it.
>
> (Marguerite Duras, *The Lover*, 18)

James's *What Maisie Knew* has something to tell us about "familial
eros" – largely because Maisie is so utterly devoid of a natural family.
In fact, Maisie is a kind of test of our human capacity to symbolize
desire even without benefit of the "real" family to "pre-figure" it: to
want. Maisie's parents Beale and Ida Farange have already decided,
when the book opens, that since they are only ordinary when they
are together, "they would be much more striking apart," indicating,
perhaps, the primary modality that frames erotic relations in modern
bourgeois culture: *uncoupling*. (James is indeed predictive of the way
the whole process of conjuring fictive relations to others and then
eradicating them accelerates in the Regime of the Brother: the manic
coupling and uncoupling I have described above.) It is a process that
also tries to split their child in two, reversing Solomon's ancient judgment: Maisie is to live with each in turn. As a result of this bitter
divorce, her parents' relation to each other is entirely formed around
economics: mother and father are engaged – like any two unrelated
persons in our society – in an all-out financial war with each other.

While it is true that a certain excessive Oedipalism operates to
condition the terms of the divorce (Beale wishes to prevent the
mother from contaminating her daughter with her "touch"; Ida is
bent on barring the father from even so much as "looking at" the
child), the two have clearly destroyed (or perhaps accelerated) the
basic "intent" of the Oedipal paradigm, at least in its ideological
form: they prepare Maisie for no future coupling. Nor for marriage
and reproduction, nor for taking a place (a job) in modern society. If
she grows to maturity she will neither be the site of the "reproduction of mothering" nor a part of the symbolic-economic order. The
egocentricity of each parent effectively blocks any systematic practical
and/or moral instruction for their mutual child, providing nothing in
the way of a regular education. Nor does the state supplement the
nuclear family's deficiency.

The severed bond between Maisie's parents produces an
unintended effect in the child. Originally split, Maisie synthesizes
herself without recourse to imaginary identification: we have no
Maisie-in-the-mirror, neither we nor she ever (apparently) know what
Maisie looks like. She selects, that is, the radical alternative to being

denied positive identity in the fraternal order: she simply will not be there. Her way of synthesizing her "identity" is not to pretend to a substantial subjectivity no brother would ever grant her, but instead to turn herself into a term in a relation: she becomes a "sign," the means of connecting the severed parents. Shuttled from one household to the other when she is very young, Maisie is used like a trained parrot to deliver a hate message from father to mother: "He said I was to tell you, from him," she faithfully reported, "you're a nasty horrid pig!" (*What Maisie Knew*, 24). At this point she is a message, not a sign. From her mother's reaction to her faithful recitation, Maisie puzzles out that neither the content nor the act of transmission is what counts: it matters to its receiver, who has taken it to signify a desire on the part of the sender. The desire is hateful, but it is desire notwithstanding: in Maisie's connective and unmetaphorical eyes, the message's conscious function – to separate Ida and Beale still further from each other – seems to be a strong indicator of a relation between them.

Maisie also sees that it works just as much the other way, that its conscious intent is to disconnect, and she also deals with this contingency. Understanding, suddenly, "the strange office she filled" in the exchange of hate, Maisie undergoes "literally a moral revolution," in which "old forms and phrases began to have a sense that frightened her": they are, one might say, metaphorized. With the acquisition of metaphor, which again splits the child in two (inner/ outer; he/she; self/other), Maisie begins to develop something of a germinal identity, but not along, as Lacan put it, "the path of the brother" – the one that leads to a non-place in the symbolic order. Maisie experiences the metaphoric order as "a new feeling, the feeling of danger; on which a new remedy rose to meet it, the idea of an inner self, or, in other words, concealment" (*Maisie*, 25). She acquires identity, not as a non-entity, but as an "idiot," the "metaphoric" name she now takes. Thus disguised as an "idiot" Maisie begins to "learn," to know a thing or two: the operations of the signifier are especially clear to her because she knows how it has produced her own false identity.

Attention to this form of representation affords Maisie the power to read the hidden imperatives, the codes that command in the most "hidden" discourses. Maisie knows that she is expected "to know" and "to learn" – but what? The concept is epistemologically empty for her:

As she was condemned to know more and more, how could it logically stop before she should know Most? It came to her in fact as they sat there on the sands that she was distinctly on the road to know Everything.

(ibid., 195)

Maisie is, however, a different order of epistemological being from her elders, a modernized mind. Having been made by her parents into a sign, having herself embodied the phatic function, Maisie has made a hole in the normal veil of polite language, allowing her to glimpse the work of the signifier. The phallic definition of the signifier ordinarily prevents everyone, and especially the young girl, from "knowing" the interhuman relation, coupling.

Maisie has, however, already seen the naked parental relation, hateful though it may be. She is justifiably averse to going on looking at it, and like Henriette in *Julie*, is happy to latch on to a mother-in-the-phallic-mode-of-mother-substitute, her governess Miss Overmore. Miss Overmore can re-cover meaning, making the signifier very attractive to Maisie, who at first hopes to forget the coupling she has witnessed: "not by anything she said, but by a mere roll of those fine eyes which Maisie already admired" (*Maisie*, 25). Maisie will not have to tell what or that she knows – the passionate shape of the parental relation she has embodied between her parents:

> Her parted lips locked themselves with the determination to be employed no longer. She would forget everything, she would repeat nothing, and when as tribute to her successful application of her system, she began to be called a little idiot, she tasted a pleasure new and keen.
>
> (ibid., 25)

The pleasure the child feels is the shelter, the hiding afforded by the signifier-as-metaphor. The girl-child retreats into the safe room, inner space. In the post-Oedipal order, in fact, there are, according to Maisie's other (phallic) mother, Mrs Wix, only two "safe" places for little girls to be: up in heaven, or safely in the grave.[9] Maisie's wonder at this impossible structure – both buried under the ground and raised aloft to heaven at the same time – parallels her perplexities with the distinction inside=knowledge/outside=mere form structure, but she is willing to give it a try.[10]

Maisie can learn nothing from Miss Overmore about the very thing about which the family is supposed to "educate" one to proper morality and which is ultimately rooted in the restrictions placed on erotic relations. Such morality appears as the art of uncoupling (incest taboos; the base of the familial relation) in the guise of coupling (marriage, kinship, etc.); for Miss Overmore marries Maisie's father and becomes her stepfather's lover and eventual fiancée.

Yet, from her position as "poor little monkey," "idiot," "wretch," "donkey," and finally "old boy" (she is never addressed as "girl"), Maisie continually sees the shape of the interhuman relationship that words are supposed to prevent from taking place. Every "revelation," every "truth," – not just sexual – in the novel becomes not just a "metaphor" but a signifier – a drama of signification – for Maisie. For example, Maisie's mother momentously asks to speak with her daughter as she is about to abandon her (to her stepfather). Ida melodramatically announces that she is "excessively ill" (*Maisie*, 152). We – and Maisie – are supposed to accept this statement as a piece of knowledge. Because of her sub-human epistemological status (despite, or maybe because of, her upper middle class position), Maisie takes this "devastating" announcement as merely a formal declaration, one with neither performative or constative value. It simply holds a slot, a place in the conversation: "This for a minute struck Maisie as but a part of the conversation" (ibid.). It is only later that Maisie realizes she is supposed to take it as meaningful form: "she became aware that it ought to strike her . . . as a part of something graver" (ibid.).

Her exploded nuclear family has, that is, failed in the proper veiling of the erotic, passionate basis of its (and her) existence, even when that passion is not love nor sexual desire, but pure hatred. The specific failure of her family structure has put her in a position to grasp the order of the signifier (Maisie reads the raised eyebrow, the tone of voice, the rolled eyes). Thus although she is obedient, knowing that there are corridors she must walk down without opening any of the doors off them, she cannot help but understand that it is this division – partitioning – that creates the "sexuality" (or sexuality-effect) her elders imagine themselves to be hiding.[11] Much more, then, than innocence, which is a moral value, it is sheer ignorance that is at issue. If ignorance appears as knowledge (and vice versa) in and through Maisie,[12] it is only the formal condition of knowing what the characters in *Maisie* fulfill. The failure of knowledge of their erotic relations in the novel is general; the everything Maisie (and everyone else) is supposed to know is clearly nothing. Maisie's uneducated presence lays bare the devices by means of which the general epistemological failure of humanity is covered with metaphors. She tries, she makes every effort to be seduced by metaphor: once educated by and to the signifier, the bearer of value, and the bearer of meaning, Maisie acquires competency in its use. It has, after all, provided her with the kind of pseudo-knowledge all the adults have: Maisie does not know about its meaning, but she does "know" the significance of the word "compromised" in relation to a lady's virtue "since her third year": "It was the condition most frequently discussed at the Faranges', where the word was always in the air and where at the age of five, amid rounds of applause, she could gabble it off" (*Maisie*, 123).

The sexual and/or social relation can be designated only if it is already symbolically ordered, that is, given a form and a value. The term "compromised" is negative – Maisie catches this "tint." Since this value is merely formal – an effect of the signifier whose work it is to imply something other – it can always be turned inside out. And so it is, when Maisie's mother Ida is caught by her second husband Claude (and her daughter) not only in a lie, but in the company of her current lover, the Captain. Maisie is hustled off with the new lover, with whom she is previously unacquainted, while Ida and Claude argue. The Captain hastens to reassure Maisie by blocking the obvious applicability of the term "compromised." He offers, in its place, a substitute, its opposite: Ida, he tells Maisie, is "true."

It is an empty gesture, a gallant misstatement for reasons of politeness before a child who is, contractually, obligated to take the adult lie for truth:

> "I assure you she has had the most infernal time, no matter what anyone says to the contrary. She's too charming." [Maisie] had been touched already by his tone, and now she leaned back in her chair and felt something tremble within her. "She's tremendous fun – she can do all sorts of things better than I've ever seen anyone. She has the pluck of fifty – and I know; I assure you I do. She has the nerve for a tiger-shoot – by Jove I'd *take* her! And she is awfully open and generous, don't you know? there are women that are such horrid sneaks. She'll go through anything for anyone she likes." He appeared to watch for a moment the effect on his companion of this emphasis; then he gave a small sigh that mourned the limits of the speakable. But it was almost with the note of a fresh challenge that he wound up: "Look here, she's *true!*"
>
> (*Maisie*, 111–12)

Maisie knows that the content of these words is entirely irrelevant, since her mother has not only been caught with another man, but also in an outright lie (she was supposed to have been at a billiard tournament). They convey only values, in this case, positive ones. She also knows that the negative (compromised) is already the other face of the positive (true) form proffered here.

The term "compromised" covers over an interhuman relation – an arrangement recognizing two different sexes – with a verbal substitution. Maisie wants desperately to make use of this veiling to blind herself (mercifully) to the tangle of amorous relations around her (to her stepfather's affair with her stepmother; to her old governess's "crush" on her stepfather; her mother's "stepping out" on Sir Claude). If she succeeds, she will be a full-fledged "lady." She fails. And she does so because, as James writes in the preface, Maisie evokes the moral sense, "spreading and contagiously acting" (*Maisie*,

12). That is, she continues to act, or rather to act as if she were a term in a set of sexual relations. Even when the adults claim to agree with this they do not, cannot do so: for what the book makes abundantly clear is that the adults do not "know" sexuality either: they know only its forms, its values, its "effects" – and then not really that, because they literally cannot recognize its most salient one – the child. Not only Maisie's natural, biological parents openly break their relation to her; but so do their substitutes (governesses, the step-mother and stepfather) even while they proclaim how child-centered they are: quite literally nobody cares for Maisie.[13] Real others are completely absent from her life.

Maisie is not, however, fully successful in her attempt to rely on the signifier, to help her "unlearn" what she already knows. For Maisie is unable to bury her knowledge – it always comes out because it was never really in: the inner/outer dichotomy exists only in a space that is already moral space, a space organized by what was once the law of the father and now promulgated under the decrees of the brother.

Maisie makes the significant slip. Once this politely ambiguous "explanation" is given, the polite, the moral, thing to do would be for her simply to accept it. She should not ask, if she wants to be safe within the bounds of the traditional symbolic, about its passionate, interhuman meaning.[14] The act, she feels, invites her to join the social (im)moral order. Someone, that is, has finally had the decency to lie to her, just for her. For the very first time in the book she is addressed by her name ("He [the Captain] called her by her name, and her name drove it home" [*Maisie*, 113]), thus recognizing her – symbolically – as a "young lady," and giving her a "proper name." This is the *rite de passage* in a world without mothers and fathers.

> She had never, she thought, been so addressed as a young lady, not even by Sir Claude the day, so long ago, that she found him with Mrs Beale. It struck her as the way that at balls, by delightful partners, young ladies must be spoken to in the intervals of dances; and she tried to think of something that would meet it at the same high point. But this effort flurried her, and all she could produce was, 'At first, you know, I thought you were Lord Eric.'
>
> The Captain looked vague. 'Lord Eric?'
>
> 'And then Sir Claude thought you were the Count.'
>
> At this he laughed out. 'Why he's only five foot high and as red as a lobster!'
>
> Maisie laughed, with a certain elegance, in return – the young lady at the ball certainly would – and was on the point, as conscientiously, of pursuing the subject with an agreeable question.

But before she could speak her companion challenged her. 'Who in the world's Lord Eric?'

'Don't you know him?' She judged her young lady would say that with light surprise.

(*Maisie*, 110)

Maisie's proper "education" has failed. Not having been prevented from seeing the interhuman relation the words obscure, Maisie attends their meaning – what she thinks is the feeling that motivates them, the Captain's love for her mother. So she appreciates the Captain's words less for the positive construction they have put on a bad situation, but for the fact that someone – for the very first time in her life – loves her mother. And in loving her, is meeting her mother's "need for love" making her into an other to be cared for.

It is telling that her primary passion is for her (or a) mother. When the Captain exclaims, in a final escalation of rhetoric to cover up their peccadilloes in front of the little girl, "My dear Maisie, your mother's an angel!" (*Maisie*, 113), Maisie is thrilled:

It was an almost unbelievable balm. . . . She sank back in her chair, she covered her face with her hands. 'O mother, mother, mother!' she sobbed. . . . 'Say you love her, Mr Captain; say it, say it!' she implored. – 'Of course I love her, damn it, you know!'

(*Maisie*, 113)

"Damn it, you know" – signifiers that frame, deny, and justify the nonsense he has just uttered.

The function of franglais

Maisie is a decided moral "failure": she knows about relations, even if she is not permitted to express her knowledge, nor to experience them herself. What she has tried to bury is the knowledge of semiosis (the means of the production of interhuman meaning). In her relation to Claude she begins to unbury it.[15]

This is in part due to Claude's great mastery of the signifier, his ability to conceal his and everyone else's couplings. Claude is Maisie's stepfather, Sir Claude, the impoverished aristocrat who has married her mother, and he is also the paramour of her stepmother, married to Beale. Claude is the soul of smooth talk, someone at last among her relations who has "the common decency" to lie to Maisie. He seems destined to move Maisie gracefully into the symbolic relation, the traditional patriarchal role – as an "old boy" – his pet name for her.

He also does not want to. Claude is obviously attracted, that is, sexually, to the girl, though there is no question of his acting on this attraction. We might say that what happens in the text is, in part, a bit of defiance of the Oedipal symbolic and a gesture in the direction of reshaping its foundations.

Maisie's knowledge of the work of the signifier is more general than anyone, including herself, knows. For ultimately, the signifier only works as a form of relation, a differential relation between positive terms, à la Saussure. In fact, James analogizes her to language itself, although, curiously enough, to a specific language: French. The fact is that Maisie is an English child who does not really know French; she has only learned broken touristic bits of it from her false "mother," her governess. French is her false mother tongue. Reaching Boulogne with her stepfather as they flee from both his wife (Ida, Maisie's mother) and his lover (Mrs Beale, Maisie's stepmother, the former Miss Overmore), Maisie "grows older in five minutes." James tells us "[she] had, by the time they reached the hotel recognized in the institutions and manners of France a multitude of affinities and messages" (Maisie, 163).

Maisie sees herself, and especially her education by means of the signifier, in French culture. As James puts it, in France one recognizes the "strict features of a social order principally devoted to language" (ibid., 194). It is a language, moreover, that is not itself principally devoted to meaning, but to the signifier. James emphasizes the ritual, grammatical, even orthographic features of the linguistic as the mark of "French" in his text: the insistent rationality of its paradigms, the monotonous intonation of tour-guide speeches (in no way intended to be understood by the travelers; they are merely markers of the object's value). The very deadness of the ritual – like the deadness of her family – becomes a resistance to the "metaphorizing" of the differential signifier.

One speaks and learns French, even in France, not as a "mother tongue" but like a foreigner, with emphasis on the formal, grammatical, rather than the signifying aspects of the language. This estrangement opens that code to critical consciousness, making it conspicuous. And it does more: it opens her eyes to the resources of an artificial set of terms and relations for modeling her own identity. "French" – the "foreign" and non-mother tongue permits Maisie to see herself familiarly and not uncannily in it: she too has no illusions about the naturalness of her existence. She herself, that is, has neither been mothered, nor fathered.[16] In other words, there never has been such a thing as a maternal relationship in language. The matrix that is conspicuously absent in Maisie is, in addition to the maternal breast, the absence of a mother tongue. Because Maisie has never taken the signifier quite as she was supposed to, as the terms on which she may enter the phallic/symbolic order, language is not the site of the father for her either.

Maisie feels instead "affinity" with a certain song in a cafe in which one is singing about *amour*, a "foreign" word of which Maisie none the less feels she "knows something." This is to be compared with her "gabbling off" of the word "compromised" in her "native" English tongue: in the case of "compromised" she knew herself to be expressing a moral relation; but in the case of *amour* she "knows" something else. What she knows is that *amour* is a formal relation, and that "love" has always been foreign and alien to her. It is thus inevitable that it is in the "foreign/familiar" France that, out of the welter of options and pseudo-options that have been given her for her care, Maisie comes to "know" her desire.

There have been repeated, urgent, attempts to create a fictional, holy, family triangle to get Maisie "settled" (and to stop her from unsettling the symbolic order). Since she is utterly rejected by her mother, the obvious solution would be for the lovers Mrs Beale and Sir Claude to divorce Maisie's respective parents and marry each other and adopt Maisie, for whom they both "care." In this they are opposed adamantly by Maisie's old housewife-governess Mrs Wix, a pillar of the patriarchal household order. She proposes instead that she herself become "mother"/"cook"/"washerwoman" in a household established with Maisie and her stepfather, Sir Claude, somewhere in the south of France. Maisie is, of course, to be the center and the cause for unity, in other words, the sign of the decency of this little arrangement.

We might suppose this to be the perfect solution, the reconstruction, out of artificial bits, of the broken family. And yet, not only has the family as we know it always only been such a reconstruction, it can never take place for Maisie – because of what she knows she wants. What Maisie wants has a dual definition: she "wants" (lacks) a maternal model for her identity as a woman – her own mother is merely a man under her handsome clothes. Miss Overmore can only play the "feminine" part, rolling eyes and being the sexual hypocrite. And Mrs Wix's relation to Maisie, organized by declarations, statements to the effect that everything she does is for the child, must be read in the light of her adoration of the Madonna, whom she adores because she sees in her a mother like herself, one whose child dies. Ultimately the only portion given to a "mother's desire" in this book is to Mrs Wix, who faithfully, dutifully, does the work not of meeting Maisie's or her own needs, real needs (nurturing the body), nor of eros (keeping the other alive – her daughter dies), but the weary old phallic one: eliminating the daughter's desire. Thus even though Mrs Wix seems to promise a "satisfying" maternity, she never delivers.

Is there a mother's desire that is not that of alienating, narcissistic desire, nor the brother's entirely negating one? The real function of a mother – practical, animal, and human – is to relate to the real needs and demands of real others. Such a real mother is absent from this scene. Even that proves no final obstacle to the resourceful Maisie.

Maisie elects the other definition of what she "wants" and it is more a sexual than a maternal or parental relation, although it has elements of both. Maisie declares decisively: "Him alone or nobody" (*Maisie*, 213).[17] She rejects the (pseudo)family in favor of the sexual relation – with her stepfather, Claude. If she cannot have that, if the symbolic order precludes it absolutely, she will have nobody – in the "positive" form of Mrs Wix: "'Not even *me*?' cried Mrs Wix. Maisie looked at her for a moment, then began to undress. 'Oh you're nobody'" (ibid.).

Maisie adamantly insists that she wants Claude without the intervention of either Mrs Wix or Mrs Beale: him alone. Her decision is consistent with Mrs Wix's complaint about her that she is deficient in the moral sense her childhood condition evokes in others. Attempting to apply the moral lessons "infused" in her by Mrs Wix while contemplating the Madonna together, Maisie responds to Mrs Wix's inexplicit condemnation of the adulterous liaison of Mrs Beale and Claude "in the name of" religion – a crime, "Branded such by the Bible" (*Maisie*, 197) – by offering to kill Mrs Beale (ibid., 199) if she reappears with Sir Claude: "That at least, she hoped as she looked away, would guarantee her moral sense" (ibid.).

Why choose Claude, who is as smooth a manipulator of the signifier as anyone in the text? Well, Claude is an interesting case. He emphasizes his own maternal side – a side which horrifies the moral Mrs Wix who wants him to play the traditional manly social role as figure-head of an ideal family. More importantly, Claude slips in his grammar of polite lying, and he errs on the side of expressing a bit of desire: he tells Maisie (in the presence of his lover, Mrs Beale!) that he would give Maisie up if only she were not so beautiful, opening his relation to her to an erotic reading. Mrs Beale immediately intervenes at this point to reframe and redefine what he has just said as meaning that Maisie is morally beautiful, having "plain dull charm of character" that lacks "personal loveliness" and "*that* vulgar beauty" (*Maisie*, 98). The most amoral people do the work of the moral order, which demands separation: Mrs Beale is jealous, of course, but her intent goes beyond desire or love: she merely feels she must interrupt any budding relation other than the pseudo-familial one between the man and the girl.

Without the cover-up of his role as pseudo-mother, the basically incestuous nature of the father–daughter relation would be apparent. But then, Claude is not her father, really, and Maisie is, clearly, by the time of the French voyage, no longer a very "little" girl. Dressing Maisie for the momentous occasion of her decision about her future Mrs Wix gives "an almost invidious tug," as she made "a strained undergarment 'meet'" (*Maisie*, 214) – Maisie is growing (breasts).

Maisie defeats or deconstructs the command (inherent in a "common language," the word, metaphor) to prevent connections and deny relations to the other. What matters is that, whereas Maisie can use one language or another to represent her needs – let alone her desire – for a relationship with someone to a third party, when it comes to expressing want to its subject, Maisie must use an inter-lingual form: *franglais*. It becomes the marked "thirdness" which allows the sharing of desire by its means.

Deferring the final decision that will necessarily force something to come between them definitively – time, space, Mrs Wix or Mrs Beale – Maisie and Claude silently agree to prolong a walk without the others. They arrive (unawares?) at the railroad station, where a train for Paris is about to pull out. In arriving at this railroad station Maisie is not arriving at the categorization (Lacan's "ladies and gentlemen" rubrics on the separated bathroom doors). Maisie ends here. There has, however, been a momentary stay of execution.

Claude asks the porter in French about the Parisian train, the price of the tickets. Rather short of funds, and weighted with the moral order, he hesitates to take the plunge and purchase the two seats. Maisie waits with him, and although she does not, we know, have any real ability to speak French, miraculously, understands the conversation. She is practiced in understanding, that is, the desires and the passions which conversational forms mediate and hide. With great excitement she calls out to Claude in a pidgin tongue, "Oh prenny prenny," the franglais for "take them, buy them."

What Maisie has "understood" is the meaning of the words, the realm of needs – she wants to survive. And she is aware that others are equally in need. Claude and Maisie momentarily and mutually retrieve this understanding from the disconnecting order, and this understanding is shared and not divided by the two. That the moment does not last, is not sustained into a break with the order, does not negate its importance as a kind of resistance, or perhaps rather an expression of "lack." Claude especially cannot sustain the resistance: he is a man, after all, he cannot be nothing – even though the only "mirror" in which he, like she, recognizes himself is the frightened face of the young girl. He will go back to Mrs Beale – though he now hates her and their marriage will be as much of a sham, as much as an example of the incompatibility of marriage and sexual pleasure as any formal marriage has ever been.

Maisie's final words in the book, replying to Mrs Wix's sour "revelation" to the child of Sir Claude's liaison with Mrs Beale of which Maisie has been perfectly aware, is "Oh, I know!" (*Maisie*, 248). As she goes off with a not-quite triumphant Mrs Wix, who gets the child but not the man, the phrase is disturbing: "Mrs Wix gave a sidelong look. She still had room for wonder at what Maisie knew" (ibid.).

What she knew, and what we learn from her is that familial eros, with no pre-figurations to guide us – can be reinvented post-Oedipally not by imitating the traditional father/mother relation, but by taking on the subject position of one who lacks, one whose identity can none the less be affirmed by the nature of the desire in question. Hers is in a sense one of its only positive forms (or rather, Maisie takes it that way): rather than permitting the accusation of lack (launched by Oedipus and completely ignored by the brother) to further negate her identity, Maisie makes it into the basis of one of the most complete identities a fictional character has seen. She exploits the "qualities" or "anti-qualities" of lack, just as the language she feels so close to exploits the difference without positive terms in order to create meaning (*à la* Saussure). This strategy is only partly successful, I think, because in spite of Claude's fulfilling the function of standing in for the mother's desire, Maisie ultimately lacks a model for the mother's desire, the mother's pleasure. The mother, that is, who is not the bitter reject of the modern brotherly Oedipal paradigm.

The next text I turn to does bring forward a more concrete "mother's desire." For it is a desire which is not entirely shaped by the phallic order of either the father or the brother, although it is to a great extent. What the mother in Marguerite Duras's *The Lover* does is both to license and to model her daughter's desire, even while she herself is never satisfied (or rather only satisfies the orders of the Brother).

The Lover

> I wanted to kill – my elder brother, I wanted to kill him, to get the better of him for once, just once, and see him die. I wanted to do it to remove from my mother's sight the object of her love, that son of hers, to punish her for loving him so much, so badly, and above all – as I told myself, too – to save my younger brother, my younger brother, my child, save him from the living life of that elder brother superimposed on his own, from that black veil over

the light, from the law which was decreed and represented by the
elder brother, a human being, and yet which was an animal law,
filling every moment of every day of the younger brother's life with
fear, a fear that one day reached into his heart and killed him.

(Marguerite Duras, *The Lover*, 7)

I return now to Duras. While in Part II my concern was with the
brother's production of the ultimate woman, the egocentric Riva, of
whom Duras is very critical, here I will look at her other women,
those who resist deeply, if not always overtly, their negative determination by the fraternal Oedipus. *The Lover* is an extraordinary book,
all the more extraordinary for its being (much like *Hiroshima, mon
amour*) a popular bourgeois romance. It deals with a young girl's
adolescent, teenage (perhaps pre-teen) sexuality in a way that no
bourgeois frame – from *Teen* magazine to the current wave of "free"
teenage sex movies (*Fast Times at Ridgemont High*) – would ever really
do, although James's text (like Freud's analyses) hint at it. As the
story of an adolescent girl who takes an inter-racial lover freely, with
knowledge, without being seduced, it is a deeply amoral book, and
it tests how far we subscribe to the white morality of the Regime of
the Brother ("law which was decreed and represented by the elder
brother" [*The Lover*, 7]); as well as the "colored morality" of the
traditional "native" father: "the one who owned the money. . . . He
won't let his son marry the little white whore from Sadec" (ibid., 35).

Like Maisie, Duras's "Marguerite" explains that her family has
exploded, fallen apart: "I say we lived out of doors, poverty had
knocked down the walls of the family and we were all left outside,
each one fending for himself" (ibid., 45).[18] Her father is dead, and
as we have seen, her brother is in charge. She characterizes her elder
brother as a thief, a cruel killer and hunter (although he does not
literally murder anyone), stupid, utterly destructive, and completely
empowered, without his ever having to say a word, or lift a finger.
This mother of the fatherless family in colonial Indochina, composed
of two brothers and one sister, does his bidding. The son's usurpa-
tion of the patriarchal function is made completely clear when he
makes common cause with a traditional Chinese capitalist – the father
of his sister's lover – against the sexual alliance of the two.

He dominates his younger brother in particular:

All three of us are eating at the dining-room table. They're seventeen, eighteen. My mother's not with us. He watches us eat, my
younger brother and me, then he puts down his fork and looks at
my younger brother. For a very long time he looks at him, then
suddenly, very calmly, says something terrible. About food. He
says he must be careful, he shouldn't eat so much. My younger

brother doesn't answer. The other goes on. Reminds him the big pieces of meat are for him, and he mustn't forget it. Or else, he says. I ask, Why are they for you? He says, Because that's how it is. I say, I wish you'd die. I can't eat any more. Nor can my younger brother. He waits for my younger brother to dare to speak, just one word, his clenched fists are poised ready over the table to bash his face in. My younger brother says nothing.

(*The Lover*, 80)

"Or else." When the sister objects, "Why?" he feels he need give no response, he issues demands. Once more the grandest lie, alibi, and excuse of modern brotherhood is laid bare in this passage: fraternal "similarity" yields before the aggressiveness of the elder brother's ego, which alone exercises power and authority.

What is more, he can have his cake and eat it, too: he can act like a father without having to give up being the beloved son. Duras tells us he is also "the favorite child," the one to whom the mother feels compelled to sacrifice everything (especially her other children). He reigns supreme, father and child rolled into one.

It is, however, less the strangely liberated daughter (we shall see why she is), and the dominated younger brother, than a certain difference in the figure of the mother that interests me here. This mother is motherly enough in the bourgeois sense: she is not destitute nor utterly despairing like Rhys's Annette Cosway Mason, and she is competent to keep her children despite her poverty, isolation, and widowhood. Sometimes she simply does not, she despairs: head of a fatherless family, she is sometimes suddenly "ashamed to live":

all three of us are our mother's children, the children of a candid creature murdered by society. We're on the side of the society which has reduced her to despair. Because of what's been done to our mother, so amiable, so trusting, we hate life, we hate ourselves.

(*The Lover*, 55)

Done what? "Their mother never knew pleasure"(ibid., 39).

Though this is the first person narrative by the daughter it is really the story of the mother, the mother forced into the world of the brother, the family that develops after the death of her own father and of the father of her children. (She sees them both as apparitions the day they die.) In the brother's world, the mother is at least half mad, for she is ruled by alternate terror of and indulgent love for her son, "the only object of her love" (*The Lover*, 7). The son is projected for the mother as the exclusive focus of her libidinal attention in this post-patriarchal family.

And only the elder son; the mother never has time for the younger son, does not attend to him, although he is in fact the equal of his elder brother:

> Battles break out regularly between my brothers, for no apparent reason except the classic one by which the elder brother says to the younger, Clear out, you're in the way. . . . They both have the same talent for anger. . . . When they fought we were equally afraid for both of their lives.
>
> (*The Lover*, 60)

Nevertheless she tends her daughter obliquely. She tells her daughter. "Perhaps you'll escape" – what? "Day and night this obsession. It's not that you'll have to achieve anything, it's that you have to get away from where you are" (ibid., 23). So the mother licenses tacitly Marguerite's liaison with her older, Chinese lover, licenses her daughter's affair with the Chinese not only in deed but in terms of desire. She goes to her daughter's boarding school and tells them not to mind if her daughter stays out all night, and at one point she questions Marguerite,

> Is it only for the money you see him? I hesitate, then say it is only for the money. Again, she looks at me for a long while, she doesn't believe me. She says, I wasn't like you, I found school much harder and I was very serious, I stayed like that too long, too late, I lost the taste for my own pleasure.
>
> (*The Lover*, 93)

The mother must be mad, of course, that's it: she is erratic, ambivalent, schizoid . . . from the viewpoint of both Oedipus and the brother. Yet at the root of her aberrations is her utter deprivation: not a single need is ever fulfilled. "It happened every day. Of that I'm sure. It must have come on quite suddenly. At a given moment every day the despair would make its appearance . . . the moodiness, the dejection" (ibid., 15). Yet out of this despair, another path – for her daughter – struggles to be formed. For after all, her mother takes back with one hand what she had given with the other. She beats Marguerite for having the affair, upbraids and berates her:

> My mother has attacks in which she falls on me, locks me up in my room, punches me, undresses me, comes up to me and smells my body, my underwear, says she can smell the Chinese's scent, goes even further, looks for suspect stains on my underwear, and shouts, for the whole town to hear, that her daughter's a prostitute, she's going to throw her out, she wishes she'd die, no one will have anything to do with her, she's disgraced, worse than

a bitch. And she weeps, asking what she can do, except drive her out of the house so she can't stink the place up any more.

(ibid., 58)

So here the mother is acting the moralist, obeying the superego, fulfilling a certain desire of the Other – or more concretely – the elder brother's wishes:

Outside the walls of the locked room, my brother. He answers my mother, tells her she's right to beat the girl, his voice is lowered, confidential, coaxing, he says they must find out the truth, at all costs, must find out in order to save the girl, save the mother . . . the mother hits her as hard as she can. . . . I know my elder brother's glued to the door, listening, he knows what my mother's doing, he knows the girl's naked, being beaten and he'd like it to go on and on to the brink of harm. My mother is not unaware of my elder brother's obscure and terrifying intent.

(*The Lover*, 59)

Marguerite's mother is histrionic in her moral indignation – she, too, knows how to "act." She is not "mad" in either the psychic or emotive senses of the term, from her daughter's point of view. She is acting out the brother's desire for his sister. The brother, crouching at the door, knows that the sister will never have a place in society, what her mother fears and desires most for her daughter: "Maybe she'll escape" alternates with "Her daughter's in the direst danger, the danger of never getting married, never having a place in society, of being defenseless against it, lost, alone" (*The Lover*, 58).

It is, we must note, the elder and not the younger brother who must repress the sister, come between her and her mother. "The younger brother shouts at the mother to leave her alone. He goes out into the garden, he hides, he's afraid I'll be killed, he's afraid, he's always afraid of that stranger, our elder brother. My younger brother's fear calms my mother down" (*The Lover*, 59).

The mother wants her daughter to study math. She'll escape: what? The fate of the sister-destined-to-be-mother, the one who "never knew pleasure." Marguerite does not go with the mathematical solution. She will write. "I answered that what I wanted more than anything else in the world was to write. . . . Jealous. She's jealous. . . . But this one, she knows, one day she'll go, she'll manage to escape" (ibid., 22).

And she will write to try to define her own desire, her own pleasure, the one she got to know, against all odds, as a girl of fifteen. In the long run, her brother's final equation of her with her exchange value is decisive. While the mixture of races, sexes, and classes involved in "Marguerite's" relation to her lover is an abomination to her brother, he permits and tolerates it, and does not care if she sleeps with her Chinese – if she gets money from him. The brother as pimp. He does not think to bar their physical relationship: is not he "modern," after all? His permissiveness does not extend to the recognition of the humanity of his sister's trick: he refuses to acknowledge the Chinese as a person in either the legal or humane senses. Thus, "Marguerite's" relation to her lover is licit purely because it is an economic relation, the exclusive criterion of morality:

> It's taken for granted I don't love him, that I'm with him for the money, that I can't love him, it's impossible, that he could take any sort of treatment from me and still go on loving me. This because he's a Chinese, because he's not a white man. The way my elder brother treats my love, not speaking to him, ignoring him, stems from such absolute conviction it acts as a model. We all treat my lover as he does.
>
> (*The Lover*, 51)

She knows it in part because she has, like Maisie, escaped linguistic positioning, the flight into intensive metaphoric contradiction:

> He calls me a whore, a slut, he says I'm his only love, and that's what he ought to say, and what you do say when you just let things say themselves, when you let the body alone, to see and find and take what it likes, and then everything is right.
>
> (ibid., 43)

The couple give up even this poetic language: "Perhaps he realizes they never have spoken to each other, except when they cry out to each other in the bedroom in the evening. Yes, I think he didn't know, he realizes he didn't know" (ibid., 99). When she is making love to her Chinese, Marguerite describes the room as caught up in the city, a city of "pleasure": there are "no panes in the windows, just shutters and blinds" (*The Lover*, 40). It is penetrated by the noise, the "incredibly foreign language" that is Chinese – "a language that's shouted the way I always imagine desert languages are" (ibid., 41), permeated with the "sound of more and more passers-by, more and more miscellaneous." Even visually the others are there in the bedroom with the couple: she sees their shadows, even though cut by the shutters, on the blinds, "There's nothing solid separating us from other people. They do not know of our existence. We glimpse something of them, the sum of their voices, of their movements." Sight, sound, movement – even smell: "the smell of the city is the smell of the villages upcountry, of the forest" (ibid., 41).

Compare the situation to that of the brother, crouching outside the door, imagining what is going on within: he overhears, eavesdrops, probes mentally, but in the end he ("the rummager in closets" (*The Lover*, 79)) can only invade the separated space – the locked room – with his imagination. Perhaps Marguerite's mother is, after all, really only acting for the brother's benefit; the door is locked so that he cannot see that she is not really attacking the girl. Here, a bedroom that is not known to the outside does not invite imaginary aggression by others; it invites them in . . .

The truth of the matter is, this daughter needed her mother in order to be able to find her own identity – needed her not as a model to imitate, for her mother never knew pleasure – but as a model none the less, when her elder brother is not there, when the two have a tête-à-tête really alone, without the brother. The model is there when the mother cleans the house, not according to the norms of the western housewife, but by ways and means she has devised in her "to-ing and fro-ing," her nomadic at-homeness in a foreign land. Hers is not a closed-up household, but the analogue of a garden:

Because the house is raised like this it can be cleaned by having buckets of water thrown over it, sluiced right through like a garden. All the chairs are piled up on tables, the whole house is streaming, water is lapping around the piano in the small sitting room, the water pours down the steps, spreads through the yard toward the kitchen quarters. The little houseboys are delighted, we join in with them, splash one another, then wash the floor with yellow soap. Everyone's barefoot, including our mother. She laughs. She's got no objection to anything. . . . My mother's very happy with this disorder, she can be very happy sometimes, long enough to forget, the time it takes to clean out the house may be enough to make her happy. . . . I remember, just as I'm writing this, that our elder brother wasn't in Vinh Long when we sluiced the house out.

(*The Lover*, 61)

Consciously, conscientiously, of course, the mother worries about everything ("an accident, or a fire, or a rape, or an attack by pirates, or a fatal mishap on the ferry" (ibid., 9)), cares most conventionally, in the finest bourgeois fashion, for her daughter. Yet the mother knows, "If I want to keep her I have to let her be free" (ibid., 71). To do so, in the brother's world, she must act unconsciously, not be conscientious. She's the one who buys Marguerite gold lamé high heels, a man's fedora (at bargain prices), gives her her old silk dress to wear to school in an act of unaware knowledge: "Not bad, she says, they quite suit you. Make a change. She does not ask if it's she who bought them, she knows she did" (ibid., 23). Her mother gives her daughter the opportunity to put her desire into circulation, to let it out into the streets. The hat frees Marguerite:

> Beneath the man's hat the thin, awkward shape, the inadequacy of childhood, has turned into something else. Has ceased to be a harsh, inescapable imposition of nature. Has become, on the contrary, a provoking choice of nature, a choice of the mind. Suddenly it's deliberate. Suddenly I see myself as another, as another would be seen, outside myself, available to all, available to all eyes, in circulation for cities, journeys, desire.
>
> (*The Lover*, 13)

A streetwalker, the "little white whore from Sadec": yes, from the perspective of the Chinese father, the elder brother, but not the mother. She has put Marguerite's desire into circulation, into the social, public relation without demanding it do so only if it takes part in the economy of the brother's desire, the "frozen dialectic" of exchange. For though Marguerite will claim to her brother and her mother that she does it for the money, she really does it because she "loves love" (ibid., 42). She even loves her lover along with it.

Which is to say, that Marguerite, who has no inherent or inherited identity – not even the old one the patriarchy assigned her (domestic woman, angel in the house, whore, mother, etc.) is using this absence to create another one, on a different model from the narcissistic one of the brotherly paradigm. Like Maisie, she will found her identity on nothing more than being a term in a relation. Out of this nothing comes the strength to escape (as her mother obscurely wanted) the patriarchal/fraternal ordering of her mind, her sexuality, and her body. Her body, indeed, like her attire, loses its figure, its figurality, its form:

> Less and less clearly can he make out the limits of this body, it's not like other bodies, it's not finished, in the room it keeps growing, it's still without set form, continually coming into being, not only there where it's visible but elsewhere too, stretching beyond sight, toward risk, toward death, it's nimble, it launches itself wholly into pleasure as if it were grown up, adult, it's without guile, and it's frighteningly intelligent.
>
> (*The Lover*, 99)

Body/mind, child/adult, self/other: the distinctions brought into being by the cutting of metaphor are rendered nil by the addition of the mother, the one who frees a woman's desire. Metonymized, the child's body forms a continuum with that of the adult, with the mind.

Marguerite writes. She makes her mother, she tells us, into "cursive writing" – a different kind of "figuring" the continuity of metonymy. By writing the mother Marguerite has also given her what Freud did not: an active role in the symbolic. The symbolic has not remained unaltered by this addition: it is no longer restricted to the patriarchal/fraternal and negational mode, it is not a simple dialectic of articulation (cutting = joining) but of coupling in a sexual, limitless, mode.

The Ravishing of Lol V. Stein: rewriting the daughter's desire

The Ravishing of Lol V. Stein is the story of a young girl, Lola Valérie Stein, who becomes engaged, is jilted, becomes deranged, is "cured," marries and settles down . . . and then . . . The night of rupture with her fiancé Michael Richardson, though seemingly traumatic, was not the "cause" of her "madness." So her best friend, Tatiana Karl, explains. Tatiana witnessed it all: she saw how the mysterious woman in black (Anne-Marie Stretter) captured Michael's heart with one glance at the Town House Ball, and Lol watched the pair dance all night, hypnotized. Yet, Tatiana recounts that Lol already had the seeds of madness within her, before the Ball.

A straight, common girl's story. But not quite. It radicalizes how absent, how completely not there the girl is under the Regime of the Brother. The patriarchal system, in which women have some exchange value is altered so that any woman (the empty mannequin woman-in-black figure, Anne-Marie Stretter, can supplant Lol in a minute) can be immediately exchanged for any other, the woman now has not even a minimal value. And no place at all – swirled on and off a dance floor.

Like Julie, the young Lol has had a close girl friend – Tatiana Karl. As children on the playground the pair did not follow the rules the other girls did, but stayed away to dance together on the empty school playground on the Thursday holiday: "Shall we dance, Tatiana?" (*Lol Stein*, 2). The playground is converted from its normal use as ritual release from school discipline into an enlarged space for "freeplay" – this is Lol's first dance: "Come, Tatiana, come, let's dance, Tatiana, come on" (ibid.). Tatiana's lack of harmony, lack of comprehension are evident: "It seemed as though she were going nowhere" (*Lol Stein*, 3), Tatiana reflects as she helps the narrator reconstruct Lol's psychobiography. There was, Tatiana explains, always something lacking in Lol, "something which kept her from being, in Tatiana's words, 'there'" (ibid.). When the narrator presses her, wondering if it was "her heart that wasn't there," Tatiana "apparently inclines toward the opinion that it was perhaps, indeed, Lol Stein's heart which wasn't – as she says – there . . . she, Tatiana, had never seen any sign of it" (ibid.).

Tatiana never suspects that Lol's lack, her failure to "be there" results from her modern position. There is no "ground" on which Lol could ever "be there": her realm, as modern young lady, is the realm of the stage, play. Lol's life sequence moves her from one playground to another. From the schoolyard and childhood friendship she moves on to her engagement with Michael Richardson, whom she meets during summer vacation "at the tennis courts" (*Lol Stein*, 2). And her adolescence ends at the great palace of play, the municipal casino of Town Beach, where "the biggest ball of the season was held" (ibid.). It is here that Michael Richardson "exchanges glances" with Anne-Marie Stretter without exchanging a word and literally waltzes off with her into the sunrise, jilting Lol.

A series of clichés brought to novelistic life ("they danced until dawn"; Cinderella at the ball; love at first sight; mysterious and fascinating woman in black, etc. *ad nauseam*), Lol is still, in her most traumatic moment, a character in an old, classic drama. Duras keeps alluding to how each of the characters fits into an old or new tale. Lol does not, even here, quite fit the traditional narrative patterns, or play the expected part:

> As the evening wore on, it seemed that the chances that Lol might suffer were growing increasingly slim, it seemed that suffering had failed to find any chink in her armor through which to slip, that she had forgotten the age-old equation governing the sorrows of love.
>
> (*Lol Stein*, 9)

The others, all of them, slip further and further into ancient, prescribed narrative patterns:

> They had failed to realize that the orchestra had stopped playing: after the break, at the moment when it should have started in again, they had moved back together, like robots, deaf to the fact that there was no longer any music. It was at this point that the musicians filed past them one by one, their violins enclosed in funereal cases.
>
> (ibid.)

Lol begins screaming as Richardson and Stretter leave her; since we have been told she is "mad" we hardly notice that the narrator ascribes to the content of her screaming "perfect sense" (*Lol Stein*, 10), and the same can be said of her long illness and convalescence. She now seems to suffer, never leaves her room, and she complains of being unbearably tired of waiting:

> She was bored, so bored she wanted to scream. And, in fact, she

did scream that she had nothing to think about while she was waiting, she demanded, with childlike impatience, an immediate remedy for this deficiency. Yet none of the distractions that had been offered her had in any way affected this condition.

(ibid., 14)

What we are witnessing is the girl's decline into "madness" because she does not fit the narrative pattern, the stereotype set-up of female adolescent attitudes toward her "desire." She is supposed to "desire" to continue to be the thing Michael Richardson desires, to want to go on dancing herself with Michael Richardson, to be devastated by his departure. By failing to be devastated as expected something else is happening; this she will develop. But only later. For now, she complains – no one listens – that their construction of her "story" is wrong: it is not that he has left her, but that they have left her out. Her complaint, then, is that once she has rejected the narrative position offered her (to be "love-sick" and jilted) she is granted no other – not in reality, not in fantasy. She has no options: "she did scream that she had nothing to think about while she was waiting." This is her lack – the one she is acutely aware of under the regime: hers is a narrative deficiency. When nothing comes to "remedy this deficiency" Lol finally speaks: to complain even more deeply. About her name, about herself:

The only times she did speak was to say how impossible it was for her to express how boring and long it was, how interminable it was, to be Lol Stein. They asked her to try and pull herself together. She didn't understand why she should, she said.

(Lol Stein, 14)

Madness? – or the realization that the role of "aesthetic supplement" is a dead end, nothing, nowhere for the woman. This is a role that Anne-Marie Stretter, vogue-like model, the thingified woman plays: Stretter is the bored emptiness of the ideal-woman, the womanly ideal, a classic. (Stretter is like Riva, in *Hiroshima, mon amour*, to whom the Japanese has been attracted, he tells her, by how bored she looks.[19]) In this narrative she is perfectly dumb, without character or characteristics of her own – she is a figure, who "looks exactly the way she wanted to look." "Tatiana thought, nothing more could ever happen to that woman, nothing. Except her death" (*Lol Stein*, 6).[20]

Let us take up Tatiana's remarks once more – that Lol had no heart, no thereness, no destination. Let us ask these things more seriously: what adolescent girl is ever "going anywhere" under the old – and new, post-Enlightenment – narrative regime? Is she not growing up to "be" Anne-Marie Stretter? The ideal woman? After the Town Beach Ball Lol breaks with this itinerary, despite her family's and doctor's incessant efforts to recuperate her within well-worn narrative formulae. Even the very latest in narrative fashion – the psycho-biographical profile, the "case" history – is a flop: "Her condition was easily explainable: Lol was suffering from a temporary inferiority complex for the simple reason that she had been jilted by the man from Town Beach" (*Lol Stein*, 15). Not quite. "She had become a desert into which some nomad-like faculty had propelled her in the interminable search for what? They did not know. She did not answer" (ibid., 14).

What Lol seems to me to be doing is re-evaluating the fact that being a woman means there is no "there" there; that woman "isn't going anywhere" in particular, lacks a destination, if not an anatomical destiny. She is slowly freeing herself not by becoming more real, longing to be anchored in place, in nature, in a "self," but by increasing her fictionality, by making her freeplay supremely free, exploiting the nomadic. By becoming the subject of desire. Her first steps are tentative: "The first time she went out was at night, alone and without telling anyone she was going" (*Lol Stein*, 15). Seen by her future husband, John Bedford, Lol takes pleasure in "sauntering" in the night-time streets. Bedford plays the gallant part of protecting her. When he realizes that "she was not headed anywhere in particular," however, he is not only intrigued, but his first and automatic gesture is to command her to follow a path, any path. (Later on, married to him, she will create garden paths that radiate out in all directions from her house, none of which intersect.) He wants her to have a purpose, a direction, an object. Lol does not follow him, however: he finds, to his surprise, that he can only follow her. He is wily. Intuiting her name, he identifies her: and tell-ing her he knows who she is does the trick: "meekly, she followed him home." He asks the classic question, "What do you want?" (ibid., 19). A mini-drama of the rise and fall of the leadership of the "romantic" woman has been played.

> Lol was thus married, without wanting to be, in the way that she wished, without her having to resort to the grotesque incongruity of a choice, or to repeat in what, in the eyes of some people, would have amounted to a kind of plagiarism, the crime of replacing the man from Town Beach who has just been jilted with some unique person of her own choice, and above all without having betrayed the exemplary abandon in which he had left her.
>
> (*Lol Stein*, 21)

Lol becomes, like Julie d'Etanges, an absolutely model wife. She not only creates a perfect domestic order, she arranges so perfect a model domestic establishment, that the place runs itself without the least mental or other energy on her part. Her husband, indeed, calls her his "Sleeping Beauty," and is supremely happy (although he has a few affairs on the side). Thus Lol resembles Julie in being a super-domestic wife, and in having lost her adolescent love, not of her boyfriend so much as of herself. She gives up on trying to unmake the "boring" Lol V. Stein, and instead intensifies that condition of her being. She, too, succumbs to the societal – but more importantly, the narrative definition of her erotic and other identities. Bracketed between Cinderella and Sleeping Beauty what else can she be except the cipher she is in her marriage?

Re-encountering Tatiana Karl, Lol tracks her down, really, after having seen her in a furtive, passionate embrace with a man, Jack Hold, not her husband.

Even though Tatiana has absolutely no comprehension of Lol, and is herself everything Lol is not – an adulterous wife, free and easy in her conventionally "unconventional" sexual liaisons – she is an important factor, their girlish friendship eventually models Lol's desire for a continuing relation to the others – all she wanted was to be *with* Anne-Marie Stretter and Michael Richardson, while they made love to each other. This desire she had not been permitted to express, and she indeed finally stops trying to express it, in words. Instead she becomes, as it were, a dramatist, and uses Tatiana and Jack Hold to do so.[21]

Tatiana is a key element in the new drama. She is crucial because she was with Lol the night of the fiancé's defection, she stayed with Lol to the end, and witnessed everything with her. She doubled Lol's consciousness. She is also crucial because, as a "partner" in an "illicit" relation – one in which "sexuality" should be licenced and expressed, she instead symbolizes the very solitude of the modern lover: her "affair" with Jack Hold, set up so perfectly it too is a dramatic, or rather daytime soap opera cliché (Lol watches their tryst through the frame of their cheap hotel window, as she lies in a field – and she is watching "television" after all for only the "upper parts" of their bodies show). It is, Duras tells us, the perfect modern union, "constructed upon indifference" (*Lol Stein*, 51).[22]

Other ties bind them in a grip which is not one of sentiment or of happiness, it is something else which bestows neither joy nor sorrow. They are neither happy nor unhappy. Their union is constructed upon indifference, in a way which is general and which they apprehend moment by moment, a union from which all preference is excluded. They are together, two trains which meet

and pass, around them the landscape, sensuous and lushly
green. . . . By opposite paths, they have arrived at the same result
as Lol Stein.

(ibid.)

The "ties" here are the libidinal bindings of the fraternal, "universal"
love that are now so deep that they use the sexual couple to prevent
"sexuality." Lol ecstatically takes pleasure in the revelation that
binary, "normal" illicit sexuality is no relation – *rapport sexuel* – at all,
any more than is her relationship to John Bedford in legal marriage.

It is this alone that makes Tatiana critical to Lol's desire, not the fact
of their having once shared a common past, a communal memory, a
common ground. True, they had enjoyed each other in a semi-official
space (the playground at off hours), but anything "unofficial" or
unprogrammed (by narrative?) about their lives has been progres-
sively organized into officialization. All "play" spaces (Kant's
"aesthetic" freeplay just does not hold) in their lives have actually
been part and parcel of the process of denying the identity of the
woman who could be the subject of desire. She met her fiancé on
another formal playground, the tennis court; the Town House Ball
sites her official engagement – and dis-engagement – from her fiancé.
Finally, the streets of S. Talma, which might seem to be the last
refuge of a kind of nomadic (à la Stendhal) desire – harbor the man
who stops all that as soon as it begins – her future husband. Lol may
have danced a little wildly with Tatiana on the school ground, but in
the subsequent sequencing of her life from playspace to playspace we
witness her growing imprisonment.

Lol has to be more methodical: "In what lost universe has Lol Stein
acquired this fierce will, this method?" (*Lol Stein*, 63). She cannot rely
on "aesthetic space" any more than Benjamin's *flâneur* can freely
walk the streets of post-communard Paris if she wishes to locate, and
voice, her place as a subject. These spaces – the "playground" as
well as "the streets" – have been co-opted by the spread of social
exchange, absorbed into the extension of imaginary space. And it is
the popular tale, the romance version of desire that has led the
repression.

Lol remakes space. She does not fight the imaginary directly either
with the symbolic or the real – what are these to the likes of her? –
but with an other imaginary. She begins to conceive of her "place"
– to reconstruct the Town Beach Ball, "the dwelling place that is truly
hers" (*Lol Stein*, 36):

In the distance, with fairy-like fingers, the recollection of a certain
memory flits past. It grazes Lol not long after she has lain down
in the field, it portrays for her, at this late evening hour in the field

of rye, this woman who is gazing up at a small rectangular
window, a narrow stage, circumscribed as a stone, on which no
actor has yet appeared. And perhaps Lol is afraid, but ever so
slightly of the possibility of an even greater separation from the
others. She is none the less fully aware that some people would
struggle – yesterday she still would have – that they would go
running home as fast as they could the moment some vestige of
reason had made them discover themselves in this field. . . . They
would bravely destroy it within themselves. She, on the contrary,
cherishes it.

(ibid., 54)

Lol wants to invent a new form, something so outrageous that it
reaches beyond legislation by the mirror. She does so by remembering what her desire was on the night of the Town Beach Ball: the
desire to see Michael Richardson and Anne-Marie Stretter making
love, to see Anne-Marie after her dress is off. What Lol remembers
is that what she had desired, had been on the verge of having at the
Town Beach Ball, was a relationship to the other, in an unheard-of
mode.

To get to it, to get into it, she uses the resources of narrative, of
the narrative she has always lived in. She rewrites not just her past,
but the present, slowly weaving both Jack Hold and Tatiana into her
outrageously conceived new narrative form. Whatever else *Lol V. Stein*
might be it is not – at least not yet – the stuff of the soap opera. She
begs Jack Hold *not* to "give up" Tatiana for her – the cliché – and
she calls herself alternately Tatiana and Lol as she and he make love.

At the end, Lol has assumed a new, a narrative power:

Lol dreams of another time when the same thing that is going to
happen would happen differently. In another way. A thousand
times. Everywhere. Elsewhere. Among others, thousands of others
who, like ourselves dream of this time, necessarily. This dream
contaminates me. I'm obliged to undress her. She won't do it
herself.

(*Lol Stein*, 177)

While the tales of Perrault exercise hegemony over the erotic life of
the young girl, displacing her mother as model, we can see in Duras
and even James the effort to displace them as "origin" myths for the
bourgeois woman, her no-thingness, her lack – and her desire. In her
"madness" what Lol discovers, what she tries to express and what
no one will hear her saying, straight out as she says it, is that it is
boring to be "Lol V. Stein" – to be a modern adolescent girl, whose
desire is supposed to take the shape of an object in an imaginary

coupling, product of a man's imagination (the Brother's denial of her existence). Which is to say, not to exist at all. Lol makes it clear that it is not the lack of satisfaction of her desire that maddens her (not at all; she feels "left out") but her consignment to a role in which she cannot be the subject of her own desire. What she discovers she had wanted, actually, was to participate in the triangulation of desire, not as object of a patriarchal programme, nor that of the brotherly-husband (the complaisant John Bedford), but as the subject who writes the programme: she will become the Other who can state her desire. She wants to go with them, to be a part of and apart from their coupling. She wants to watch. She wants to write.

Lol rejected her natural mother at the Town Beach Ball; Maisie had only mothers made by art and not by nature. Their mothers are not upholding a traditional order (Lol's mother expresses no indignation at her future son-in-law's defection, obscurely seeming to blame the girl); Maisie's mother rejects the traditional fantasies of motherhood (she is not madonna-like and pure), yet at the same time her utter self-seeking is perfectly in tune with the modern regime, and she refashions herself on a male model – dress, sports, rapid liaisons). What the narratives make clear, however, is the utter shabbiness and dreariness of the "moral order" these mothers have been invented to support. Thus, what their two daughters have in common is a sort of primary *bricolage* in which, constructing themselves out of the debris of the phallic Oedipus and his version of the mother, they manage to protect themselves from absolute submission to the new order by refusing to accept the negative value placed on their "not-thereness" by that order. In both cases theirs is a more or less cogent, more or less aware anti-programme for assuming their subjectivity. Duras's more fantasmatic – less absent, less artificial, but no less unreal – mother in *The Lover* acts on behalf of her daughter (in *The Seawall* she acted for Joseph). She has provided her and provides us with an (oblique) code in support of her daughter's subjectivity. She seems to me to characterize something slightly different from either of these others, articulating the difference between the fraternal and the symbolic subject as it might become. In a way, "Marguerite's" mother exercises the very old-fashioned dream of a paternal function – the one displaced completely by the Regime of the Brother. This other mother would give back more than the minimal identity the woman had under the patriarchy and had lost completely under fraternity, one that is not entirely conditioned by man's fantasy. She is rare, indeed.

Chapter 7

After the new Regime

Even though psychoanalysis has uncovered the degree to which the narcissistic ego denies that *in itself* it is also a collective form, this denial is a structural feature of a democracy lived mythically, according to a myth which is no longer fully Oedipal in character. Oedipus is not a bad name for this myth, but it needs redefinition and a change of name for modern times. We can no longer assume the traditional parental roles Freud saw as modeling the superego (the mother or the father) as determinative for its modernized form. I have looked back past Oedipus to *Totem and Taboo* to find a model for the Regime of the Brother: the neo-Totemic. I have also, in the literature I have read here, uncovered its primary taboos: its parents, its women – mothers, sisters, daughters – and its children.

In bringing this book to a close I want to ask one more question: what kind of art would provide the necessary critical counterpoint to the modern regime? Is there an art that could present us with the modernized cultural consciousness? In Hélène Cixous's new "epic theater" I glimpse a certain renewed artistic effort to recognize the double sublimation in the art (and politics) of our time – both that of the parents and that of real, historical subjects. The play I will speak of is her historical epic, *L'Histoire terrible, mais pas encore achevée de Norodom Sihanouk, roi du Cambodge.*

Modern forms: art and politics

In traditional society, narrative is a mode of production, it forms and defines a collective (tribe, clan, family). In modern society this lot falls to artificial myths (Oedipus, totem and taboo, etc.)[1] not to narrative *per se*, which increasingly names those who "are" not. It has become apparent that the form of collective consciousness/conscience (the modern superego) that has developed under the conditions of modernity is a failure: a fantasm. We have insufficiently attended to its construction and development, preferring to assume that the ideals of *liberté, égalité, fraternité* would somehow be born of themselves – which is to say, without parents – and with no further formalization than that produced in fact by the letter of the law. We seem blandly to have assumed that the overthrow of monarchism in the revolutions of the seventeenth and eighteenth centuries would yield a general form of the collective: through universal equality before the law, the substitutability of each for everyone else, via imaginary (chiefly literary) and concrete political (the vote) identification of our will with that of others. In short, through the installation of democracy, or the dream of collective freedom, equality, and universal relation – as a brotherhood.

In democracy, after all, it has been amply proven. *Any* one can grow up to be President, and any one can see himself in the role, in the place of the leader.[2] Ever since Kant (mis)read Rousseau as rooting the collective in an imaginary, ideal and infinite projection of the "I" – the general self – we have had only one way of forming collective identifications: We can exchange places with an other, equal, "I." But that "I," recall, is formed from the repetition or doubling of "self."[3]

There is, then, a paradox, and it is the paradox of Narcissus, of the mirror and its stage. For what is licensed by the mechanism of identification and exchange as the exclusive collective form in democracy also fosters the greatest of inequalities. It is in the interests of an ego that identifies itself with its own ego-ideal for there to exist an objective, ideal ego: a greater Other, a leader, a focal point. As a relay of the self the greater he is the greater one's own self-esteem: if one could also at any moment fill the leader's (the "father's") shoes, perform the same role, so much the better for him to be all-powerful, the greatest of ideal egos. This is also, I might add speculatively, what undermines even the most tenuous forms of fraternity that sometimes appear in a "traditional" world, and replaces them with the narcissistic drive.

We have been insufficiently vigilant: in the guise of the ego modernity has permitted the return of what Stendhal once called the "monarchical principle" in an unconscious form. It "forgot" the father, and its own lack. It did not "sublimate" him as he had sublimated the mother: for it forgot him in the mode of sublation, saving him as a figure. Thus the modern *individual* imagines himself in the place of the sovereign subject, a minor or major despot, a sum of his wills. The modern political subject is one who represses not just the mother but the father for the benefit of the son. Or rather, the brother.

The passage from monarchy to democracy as the primary form of governance in modernity could be characterized formally as a passage from a "metonymic" (more precisely, a synecdochical) to a metaphoric mode: the king, as part, stands for the whole, whereas it is only the power to exchange anyone for anyone else that grants modern democracy its "collective representation."[4] In their essential, political being all men *resemble* each other and can be exchanged for each other.[5]

Metaphoric power liberates major creative forces in the "I": already an empty form, free for substitution, it is permitted unlimited democratic fantasies of where "I" might fit into the life of the collective: "all men are created equal" so any one of them can be substituted for any other to wield power and make decisions – "anyone can grow up to be president." For us moderns a newly sovereign "I" (Freud (*SE XIV*, 297), speaks also of "the autocratic ego") both frees us from and bars access to a fatherly superego.

Nevertheless, at times that ego is too much for us to bear, and our collective consciousness can no longer find a way of conceiving itself: times when clinging to the past or moving reflexively with the current just do not work. The "old ways" suddenly lose effectiveness as comfort or as resource for modeling what is yet to come; and the present becomes so unfathomable, or so deplorable, that to "experience" it is to be unable, properly, to bear full consciousness of it. At moments of great social and cultural change history, our own history, can become the subject of our experience only if it is marked *as something else* – as a merely "artistic" or "ritual" form. Indeed, Lacan once wrote,[6] the derivation of consciousness (as of conscience) is "ungraspable, indeterminable historically."

More and more often it appears as a story, even someone else's story. A story that has not got an ending, a history that is nevertheless not a "past": like Hélène Cixous's terrible but not yet finished his/story of Norodom Sihanouk,[7] which is, I think, a step in the formulation – the formation, really – of a collective, contemporary *modern* consciousness. The world has turned on its axis, so that its orienting polarities are no longer east versus west – spatially and politically. Instead, traditional and modern shape our fundamental opposition. This reversal has been in effect since the invention of modernity sometime in the eighteenth century, and modern artists and writers who have articulated it are not only rare, but highly resisted as well: especially Rousseau.

In their place, scientists, economists and political scientists (and some philosophers[8]) have been granted the last word on the attitude we are to take toward traditional forms: here again is a highly praised quote from the nuclear physicist, architect of the uncertainty principle, Werner Heisenberg, taken from his book, *Physics and Philosophy*:[9]

[M]odern science . . . penetrates in our time into other parts of the world where the cultural tradition has been entirely different from the European civilization. There the impact of this new activity in natural and technical science must make itself felt even more strongly than in Europe. . . . This new activity must appear as a decline of the older culture, as a ruthless and barbarian attitude that upsets the sensitive balance on which all human happiness rests. Such consequences cannot be avoided; they must be taken as one aspect of our time.[10]

You might say that Heisenberg's "must" inspires me here: what *is* the source of this imperative?

The priority of modernity over traditional forms is one of our most cherished assumptions – it almost goes without saying. Its counterweight is an equally cherished nostalgia for the "old forms" as superior, in their simplicity and closeness to nature and/or innocence, to the modern. Thus, those human groups and epistemological forms that the Heisenberg paradigm both explicitly and implicitly (but absolutely) disenfranchises – family, tribe, clan, also the woman – are those about which we moderns have the most obviously guilty (and reparational) consciences. But liberal modern efforts to accommodate them are almost always rooted in the assumption that they are "simpler," a more primitive stage, closer to innocence, or paradise or something we know we have given up, or "lost," willingly or not. To "bring them back in" has a false air, a bad conscience, it sentimentalizes: woman becomes "the eternal" or "the maternal" just as we have eliminated matriarchy; indigenous peoples who have been done away with are commemorated in monuments where they will remain, dead but idealized, ennobled by their troubles.[11]

Let us take a detour through the specificity of modern history, the modern instance of forgetting *vis-à-vis* traditional social forms – forgetting in the traumatic "modern" mode first described by Rousseau, and not in the mode of marked "remembrance" delineated by Tönnies. When Ferdinand Tönnies defined "custom" as the basis of traditional groups he did so specifically within the terms of a memory that could not be located: customs are ritual forms deep in and dear to the heart of a people, but they are not "historical." They mark a blank. "Remembrance" in "traditional" societies is a simple dialectic: we do not even attempt to remember what cannot be remembered, in other words, what we have come from, what we have supplanted. Custom "consists in replacing an earlier, more natural (because cruder) practice and in restraining it,"[12] thus partaking of the paternal "sublimation" (to use Lacan's term) of natural or maternal engendering. (The mother's genitals are unseeable and "recalled" only uncannily and unconsciously.) But what modernity cannot recall is something else.[13]

Ritual remembrance, a reverence for the power to replace a lower, cruder "natural" practice by transfer to "unseen spirits" implicates the dead who are imagined to be continuously living and acting, and who have claims on the living: we owe them for our very life. (How unwelcome such ritual recall is in modernity is made clear in Freud's opening chapter of *Totem and Taboo*, where he demonstrates again and again our denial of the life of the spirit in contemporary life, though we are unable to do so without compulsive ritual actions – especially unconscious taboos – which, finally, indicate a continued but disavowed belief in them.) In simple settings, simple rituals grant the dead food, drink, sacrifices.[14] Gratitude, grief, admiration for the dead are always elements in this spirituality, but the manner of expression varies with each group and each considers only its way proper. The ritual repetition of a "custom" thus has the secondary advantage of giving a group the means to distinguish itself from other groups: adherence to its own customs enables the traditional group to see itself as civilized "before barbarians among whom the more wicked custom is practiced."

Now in the modern case, deritualized, de-spiritualized, the ascription of "wickedness" to others is potentially infinite: since we can remember nothing of our parents, our past, without trauma, without horror, our distinction from and superiority to others knows no limits.

Great big modern countries[15] – the US in Vietnam, the USSR in Afghanistan, both in countless, secret little "wars" – have seemed compulsively driven to bringing their might to bear on traditional societies, for reasons that remain largely unfathomable from known political-analytic viewpoints. Yet they clearly participate in the imaginary, in phantasms of "traditional" cultures, and, more significantly, phantasms of their own collective being or more precisely, collective identity. Our "collective identity" has ever more tenuous links to a rational and objective character (yet the great achievement of modernity was supposed to have been the demythification of social being in favor of a scientific, economic or *reality* principle in social formations) and ever closer links to a fantastic superego: what I have called the new cultural unconscious, *It*. The cultural unconscious, not collective, not racial or historic, but contemporary, is at work, shaping and shaped by an ego-ideal.

Will we ever get over the *ancien régime?*

The advantage that the actual *ancien régime*, the traditional rather than the phantasmatic monarchy[16] has over ours is its real lack of reciprocity: the peasant, structurally, cannot exchange places with the king. But there is nevertheless identification – and if Freud is to be believed about group psychology there must be. But in the traditional societies it is supposed to be a two-way street: we accept the father/king's (and in Cixous's play it is always a matter of "Monseigneur Papa")[17] rule not only on the condition that he "love" us but instead to the degree that he is conscious that, apart from us, he simply does not, cannot exist. When Cixous has Sihanouk at his most egotistical-seeming, his most improbable, most exasperating he is always redeemed by this identification in reverse. Not "l'état c'est moi" but the opposite: his is a strict awareness of the multiplicity of selves – his people, Cambodians, Vietnamese, men, women, children, trees, rivers, plants, cities, even and especially the dead – that go into making up his "identity" as monarch. He is lack, the classical Other as the site of desire.

Cixous's play deals directly and with great forthrightness with the clash between traditional and modern. We love the old women, so down to earth and so charmingly flighty at the same time, aristocrat and petty bourgeois, Cambodian royalty and Vietnamese immigrant shopkeeper, Queen Kossomak and the fishmonger Madame Lamné – we love them for each other – because they love each other. We grow passionate for and with Sihanouk because he is the King, and to be a King means for him precisely not to be a despot, arrogant, and egocentric.[18] It means embodying by taking into himself all the people, and not just the people of Cambodia, not just "real" Cambodians, but all the immigrants, the whole of the population – and also the elephants and trees. . . . And we hate the character of Henry Kissinger, admirer of Metternich and practitioner of "Realpolitik," as he grows mad with a lust to "sanitize" Cambodia; and we hate Saloth Sâr/Pol Pot for his like determination to "purify" – to purge – Cambodia of its non-Communist, traditional past. The result, as we know, was the slaughter of millions, by this Khmer Rouge "with a mouth full of teeth" whom Mme Khieu Samnol describes as looking like he "eats men": he eats them, then purges their dead bodies, spits them out. And we especially hate Lon Nol, whose anti-Vietnamese campaign begins an anti-foreigner pogrom for political reasons that ends by opening the door to the Khmer's total genocidal reign over the Cambodians themselves.[19]

The evacuation of the self, this emptying it of all others, is the final moment of the narcissist: the incorporated other is no longer necessary to reassure the narcissist of his fullness, aliveness, like Riva. He has become, like Pol Pot, the living dead. He has exorcised the traditional, ghostly – Oedipal – past as well as his contemporaries, those who would dwell with, relate to, and remind him of their difference from himself. It is precisely this that Sihanouk, Sihanouk *as* King, Sihanouk *as* Papa, refuses to do. He is Cambodia, and he is all of it. Although he is an artificial "Papa" he has at least – as brother Pol Pot has not – grasped the essence of the good paternal function, saving and protecting the other.

Thus while democracy still has much to offer that is new in our collective history, fulfilment of the democratic promise waits. Locke's *Treatises on Government*, after all, celebrated the freedoms that accompanied the overthrow of a specifically patriarchal order, and Rousseau, too, thought that freeing society from the paternal model could be a major gain. To remedy the defects of modernity, however, we will have to complete the liberation from the patriarchy not by "forgetting" it, but by remembering it. Possible, but we will need a new art, a new form of "epic" memory.

Epic again

Polyglossia, heteroglossia, and the anti-epic stance of the novel made it, Bakhtin says, the "hero of our times." Heir to the epic's role but not its cast of characters (low rather than high personages), the novel's chronotope (its spatio-temporal coordinates: the "low contemporary" versus the "high past"), brought it to the fore (and to the rescue) of the diverse groups making claims, voicing their desire in the Enlightenment: it spoke "the people." Like the disreputable nephew of Rameau Hegel saw as the first hero of the modern spirit, through the novel "people" sought to declare their lack, their need, their material desires. The first modern hero of the novel, Hegel told us, was Rameau's nephew: the one who revealed that everyone in his society desires: except the sovereign.[20] "In the whole of a kingdom there is only one man who walks, and that is the Sovereign. The rest take up positions."[a]

Rameau freely admits to being the subject of desire. Pointing his finger at his open mouth, the nephew ("He," *Lui*) tells us not to forget that "It is natural to have an appetite."[b] Such expressions, together with his outrageous demands not merely to live, but to live well (and not from his labor, but from charity), jar us as they did his interlocutor, "I" (*Moi*), who sees Rameau as the last of a long line of parasites, and the first of what will become greedy self-seekers in the modern, capitalist era. But close attention reveals that what disturbs "I" is *Lui's* enunciation of his desires – just what the ego can never do. Rameau functions like an unleashed *id* for this "I," permitting him to make a fundamental critique of an economy that satisfies the desires of a few at the expense of the many who are not allowed to express their desire. He complains about what he terms the "devil of an economy" under the *ancien régime*:

> It is natural to have an appetite. . . . I find that it is not in good order to not always have something to eat. What a devil of an economy, men who stuff themselves on everything while others, who have an importuning stomach just like theirs have nothing to bite down on.[c]

Thus, while "lui" sounds as if he is about to prefigure the late nineteenth century's egomania this "he" who desires is not an ego: every creature, he tells us, seeks its well being at the expense of others – not, however, just any and every other but specifically at the expense of "whoever is *in possession of it.*"

It slowly dawns on *moi* and on the reader that *lui* is becoming the new sovereign, that the king is gone, and it is up to "the people," to make their claims explicit, articulate their desires. When they do, they become – as Rameau does – the new epic hero. Rameau repeatedly characterizes himself as "Sir Belly," a phrase that recalls the *Odyssey*. It is as a "beggar" that Homer's hero returns to be once again master of his own house, though he must fight to turn out those in possession of his well-being. This rise of the people was to be the ground of the novel.

When speaking their desire, their lack falls again under a ban, a taboo; however, the "people" will become a new id, for which no art but a critical one is suitable. Modernity and its failure of consciousness, failure of nerve, is both cause and effect, then. Our story, our modern history is replete with events so shocking to consciousness that they cannot be faced: even to enumerate them is in a way to be complicitous with them. The principal forms of artistic representation fail specifically to render the horror of horror, and they also fail, collectively, to form our consciousness. When they are reproduced or represented their horror is dulled, made into something different, even something attractive, something that secretly supports the conditions that made the horrible event possible: imaginary exchange with and phantasmatic replacement of self for other. Beginning with Cixous's new epic theater, one might work to transform these mythic ways and means of representation, opening thoughts of others which should be available to "post-modern" artistic representation.

Finally, I repeat that the literary modeling of the social, the rooting of the social in egomimetic desire, or narcissism, have to be criticized by reforming the primary model we have of the symbolic, i.e., Oedipus.

It should by now be clear that I have not undertaken to do an "anti-Oedipus" as much as to make the case that the post-Enlightenment version of Oedipus, which consists in the Brother's imaginary adoption of the "name of the father," is too narrow a version of a symbolic order. A pseudo-Oedipus stands in the way of reform-(ulat)ing the symbolic under new material and political conditions, conditions which include the technological changes in reproduction (control, cloning), the nuclear framing of internationalism, and the transformations of "manhood" and "womanhood" in the post-colonial world-setting. Under these terms, Oedipus is no longer an adequate mythic, or rather, dramatic, form for programming a Symbolic for our time.

Notes

INTRODUCTION: THE STRUCTURE OF THE BOOK

1 In narcissism, Lacan tells us, the ego has only a phantasmatic relation to the object, modeled on its relation to the "mirage" of its own "Ideal ego" (in *Ecrits*, Paris, Editions du Seuil, 1966, 552; English tr., *Ecrits: A Selection*, tr. A. Sheridan, New York, Norton, 196. In *Séminaire II*, Paris, Seuil, 1978, 207–21, Lacan develops the notion of egomimies, in reference to the game of odds and evens in Poe's "Purloined Letter."
2 Lacan, *Séminaire VII*, Paris, Seuil, 1986, text est. by Jacques-Alain Miller.
3 *The Sociology of Georg Simmel*, tr. Kurt Wolff, Glencoe and London, The Free Press and Collier-Macmillan, 1950, 69–70.
4 He insists on the difference between the patriarchal pattern for society and the one he will elaborate in his social contract in the first version of the *Contrat social*.

1 THE PRIMAL SCENE OF MODERNITY

1 *Standard Edition* (referred to hereafter as *SE*) *XIX*. All volumes of the *Standard Edition* are tr. and ed. James Strachey *et al.*, London, Hogarth Press and the Institute of Psycho-Analysis, 1953–74.
2 Jacques Lacan interpreted psychosis as the refusal of the name of the father, "le nom du père," in his reanalysis of Freud's "Wolfman" in *Séminaire III, Les Psychoses*, Paris, Seuil, 1981; "La grand'route et le signifiant être père," 321–32.
3 In wartime, of course, Uncle Sam wants soldier males: his concrete response appears in First World War recruiting posters where his finger points directly at the viewer and the legend reads, "Uncle Sam wants You!"
4 Freud set up the problem in *The Ego and the Id* (*SE XIX*), when he allied the once erotic-seeming id with the death drive. Lacan expanded *Its* scope dramatically as the question of the desire of the Other.
5 In "Kant avec Sade," *Ecrits*, Paris, Seuil, 1966, 755–92, Lacan warned us that uncovering the desire of the Other – what *It* wants – will not bring us comfort. The *jouissance* of the Other comes at our expense.
6 See my essay on "Resistance to sexual education," *Strategies: A Journal of Theory, Culture and Politics*, vol. 2 (1989), 92–113. There I show a dialectic of "sexuality" in Lacan's double unconscious.
7 Ferdinand Tönnies, *Custom: An Essay on Social Codes*, tr. A. F. Borenstein,

Chicago, Gateway/Henry Regnery Books, 1961.
8 "Group psychology and the analysis of the ego," in *SE XVIII (1920–2)*, 67–144.
9 *Totem and Taboo: Some Points of Resemblance Between the Mental Lives of Savages and Neurotics*, tr. James Strachey, *SE XIII (1913–14)*.
10 For a criticism of postmodernism's abuse of the "innocent" image of the neolithic, see Dean MacCannell, 'Introduction to the 1989 Edition,' in *The Tourist*, New York, Schocken Books, 1976/1989.
11 Freud demystified what passes for civilization as a kind of barbarian group, often with a touch of bitterness and irony. For example, in "Thoughts on war and death" (1915) *SE XIV*, 273–308 (orig. "Zeitgemässes über Krieg und Tod," in *Imago*, Bd. IV, 1–21). He characterizes "the world-dominating nations of white race" as palming off their own group as if it were identical to "civilization" in the widest sense, while leading that group into the conscience-less barbarities of The Great War:

> We had expected that the great world-dominating nations of white race upon whom the leadership of the human species has fallen, who were known to have world-wide interests as their concern, to whose creative powers were due not only our technical advances towards the control of nature but the artistic and scientific standards of civilization – we had expected these peoples to succeed in discovering another way of settling misunderstandings and conflicts of interest.
>
> (*SE XIV*, 276)

This is in contrast to the way we imagined our difference from "races who are divided by the colour of their skin" or among nationalities of Europe whose "civilization is little developed or has been lost" – such "primitive" peoples might war on for a considerable period – but not us (ibid.).
12 Hélène Cixous's play *L'Histoire terrible mais pas encore achevée de Norodom Sihanouk, roi du Cambodge*, Paris, Théâtre du Soleil, 1987, demonstrates this possibility, and shows how it is no match for the new order. I will discuss it in chapter 7.
13 Freud's eloquent "Thoughts on war and death," op. cit., explains the general disillusionment with "civilization" attendant on the Great War as attributable to the perception that the highest models in civilization, state governments and their leaders, were doing the very things that civil order demanded they as individuals not do: lie, kill, steal, etc.
14 I disagree with those who are calling for those of us at some remove from the events to "forget" it, it was not *our* problem. It is.
15 There is much specific reconstructive work to be done on the symbolic before we can, in the wake of Lacan and with Jean-Luc Nancy, answer whether there is a way for the speaking being – ego, Narcissus, etc. – to be "not-alone." Nancy writes, "How are we not alone when we are neither before the gods nor within the bosom of the community" i.e., submitted to the father or enfolded by the mother? Nancy tells us we need to learn the shape and form of a "community without communion, a face to face encounter with no divine countenance" – one symbolized, in short, in unheard-of ways ("Of divine places," *Paragraph* 2 (1986), 39).
16 *SE XIV*, 141.
17 Even Norman O. Brown accepts without reservation the religious and

anthropological definitions of social groups as "fraternities" or "moieties or segments of one body" (*Love's Body*, New York, Vintage Books, 1966, 21).

18 J. Lacan, *De la psychose paranoïaque dans ses rapports avec la personnalité*, Paris, Seuil, 1975 (orig. 1932), 259–60).

19 Here see L. Irigaray's section on Hegel and Sophocles regarding the sister in *Speculum of the Other Woman*, tr. Gillian C. Gill, Ithaca, Cornell University Press, 1985, 214–20.

20 M. Horkheimer and T. Adorno, *The Dialectic of Enlightenment*, tr. John Cumming, New York, Continuum, 1982, 215.

21 ibid., 216.

22 See Freud, *SE XIV*, 69:

> only rarely and under certain exceptional conditions is individual psychology in a position to disregard the relations of [the] individual to others . . . . The relations of an individual to his parents and to his brothers and sisters, to the object of his love, and to his physician . . . may claim to be considered as social phenomena; and in this respect they may be contrasted with certain other processes, described by us as "narcissistic," in which the satisfaction of the instincts is partially or totally withdrawn from the influence of other people.

23 Denis Hollier points out that the theme common to members of the "College of Sociology" (*The College of Sociology, 1937–39*, tr. Betsy Wing, Minneapolis, University of Minnesota Press, 1988 (orig. French 1979), xiv ff.), is admiration for models of a social unity which would "remedy" bourgeois fragmentation and revolutionize it: male-subgroups. They were thus fascinated by ideas of "regenerative expulsion" (xv); Roger Caillois is reported by Hollier to have admired "monastic and military orders, Templars and Teutonic Knights, Janissaries and Assassins, Jesuits and Freemasons . . . even . . . the Ku Klux Klan and the Communist Party" (Hollier, xv).

24 L. Irigaray, op. cit., 355 ff.

25 Marginal notes on *Les Liaisons dangereuses*, Baudelaire, *Curiosités esthétiques*, ed. Lemaitre, Paris, Editions Garnier Frères, 1962, 828–32. The sense of a deepening of a crisis in desire is apparent in literature, where a feeling of loss of the object of desire is accompanied, at the beginning of and late into the nineteenth century, by a nostalgia for the clarity of active desire under the *ancien régime*. Describing *Les Liaisons dangereuses*, "ce livre qui brûle comme de glace" (this book that burns like ice), Baudelaire claims it is the last work where there is no divorce between consciousness and desire, desire and act. The equation of desire and consciousness had, to him, political power: "The French Revolution was made by voluptuaries; libertine books comment on and explicate the Revolution." But not all later writers assign the active libido a male character: for Stendhal, it was women who exercised desire and who lost this power under the bourgeoisie.

26 Samuel Richardson, *Clarissa: Or the History of a Young Lady*, Harmondsworth, Penguin, 1985 (orig. 1747–8). Citations are from the abridged Riverside edition, Boston, Houghton Mifflin Company, 1962, 75.

27 Jean-Jacques Rousseau, *Julie, ou la Nouvelle Héloïse*, OC II, ed. Bernard Guyon, Jacques Scherer, Charles Guyot, Paris, Pléiade, 1964, 5–796.

28 Many writers believe there is a real division: Balzac, Kierkegaard, Vigny

treat the French and other anti-monarchical revolutions as marking two ages, distinct epochs in desire – unalienated and alienated. See Kierkegaard's "Preface" printed, pp. 153–4, as an appendix to his review of the book *Two Ages*. *Two Ages: The Age of the Revolution and The Present Age, A Literary Review*, tr. Howard V. and Edna H. Hong, Princeton, Princeton University Press, 1978 (vol. XIV of *Kierkegaard's Writings*). See Balzac, "Madame de T. . ." and Alfred De Vigny, a political reactionary, who mythifies and mourns the loss of aristocratic desire in his unsuccessful play, *Quitte pour la peur*.

29 In the special "catharist" mode that Stendhal tried to retrieve in his *De l'amour* and Lacan cites in relation to Duras's *Lol V. Stein* (*Duras on Duras*, San Francisco, City Lights Books, 1987, 128). See chapter 3.

30 See Freud's metapsychological essay, "On instincts and their vicissitudes," *SE XIV*, op. cit., 109–40, esp. 122–3.

31 In *The Dialogues*; see my 1977 article, "Nature and self-love: a reinterpretation of Rousseau's '*passion primitive*,'" *Publications of the Modern Language Association*, vol. 92: 5 (October), 890–902, as well as "Fiction and the social order," *Diacritics* vol. 5: 1 (Spring, 1975), 7–15. These concern the change in desire as part of a theological shift from a traditional God who exists "above" us (and is supposed to be the aim of all desires) to a God who makes us the aim of His desire. The first is the line of theologians from Augustine to Malebranche. In this frame, the "feminine" object is able to provide a model or means of access, a means to ascent. The paradigm of the post-reformation God has God's "love" inclined to descend to us. If we become the aim, the feminine "object" has no special status; virtue does not appeal or call us on high in her form. The spatio-temporal dislocation of our desire has yet to be sorted out in the wake of this revolution: at best, one can say, with Hegel and others after him, that the "aim" of "our" desire is pretty definitively lost, or is consigned only to the imagination.

32 See *SE XVIII*, 90. Freud lists self-love, love for parents and children, friendship and love for humanity in general, devotion to concrete objects and to abstract ideas, which even though all have sexual love as a "nucleus" and are diverted forms of it, nevertheless are integral to human life.

33 Anthony Wilden, *System and Structure*, London, Tavistock, 1972/1980, 22: "Behind the symbolic lies the notion of mediated (unconscious) desire . . . Freud points out that there are no 'instinctual impulses' (*Triebregungen*) 'in' the unconscious, only 'representatives of desire' (*Tiebrepräsentanz*)."

34 A. Wilden, op. cit., 30.

35 Culture, by recycling the past, is to exploit itself and leave human labor and love aside from the process: this is Lévi-Strauss's vision at the end of the *Scope of Anthropology*, London, Jonathan Cape, 1967, and it is at the heart of the postmodern vision as well. Wilden assures us that hunters and gatherers – because they lacked possessions and material wealth – were among the most egalitarian societies, except as far as the sexes were concerned, ever to appear on the face of the earth. *Man and Woman, War and Peace*, London, Routledge & Kegan Paul, 1987, 69.

36 After I had completed writing this book I came across Carole Pateman's *The Sexual Contract*, Cambridge, Polity/Basil Blackwell, 1988, which also refers to her previous work on the "fraternal social contract." This latter is republished in her *The Disorder of Women: Democracy, Feminism, and*

Political Theory (Stanford, Stanford University Press, 1989). It is extremely gratifying to a literary critic like myself to find confirmation of my hypothesis, drawn mainly from literary sources, in the work of a political theorist. But while there are great areas of agreement between Pateman's *Sexual Contract* argument and my own, I find certain areas where we do not concur, largely because our interpretation of certain authors and texts, especially Rousseau (*Sexual Contract*, 55–6) and Freud on feminist questions, differs radically. My method is to develop exactly how and where political ideologies and 'contracts' touch on fundamental unconscious desires through fantasies and fictions. For this reason, and also because we begin in different places, I thus see literary works as playing a more crucial role in the political process than Pateman does. They not only merit attention, but they must be read with analytic precision, in both the psychical and literary senses of the term "analysis."

37 See John Locke, *Two Treatises of Government: In the Former, the False Principles of Sir Robert Filmer and His Followers, are Detected and Overthrown* (*First Treatise of Government*), Critical Edition by Peter Laslett, New York and Scarborough, Ontario, New American Library (a Mentor Book) 1960. (orig. 1678?), 260. He criticizes Filmer's principle that Adam's posterity are not only rulers by right of descent, but that

> *such Heirs are not only Lords of their own Children, but of their Brethren,* whereby, and by the words following, which we shall consider anon, he seems to insinuate that the Eldest Son is *Heir*: be he no where that I know, says it in direct words, but by the instances of *Cain* and *Jacob* that there follow, we may allow this to be so far his Opinion concerning Heirs, that where there are divers Children the Eldest Son has the Right to be *Heir*. That Primogeniture cannot give any Title to Paternal Power we have already shew'd. That a Father may have a Natural Right to some kind of Power over his Children, is easily granted, but that an Elder Brother has so over his Brethren remains to be proved. God or Nature has not any where that I know, placed such Jurisdiction in the first-born, nor can Reason find any such Natural Superiority amongst Brethren.
>
> (111, ll. 37–51)

38 *SE XVI*, 312.

39 *Séminaire II, Le Moi dans les écrits techniques de Freud*, "Pair ou impair: au delà de l'intersubjectivité," Paris, Seuil, 1978, 207–21.

40 Lacan, *Séminaire III, Les Psychoses*, "Qu'est-ce qu'une femme?", Paris, Seuil, 1981, 98.

41 L. Irigaray, op. cit., 55 ff.

42 Freud asked his famous, "What does a woman want?" in a letter to Princess Marie Bonaparte, who was convinced, ironically, that woman's biological possession of the clitoris was "supernumerary," too much, not lacking enough.

43 The chain of fear, castration, and penis envy (a misprision, since it is the brother's error that launches the event) is begun. The secondary association, so controversial in Freud, is less important here than the "discovery" (="disavowal") of the sister's genitals. Also, *SE XIX*, "Infantile genital organization of the libido": "Little boys never discover 'real female genitals.'"

44 See L. Irigaray, op. cit., 217: "Hegel . . . affirms that the brother is for the

sister that possibility of recognition of which she is deprived as mother and wife, but does not state that the situation is reciprocal. This means that the brother has already been invested with a value for the sister that she cannot offer in return.''

45 There are numerous brother–sister incest fantasies in early romantic literature, starting with Montesquieu's *Lettres persanes*, where the central tale concerns the tribulations of a brother–sister pair whose marriage is considered normal in one culture, but not by the one in which they find themselves. See also Chateaubriand's *René* and more indirectly, George Eliot's *The Mill on the Floss*, etc. In romanticism, the new taboo on the sister-figure (enunciated positively in the fiction of the Enlightenment – *Clarissa, Manon Lescaut, Julie, Wuthering Heights*), seems to be lifted once she is definitively eliminated as a threat. The Enlightenment's demythologization of the biblical parents of the human community, which makes them irrelevant to the formation of modern society and ''frees'' us of ancestral obligations, unfortunately leaves any (sexual) relation to the other out of the new, modern social contract, throwing the role and place of woman precariously into doubt. See Carole Pateman and Teresa Brennan ''Women and the origins of liberalism,'' *Political Studies*, vol. xxvii, 2, June 1979, 183–200.

46 Denis Diderot, *Le Neveu de Rameau*, Paris, Flammarion, 1967.

47 Gilles Deleuze and Félix Guattari, *A Thousand Plateux: Capitalism and Schizophrenia*, tr. Brian Massumi, Minneapolis, The University of Minnesota Press, 1987 (orig. 1980).

48 *The Marriages Between Zones Three, Four, Five (As Narrated by the Chroniclers of Zone Three)*, New York, Vintage Books, 1981.

49 See Terry Eagleton (who dissents from this tradition) in *The Rape of Clarissa: Writing, Sexuality and Class Struggle in Samuel Richardson*, Minneapolis, University of Minnesota Press, 1982.

2   MODERNITY AS THE ABSENCE OF THE OTHER: THE GENERAL SELF

1 Georg Simmel, *The Sociology of Georg Simmel*, tr. Kurt Wolff, Glencoe and London: The Free Press and Collier–Macmillan, 1950, 69.

2 Benjamin, *Paris in the Second Empire of Charles Baudelaire, A Lyric Poet in the Era of High Capitalism*, London, NLB, 1973, 58–9.

3 M. Horkheimer and T. Adorno, *The Dialectic of Enlightenment*, tr. John Cumming, New York, Continuum, 1982, 216:

> Individuals are reduced to a mere sequence of experiences which leave no trace, or rather whose trace is hated as irrational, superfluous, and ''overtaken'' in the literal sense of the word. Just as every book which has not been published recently is suspect, and the idea of history outside the specific sphere of historical science makes modern men nervous, so the past becomes a source of anger. What a man was and experienced in the past is as nothing when set against what he now is and what he can be used for. . . . History is eliminated in oneself and others out of a fear that it may remind the individual of the degeneration of his own existence – which itself continues.

4 Here he differed in nuance and emphasis from his colleague Adorno. This is partly because Benjamin found the structure of the commodity itself

something he could live with: it contained, he tells us, a "frozen dialectic," or dialectics at a standstill. It is not univocally a negative structure: its hidden history embodied freedom as well. To see only its negative side is to overlook the personification of objects that takes place as technologies occult the real relations of production. And it invites a sentimentality that obscures economic and social structures of exploitation, domination, and mastery. Benjamin may have had this kind of thinking in mind when he connected the fetishizing of the worker, and labor, without concomitant rearrangements in property relations and relations of producer to product, directly to fascism ("Theses on the Philosophy of History" in *Illuminations*, tr. Harry Zohn, New York, Schocken Books, 1969, 258).

5 W. Benjamin, "Paris, capital of the nineteenth century," *Reflections*, tr. E. Jephcott. New York, Harcourt Brace Jovanovich, 1978, 157.

6 T. Eagleton, *The Rape of Clarissa: Writing, Sexuality and Class Struggle in Samuel Richardson*, Minneapolis, University of Minnesota Press, 1982, explicates comprehensively the significance of Pamela in her time, how she becomes a central moral force, the subject of sermons, the focus of libido.

7 Denis Diderot, *Eloge de Richardson*, *Oeuvres esthétiques*, Paris, Garnier, 1959.

8 *Paris in the Second Empire*, op. cit., 58.

9 "On some motifs in Baudelaire," in *Illuminations*, op. cit.

10 The Other or the leader is an ideal ego in the imaginary, rather than an ego-ideal as it is in the symbolic.

11 See Jay Bernstein, "Aesthetic alienation: Heidegger, Adorno, and the truth at the end of art," in John Fekete (ed.), *Life After Postmodernism*, New York, St Martin's Press, 1987, 86–119.

12 *L'Amour et l'occident*, originally 1939. English translation: *Love in the Western World*, tr. M. Belgion, New York, Pantheon Books, 1940. Rougemont described his own attraction to the feeling of unity in mass gatherings he witnessed in Germany. He belonged to the loosely affiliated group which called itself the "College of sociology" in pre-war France. See D. Hollier, *The College of Sociology, 1937–39*, tr. Betsy Wing, Minneapolis, University of Minnesota Press, 1988.

13 See P. N. Medvedev and M. M. Bakhtin, *The Formal Method in Literary Scholarship: A Critical Introduction to Sociological Poetics*, tr. A. J. Wehrle, Baltimore, Johns Hopkins University Press, 1978.

14 Hollier, op. cit., xv, xvi, and 272.

15 ibid., xvii–xviii.

16 See my 'Oedipus wrecks: Lacan, Stendhal and the narrative form of the real,' *Modern Language Notes*, December, 1985.

17 His twist is that he sees narrative as only once having had a perverse commonality for the bourgeoisie: each individual experiences desire as "private" – a fact that affords him access, through narrative, to that experience which is most typical of his own *class*. Private, unfulfilled desire is given collective expression in narrative. "The libidinal investments of the individual subject," Jameson writes (185), are experienced through and as "narratives of ideology – even what we have called the Imaginary, daydreaming, or wish-fulfilling text" (*The Political Unconscious: Narrative as Socially Symbolic Act*, Ithaca, Cornell University Press, 1980, pp. 175 ff.). Dialectically, then, what is most "private" takes on a public existence, granting us a collective experience, and narrative

thus has to be seen as the most important grounding for bourgeois class solidarity. For Jameson it no longer operates via desire in the postmodern condition.

18 The challenge is to distinguish Kafka's desire, in his "On the Yiddish Language," for literature to become part again of the living life of a people from the abuse of the *Folk* as a regulative artistic norm. It is imperative to do so. Bakhtin and Medvedev's eloquent depiction of the art work as the horizon of societal values (which both reflects and refracts "social reality") needs to be distinguished from demands made by a moral majority for art to reflect mainstream values in formal and critical terms. See also Medvedev and Bakhtin, *The Formal Method*. So must the defense, as in Deleuze and Guattari's book on Kafka, of the cultural minoritarian position of a societal subgroup, be analyzed for its specific difference from ethnocultural warfare. See *Kafka: Towards a Minor Literature*, tr. Dana Polan, Minneapolis, University of Minnesota Press, 1986, as well as Guattari, *Molecular Revolution: Psychiatry and Politics*, Harmondsworth, Penguin, 1984 [orig. 1972 and 1977].

19 R. Barthes, "Myth today," *Mythologies*, tr. Annette Lavers, New York, Hill & Wang, 1972.

20 Hollier, op. cit., xix–xx. Anti-feminine, oriented toward monumental phallic structures and afraid of, as Hollier tells us, the "gap" women represent, they also occasionally expressed attitudes akin to those of fascism.

21 Fragmentation and atomism are not necessarily the same; but to some of the "College" members in the 1930s the power to topple bourgeois democratic individualism lay only in fascism (Hollier, op. cit., on Bataille, xix–xx).

22 Freud does not hesitate to claim that the structure extends to any and every type of group – ethnicity, city-state, nation, religious formation, even civilization in its most general sense. The exceptions are transient, "spontaneous groups" (like those formed during the French Revolution, for example) – and the primary family.

23 As admirably demonstrated by Avital Ronell, *Dictations: On Haunted Writing*, Bloomington, Indiana University Press, 1986.

24 I stress Freud's antagonism to "love" because he is openly hostile to the term as a cultural imperative ("Love thy neighbor . . ."). The command to universal love is, for him, "an excellent example of the unpsychological proceedings of the cultural super-ego. The command-ment is impossible to fulfil; such an enormous inflation of love can only lower its value . . . . Civilization pays no attention to this; it merely admonishes us that the harder it is to obey the precept the more meritorious it is to do so" (*Civilization and its Discontents, SE XXI*, 141–3).

25 G. Rubin, "The traffic in women," in Rayna Reiter (ed.), *Towards an Anthropology of Women*, New York, The Monthly Review Press, 1975.

26 These phrases are taken from Lévi-Strauss (*The Savage Mind*), Jameson (via McLuhan in *The Political Unconscious*), Freud (*The Group Psychology – die Masse*) and Benjamin.

27 There is a neo-totemic character to many of the best-intentioned recent dreams for a "postmodern" ahistorical society: Lévi-Strauss" *The Scope of Anthropology*, Wilden's *Man and Woman, War and Peace*, Fredric Jameson's *Political Unconscious*. That there may be a darker side to this dream –

instituting it before genuine equality is achieved, and before we have actually devised ways of dealing with real, material rather than metaphysical differences, is the problem I want to enunciate here. Dean MacCannell, in his introduction to the second edition of *The Tourist* has already opened the question of the pernicious as well as the good utopian possibilities of the postmodern. Like Eco, he differs from those most critical of mass consumer society, such as Baudrillard, who appear to desire a flat rejection, without seriously attempting to consider how the postmodern may be integral to the development of social forms.

28 It must be made clear that, as Freud found in his "Thoughts on war and death," the fantasy of the "savage" world as pre- or non-Oedipal (guilt and debt-free) is just that – only a fantasy: indeed, it may be only the so-called primitive who still understands the debt we bear toward the dead. See chapter 3, "Egomimesis."

3 EGOMIMESIS

1 "These two absent gentlemen are dear to us in so many ways. They are our friends and our lovers, they are our husbands and our brothers, and they are these children's fathers." This song he attributes to his mother in Book I of the *Confessions*, in *Oeuvres complètes* I (hereafter cited as *OC* I), ed. B. Gagnebin and M. Raymond, Paris, Pléiade, 1959, 7. Her sister had married her husband's brother, in a kind of fairy-tale romance of doubles; she writes this song when both the husbands depart on commerce.

2 tr. Trent Schroyer, Evanston, Northwestern University Press, 1973, [orig. 1964], 164–5.

3 Rousseau's insistence on the ego-basis (*amour-propre/amour de soi*) of (what passes for) "sociability," prefigures Freud and Lacan.

4 Rousseau, the supposed source of the myth of primary innocence, also drew the picture of guilt, love, and reparation (to borrow Klein's phrase) more clearly than anyone before Freud.

5 In "On narcissism," *SE XIV*, 74, n. 3, and 76, this desire knows almost no limits, culminating in what Freud called "the end of the world" syndrome, in which one finally wishes that the world not outlast one's own life.

6 See J. Lacan, *Séminaire VII*, "L'Objet et la chose," Paris, Seuil, 1986, 126–7. He speaks mainly of art as aggression against the maternal body, *à la* Oedipus, citing the work of Melanie Klein.

7 F. Tönnies, *Custom: An Essay on Social Codes*, tr. A. F. Borenstein, Chicago, Gateway/Henry Regnery Books, 1961, 66, defines "Law" as that "which must be pronounced, rather than followed [like custom – JFM]." The law appears to lift a taboo of silence (custom's remembrance only through a displacement). Law is a positive, creative force, since it wills that "something comes to pass." Modern law, oriented to the future, is a means of expressing one's claims, demands, rights. Thus the structural repression of desire at the root of custom should be removed by the advent of law. Yet a secondary repression sets in. As Freud notes in *Totem and Taboo* (*SE XIII*, 84–5) the expansion of will power distances us from our wishes. "Desire" is representable ever more only in neurosis, where it manages to get represented somewhat, parapraxes, faults in behavior – and in our attitude toward the dead (mainly in our collective transgressions against them).

8 J. Lacan, *Séminaire VII*, 128.

9 ibid., 129.

10 ibid., my trans., 264.

11 See Slavoj Zizek's book on Hegel, *Le plus sublime des hystériques: Hegel passe*, Cahors, Point Hors Ligne, 1988. In going through it I note that pp. 251 ff. deal with "le peuple" in a similar way to mine here.

12 See Ernst Cassirer, *The Question of Jean-Jacques Rousseau*, tr. Peter Gay, Bloomington, Indiana University Press, 1963 [orig 1954]. Reading *Emile* apparently influenced Kant a great deal, for example. Only the Kantians consider the superegoic dimension in Rousseau, but of course they do not usually recognize his general "I" in the way Lacan did, as akin to Sade. Recall Lacan's hint that the "first" person is rooted in the suppression of another, third person, "he."

13 "Jean-Jacques Rousseau et le péril de la réflexion," 92–188, in Jean Starobinksi, *L'Oeil vivant: Essai (Corneille, Racine, Rousseau, Stendhal)*, Paris, Editions Gallimard, 1961.

14 I should specify Oedipal-onanistic-imaginary: J. Derrida, *Of Grammatology*, tr. Gayatri C. Spivak, Baltimore, Johns Hopkins University Press, 1976 (orig. 1967).

15 Peggy Kamuf, "Rousseau's politics of visibility," *Diacritics*, 1982 (a stance modified in her recent book *Signature Pieces*, Ithaca, Cornell University Press, 1989), states the case succinctly and with disapproval. Also, see Allan Bloom, introducing his translation of *Politics and the Arts: Letter to D'Alembert on the Theatre*, Ithaca, Cornell University Press, 1960, xxvii–viii, and xxx: "The vanity of woman is promoted wherever there are refined entertainments . . . adornment becomes an object in itself, and all sorts of expense and attention are devoted to it – not to mention the revolution in family life that is its result. This expense and attention must be given at the sacrifice of other things." Joel Schwartz, *Rousseau's Sexual Politics*, Chicago, University of Chicago Press, 1985, finds Rousseau's sexual politics (women modest and dangerous; men aggressive but bearers of rationality) meets with his complete approval.

16 J. Lacan, *De la psychose paranoïaque dans ses rapports avec la personnalité*, Paris, Seuil, 1975, 289.

17 E. Cassirer, op. cit., sees Rousseau as the voice of modern, liberal democracy, explaining his psychic "disorders" in terms of the Kantian distinction between the transcendental and empirical egos. Conservative Straussians like Bloom, social psychologists and literary critics often see his democratic ideals as "perverted" or authoritarian. Only certain neo-Marxists like Colletti and della Volpe read proto-Marxist critical and structural positions in his work. See Galvano della Volpe, *Rousseau and Marx and Other Writings*, tr. John Fraser, Atlantic Highlands, NJ, Academic Press, 1978 [orig. 1964]; Lucio Colletti, *From Rousseau to Lenin: Studies in Ideology and Society*, tr. J. Merrington and J. White, New York and London, Monthly Review Press, 1972.

18 Again, it is Cassirer's defense of Rousseau's liberal democratic stance that makes the division.

19 To be fair, Colletti considers Rousseau to have seen the transformation of the division of labor into a division of desire in Marx's terms: "every new product represents a new potency of mutual swindling, and mutual plundering" (Marx's 1844 manuscript on *Human Requirements*, cited in Colletti, op. cit., 161).

20 Denial of difference is the basis of our homoerotic order (desire marked with a male sign) in so far as, in Lacan's thesis, "heterosexuality" is a metaphor/symptom which marks by substitution a lack of distinction. For Lacan, as for Freud, homophobic declaratives, homosexual conjugations (*De la psychose*, 261) and hysterical defenses of fixed, natural, or permanent gender distinctions (women are like this, men are like that; they're "just naturally different") are all transformations of the root declarative sentence – that cannot be uttered – "I, a man, love him [a man]." See Anthony Wilden, *System and Structure*, London, Tavistock, 1972, 290, for a more extended comment on the "I love him" sentence.

21 J. Lacan, *Séminaire XX*, Paris, Seuil, 1975, 12.

22 Rousseau *Oeuvres complètes* III, Paris Bibliothèque de la Pléiade, 1965, 165. Cited hereafter as *OC* III.

23 English version of Rousseau's *Oeuvres Complètes* is from the translation by Donald A. Cress, *Jean-Jacques Rousseau: On the Social Contract, The Discourse on Human Inequality, and the Discourse on Political Economy*, Indianapolis, Hackett Publishing Company, 1983, here p. 141.

24 See my "Nature and self-love," *PMLA*, vol. 92: 5 (October 1977), 890–902.

25 D.A. Cress, op. cit., p. 141.

26 Rousseau has laid out the primacy of tropic language in the *Essai sur l'origine des langues*, ed. Charles Porset, Bordeaux, Guy Ducros, Editeur, 1968, in the famous passage on the invention of figurative language: a primitive man seeing another very like himself, nevertheless perceives the other as a fearsome giant, and names him such before inventing the equalizing word, "man."

27 Here see the Marxist perspective in Lucio Colletti, op. cit., and Galvano della Volpe, op. cit.

28 Cress, op. cit., p. 143.

29 The *Essai* is more explicit on this point, twinning the "charming" origin of love at the watering place with the birth of its opposing instinct, hate. Brother–sister incest predates to this first exchange in the public/market place: "On devenoit maris et femmes sans avoir cessé d'être frére et soeur"; "il fallut bien que les prémiers hommes épousassent leurs soeurs. Dans la simplicité des prémiéres moeurs cet usage se perpétua sans inconvénient", *Essai sur l'origine des langues*, 125.

30 Cress, op. cit., p. 143.

31 In "'Civilized' sexual morality and modern nervous illness," *SE IX*, 1959, 177–204 (orig. 1908). Freud calls "family feeling, derived from erotism" the first source of instinctual renunciation (187). This recourse to love is the first true step in "civilization" or the development of conscience.

32 Jean-Jacques Rousseau, *Les Rêveries d'un promeneur solitaire* in *OC* I. English translation *Reveries of the Solitary Walker*, tr. Peter France, Harmondsworth, Penguin, 1979.

33 Rousseau's emended phrase is that to become human is to "mutiler en quelque sorte la constitution de l'homme pour la renforcer." (*OC* III, n. 7, 1462 [note 7 to p. 313]). Is it possible to desexualize this sacrifice?

34 René Girard also places expulsion and sacrifice at the origin of society, (*Violence and the Sacred*, Baltimore, Johns Hopkins Press, 1977), and morality: guilt for a primal murder (as in *Totem and Taboo*) urges us on in the direction of greater civilization.

35 See especially Derrida, *De la grammatologie* (Paris, Editions du Minuit, 1967),

on Rousseau's sensitivity to the "passions." On Pateman, see chapter I, n. 35.

36 The late Ted Morris pointed out to me that the use of the phrase "flattoit ma vue" is standard French love-idiom.

37 Rousseau, *OC* I, 1037.

38 The editors of the Pléïade edition of the *Rêveries* devote no fewer than six historical and etymological notes to the Fazy episode, including historical and archeological documents, biographical dictionaries, linguistic dialects, geographical, and industrial-mechanical information. The one note on Pleince confirms the existence of a playing field at Plainpalais in southwest Geneva.

39 The role of primary narcissism as childhood innocence has already been discussed above. "Rousseauism" might seem like pre-Oedipal innocence (primitivism), but these passages grant ego-aggression full recognition. Many analysts, especially American ones, resist strongly the assignment of aggression (which Melanie Klein saw as fundamental) to the primary self of the infant, the child, yet the concept is crucial for the political and social implications of Rousseau's, as later for Freud's, thought.

40 Rousseau, *OC* I, 1037.

41 Incidentally, fiction does not operate according to the *fort/da* of revelation/hiding, presence/absence, here/not here or the effect of a logic of castration.

42 See note 6 above on Melanie Klein and Lacan.

43 For Rousseau, *law* is the relation of the whole to the whole. (*Social Contract* II, xii, 48); the most important form of the law prior to modernity is the "folkway" or custom.

44 F. Tönnies, op. cit., 47. The word is *Sitte*, or the folkway, everyday mores.

45 We may quibble about whether the law is good or bad, but we do not doubt it to be the very essence of modern society. The law has been identified as a masculine mode, and custom with traditional "women" in Tönnies, op. cit., 120 ff. Since in the entire body of his texts Rousseau set about rethinking every political and social relation (individual/society, art/republic, citizen/city, father/son, mother/child), it is perhaps wise to look much more closely than anyone has up till now at Rousseau's sexual relations.

46 Lacan, *Ecrits*, Paris, Editions du Seuil, 1966, 770.

47 Rousseau says he will take men as they are, but the laws as they might be: and lays ultimate responsibility for the character of a "people" at the doorstep of its government: "les peuples sont à la longue ce que le gouvernement les fait être" (*OC* III, 251: *Sur l'economie politique*).

48 There is also a third branch of the law, criminal law, in which the member relates neither to the Other as the whole, nor to the other as equal, but directly to the law itself. The fact of criminality is itself one of the finest indicators of the independent existence of the law.

49 Self-legislation in Rousseau means the ultimate power to suppress nature and abolish the difference between individual and collective for good: "The more these natural forces are dead and obliterated," he writes in *The Social Contract*, pt. II:vii 39: "the greater and more durable are the acquired forces, the more too is the institution solid and perfect. Thus if each citizen is nothing and can do nothing except in concert with all the others, and if the force acquired by the whole is equal to or superior to the sum of the natural forces of all individuals one can say that the legislator has

achieved the highest possible point of perfection."

These new "natural forces" ascend over mere custom and attune all to the finality of the "whole" (the product of self-governance – democracy). The death of the natural and the individual has an undeniably ominous ring. Rousseau's discussion of law has it "optimistically" overcoming fantasies of natural law as the source of moral life, but also "pessimistically" has it permit the surreptitious return of a (pre-Oedipal) relation. Because it does not adequately specify *who* plays the parental part (we believe any one can take the "first place"), our superego (*It*) is a site not of lack, but of consumption and takes on the despotic ways of the pre-Oedipal father. This is the fascism inherent as a threat in a democracy that is too forgetful.

50 The power of horror here is not, as for Kristeva, fear of engulfment, but of division, the *corps morcelé* of the mirror-stage.

51 See my discussion above on the Kantian "ego" as grounding of humanity in general.

52 Compare Erving Goffman's *The Presentation of Self in Everyday Life*, Garden City, Doubleday Anchor Books, 1959, and Kenneth Burke's well-known "dramaturgical frame of reference."

53 Rousseau tells us that we moderns need the theater because our "heart is ill at ease inside us" (16), but also that "the heart of man is always right" unless it is warped by self-interest (24). If we accept that, as inherited from Kant, the ego is the ultimate social unit, and that its *Bildung* models the collective, we miss Rousseau's dialectic. It is my argument that the theater, the modern theater Rousseau defines in the *Letter*, is not only a site for staging the ego (and its conjuring of relation) but for staging of desire as difference.

54 In the *Social Contract* pt. II: vii, Rousseau claimed a systematic relation of the overall shape of a social group to the "customs" of its members. These customs are distinct from ideals, laws and official moral doctrines, the everyday *moeurs* of its people, their habits of mind and behavior. Custom is the most important, if least recognized by the modern, form of the law (48). It is, for Rousseau, the "true constitution of the state" since it "everyday takes on new force":

> When other laws grow old and die away, it revives and replaces them, preserves a people in the spirit of its institution and imperceptibly substitutes the force of the heart for that of authority. I am speaking of *mores, customs*, and especially of *opinion*, a part of the law unknown to our political theorists, but on which the success of all others depends. (48)

That the heart of the people is not "natural" is already a part of Rousseau's structure: for whoever or whatever has undertaken to "establish a people" has already had to "change human nature" (*Social Contract* pt. II: vii, 39). In itself, custom is politically indifferent: it only becomes significant in context, in the way it is used: it becomes easy prey to ideology when it is tacit and unacknowledged.

55 Allan Bloom, "Introduction" to his translation of *Politics and the Arts: Letter to D'Alembert on the Theatre*, op. cit.

56 Of his Galatea, his Pygmalion cries, "Ah que je sois toujours un autre pour vouloir toujours être elle" in "Pygmalion, scène lyrique" (Rousseau, *Oeuvres Complètes II*, Bernard Guyon, Jacques Scherer, and Charly Guyot

(eds), Paris, Bibliothèque de la Pléïade, 1964, 1228).

57 It is only after Rousseau's *Social Contract* that the moral is seen to grow out of the *mos*, or custom, rather than natural or divine law. Tönnies' discussion of the root of the *mos* in inhibition, or a guilt toward the dead is relevant to the psychoanalytic-sociological-aesthetic synthesis Rousseau brings about in the *Contract* and in the *Letter*. Colletti, op. cit., 145, sees Rousseau as subverting both secular Christianity and the school of natural law by thus having "politics" found morality: "A morality in itself, anterior to and independent of politics, and restricted to the 'inner life' of men, is ultimately inconceivable for Rousseau."

58 Rousseau opens his reply to D'Alembert by defending the Genevan pastors whom, the mathematician claims, had told him they thought the establishment of a theater in Geneva not a bad idea. Rousseau accuses D'Alembert of using the tactics of despotic censors, imputation, and hearsay, to speak for the "feelings" of the pastors, and to imply they are basically Enlightened Socinians. Not only is D'Alembert likely to be mistaken (who can know what they feel in their hearts?), but these pastors are the "officers of morality" in their own society. Like Socinians they may indeed be humane, philosophic, and tolerant, but to make them full-fledged Socinians is to turn them into heretics and put them in dangerous contradiction with their function in the Genevan republic.

59 Rousseau associates this patriarchy strongly with Protestantism, and expects to be going "back" to a matriarchal, femino-centric world when he leaves for France to convert to Catholicism (Mme de Warens can be read as an allegory of the mother, Church, etc.). The next books are a catalogue of his disappointments on this score: from Mme de Warens, to Mme Vercellis, Mlle de Breil, Mme Basile, on down.

60 Allan Bloom thinks Rousseau entirely approves of the city-state in which the arts, and their most salient personal representative in everyday life, the actress or painted woman play a minimal role.

61 It is *not*, he asserts, a comedy (though he does not, as a later century believed, call it a tragedy either). Molière's play fails to "shake" the order of society. This is because he had to "please the public"; he "consulted the general taste and from this formed a model of contraries." Rousseau in fact finds Alceste – for all his misanthropy and railing against society – is not nearly antagonistic enough to the prevailing societal norm – self-interest. He "needed to be colder where his own interests were concerned" (40).

62 *Letter to D'Alembert*, 47.

63 *Confessions*, English translation by J.M. Cohen, Harmondsworth, Penguin, 1954, 460.

64 The *Letter* confronts the relation of art to political life (the relation to the whole) as well as to social life (the relation among members): is art on the "side" of political (cut) or social (linked) relations? We assume a certain correlation if not legislation between artistic genres and socio-political forms, whether these are understood à la Jameson (who calls genre a "social contract") or whether we think of art as revolutionary or socially conservative. In the case of the novel, for example, the eighteenth century disturbed classical generic categories, especially in regard to the separation of styles, e.g., in Fielding's preface to *Joseph Andrews*. Just as Bakhtin pointed out that the novel is the first genre invented after antiquity and

which also post-dates the art of graphic writing, so too Rousseau makes a radical claim for modern theater: in contrast to the classics, it is the first theater of love.

65 Recent efforts to analyze theatricality and representation have held little for the sexual relation-in-art. Yet this is exactly what is at issue in the *Letter*. See David Marshall, in *Representations* 13 (1986), "Rousseau and the state of the theatre."

66 See J. Lacan, *Le Séminaire VII*, op. cit., p. 134 and "L'Amour courtois en anamorphose," Paris, Seuil, 1986, 167–209.

67 Lacan sees the antinomy individual-state (from Plato to Hegel) as one which reproduces, on the psychic scale, disorders in the state (*Sem. VII*, 126). He differentiates this view from Freud's, where "society" plays the role of the "reality principle": "Les exigences de la réalité se présentent en effet volontiers sous la forme des exigences que l''on appelle de la société" (ibid.). Freud, that is, connects the powers of life as they end up in death directly to the powers that stem from the knowledge of good and evil, from moral choices, the choices that exist only with a civilized order.

68 None of the major readers of Rousseau, including the psychoanalytically oriented Jean Starobinski and Derrida, speak to the repeated incidents of homosexuality that appear in *The Confessions*. Only Lacan, as I pointed out, mentions it in a passing remark in *Les Psychoses, Séminaire III*.

69 I address a problem similar to that of René Girard's *Mensonge Romantique et vérité romanesque*, Paris, Grasset, 1959, whose central concept is mimetic desire. The account Girard gives of the relations among the self, the fictional other and desire do not adequately criticize the ego, nor permit the inclusion of the feminine subject. Girard's exclusion of the feminine has been criticized by Toril Moi, "The missing mother: the Oedipal rivalries of René Girard," *Diacritics* 12: 2, 1982, 21–31.

70 *Confessions, OC* I, Book IX, 430 and 435. References are first to the French Pléiade edition, then to the English translation by J. M. Cohen, Harmondsworth, Penguin, 1954.

71 Walter Benjamin thought love between women might, after all, be the highest form of love ("Socrates," *Philosophical Forum* XV:1–2 (Fall/Winter) 1984, 53). In any event, Benjamin, like Rousseau, felt that without sexual difference thought could only be a genuine evil.

72 When Rousseau "sees" his Julie in Sophie d'Houdetot, we suspect that he does so within the ideology of sublimation. But it is, after all, Julie who comes to "life" in Sophie.

73 Returned from the war and learning of Rousseau's love for Sophie, St Lambert and she come to the Hermitage to invite Rousseau to dinner (*Confessions*, 461).

It can be imagined how gladly I welcomed them! But I was even more delighted to see the good understanding between them. I was so pleased not to have disturbed their happiness that I felt happy myself; and I can swear that throughout my mad infatuation but especially at that moment, even if I could have stolen Mme d'Houdetot from him I should never have wished to do so. I should not even have felt tempted to try. I found her so lovable in her love for Saint-Lambert that I could hardly imagine her being so if she had loved me; and far from wishing to interfere with their union, all that I most truly desired from her, throughout my delirium, was that she should allow herself to be loved.

In short, however violent the passion with which I burned for her, I found it as sweet to be her confidant as to be the object of her love, and never for one moment looked on her lover as my rival, but always as my friend. It may be suggested that this was not really love. Very well, then, it was something more.

(Confessions, 429)

Rousseau loses St Lambert's "estime" – marked by his snoring while Rousseau reads his work aloud – but not his "amitié." He has not been a faithful depositary; he has "touched" St Lambert's capital. But he has not touched it either.

74 Here, the English translation simply fails to make the important distinctions Rousseau does: Cohen's English uses the terms "unrequited" and "returned," without the important concept of overcoming reciprocity being at all involved : "But I am wrong to say unrequited love, for mine was in a sense returned" (413).

75 By "reproduced" I mean the situation of "the two girls" and "Saint Preux" and not the sterilized courtly love triangle Wolmar permits to reign at Clarens. It redeems the Oedipal rivalry of Wintzenreid or Claude Anet and Rousseau with Mme de Warens.

76 As in the precursor to both situations, the so called "Idyll of the cherries," in the *Confessions*. See my essay, "History and self-portrait in Rousseau's Autobiography," *Studies in Romanticism*, vol. 13, no. 4, 1974, 279–98.

77 Here the I urge the reader to look at Roger Caillois's lecture, in Denis Hollier, *The College of Sociology, 1937–39*, tr. Betsy Wing, Minneapolis, University of Minnesota Press, 1988, 281 ff. on the festival. Caillois links the fiesta to the sacred revival of the ancestor-creators (in contrast to Freud's *Totem and Taboo*, where the ancestor is "remembered" as a displaced totem, but the crime of eating him is re-enacted collectively, by the totem feast that lifts individual guilt). For Caillois, it is the experience – the overturning of ordinary everydayness, an epiphany of a higher order in the chaos, debauchery, and disorder it introduces into the routine, daily round of events – that is crucial. (In Freud's terms it would be the reinforcement of the clan of the brothers.) The return of the malevolent ancestors feared in the practice of a taboo is exorcised by men acting in concert. This "festival" seems to me appropriate to a society that assumes it has no future history, one whose everyday life is entirely and boringly real. The sense that daily life is non-dramatic in character is, I think, one that neither Freud nor Erving Goffman could be accused of sharing.

Nor does the overturning and "de-construction" of Bakhtin's carnival have the same significance. It is less for him a matter of the emotional injection of festival colors into the dreariness of life than of a specific, special, temporally limited, breakdown of contemporary political hierarchies – and which finally serves to reinforce them. Another odd difference: Caillois sees the fête as "suspending" marked time, where Walter Benjamin sees the holiday or festival as what *marks time* otherwise than in daily life, because it is remembrance. (See "Some motifs in Baudelaire," *Illuminations*, tr. Harry Zohn, New York, Schocken Books, 1969, 181.)

4 FEMININE EROS: FROM THE BOURGEOIS STATE TO THE NUCLEAR STATE

1 See my review essay, "Stendhal's woman," *Semiotica*, 48:1–2 (1984), 143–68, as well as "Women in Stendhal," by Simone de Beauvoir, both of which are reprinted in Harold Bloom (ed.), *Stendhal*, New York and Philadelphia, Chelsea House Publishers, 1989, 197–217.
2 English citations are from the Penguin edition of the text, *Love*, translated by Gilbert and Suzanne Sale, Harmondsworth, Penguin, 1957; French citations from *De l'amour*, ed. Michel Crouzet, Paris, Garnier Flammarion, 1965).
3 As Derrida has argued in *Glas*, Paris, Editions Galilée, 1974.
4 Derrida, *Glas*, 146. Derrida's use of two phallic columns in *Glas* seems to allude to homosexuality as the ultimate frame around the modern couple; he follows Irigaray in seeing it repressing the brother–sister relation (*Glas*, 170 ff.). Hegel termed the brother–sister relation "peaceful, equal and general" without retaining any trace of naturalness. Derrida questions this unique phenomenon in Hegel: no conflict, no violence, no rape: absolute unity, the prestige not of Oedipus but Antigone. Hegel's esteem for *Antigone* refers, for Derrida, to his own sister. But in my reading (as in Irigaray's) it would also code the more general relationship that is being affirmed (brotherhood) as well as the one that is being eliminated (sexual difference within the same-generational tie).
5 M. de Volney used to relate how, as he once sat at table in the country house of an American, a fine well-to-do man surrounded by his grown-up children, a young man came into the room. 'Good day, William,' said the American. 'Come and sit down. You're looking well.' The traveller asked who the young man was. 'He's my second boy.' 'And where has he come from?' 'Canton' (*Love*, 164).
6 See his "L'Amour courtois en anamorphose," *Séminaire VII*, Paris, Seuil, 1986, as well as his "Love Letter," in Juliet Mitchell and Jacqueline Rose (eds), *Feminine Sexuality: Jacques Lacan and the école freudienne*, New York: Pantheon Books, 1982 (French original in *Séminaire XX*: "Encore").
7 See my review essay, "Fiction and the social order," *Diacritics*, vol. 5: 1 (Spring, 1975), an analysis of Christie Vance McDonald and others in relation to this.
8 For critics from Denis de Rougemont to Peggy Kamuf ("Rousseau's politics of visibility," *Diacritics*, 1982), Rousseau's *Nouvelle Héloïse* stands at the gateway of patriarchy: they see him approving his heroine's submission to her loveless, dutiful marriage. In *Love in the Western World* (tr. M. Belgion, New York, Pantheon Books, 1940), Denis de Rougemont lauds Julie's famous letter arguing for absolute fidelity to her marriage vows: she reasons, he tells us, like a man. Julie's sacrificial virtue seems to me to be entirely tragic for Rousseau, since its outcomes are for her purely negative.
9 The drunk scene where he attempts to arouse her with obscene proposals (*I*, l) immediately precedes Julie's invitation to her bedroom (*I*, liii).
10 This is the structure of the "new" symbolic: it does not speak in its own name but in the "name of the father," whom it has done away with.
11 Is it Montesquieu's failure to imagine a sexual nature for the bourgeois woman, or is he – author of the *Persian Letters*, after all – having an insight into male despotism in the bourgeois class? The convent and the harem are such targets of social critique by the *philosophes* that the idea of veiling and walling up women – even in the bourgeois household – ought to have been repugnant to them.

12 The children have been mixed together after Claire merges her household with the Wolmars' when she becomes a widow.

13 In "'Civilized' sexual morality and modern nervous illness," *SE IX*, 1959, 177–204.

14 The specific means Wolmar uses as a barrier to their "brother-sister alliance" is a form of figural repetition: he provides Julie and Saint Preux with a cafeteria of replays of their earlier passions, restagings which he duly oversees. He forcibly creates "screen" memories and mirror-stagings.

15 *De l'amour*, ed. Crouzet, 1965.

16 In the *Second Discourse*.

17 Freud, op. cit.

18 An American girl and a would-be suitor can be left alone together without fear for her virtue as long as a question of dowry remains unresolved. See Fragment 40 (*Love*, 225; *De l'amour*, 252) on how love has deserted America's youth.

19 Stendhal discovers it is originally "Arabian-Bedouin" (*Love*, 174–5; ch. 53), and whatever small foothold it had in Christian Europe was the result of the catharism and the culture of Provence, "before the Conquest of Toulouse by Northern Barbarians in 1328" (ibid., 165). Using "barbarian" much like the later Freud to mean the failure of erotism, he thus characterizes the Albigensian crusade. It is this fourteenth-century crusade that enables him to describe the earlier Christian crusades to the Holy Land like this: "Clearly it is we who were the barbarians when we went to harrass the East with our crusades" (ibid., 175). In aligning anti-Orientalism with aggressive invasion Stendhal shows a certain political correctness, for the great orientalist fads and fantasies of his time helped promote imperialist adventures. (See Edward Said, *Orientalism*, New York: Vintage Books, 1979.)

20 A student of Lacan's, Researcher Marie Lanfant of C.N.R.S., has said that Lacan always pronounced the term "norme-mal" (or perhaps "norme-mâle").

21 "In family relationships the deceiver is always the first to suffer. There can be no refuge for *him*; being always a lawbreaker, *he* is always afraid" (*Love*, 175 [my emphasis]).

22 Lacan began to see his way out of the word as the primary form of the symbol through a reanalysis of the psychotic President Daniel Schreber. Schreber, Lacan finds (in a seminar entitled the "symbolic sentence", or "La phrase symbolique," *Séminaire III*, op. cit., 117–32), senses a magical power in language. See note 33 below.

23 *Love*, 169–74; *De l'amour*, 190–6.

24 This is the name Walter Scott gave Gabrielle de Vergy in his *Anne of Geierstein* which must have been Stendhal's source. See also Diderot's *Paradoxe sur le comédien* where de Vergy is discussed.

25 So it is that, in Kant, while the relationship between goodness, the good father/mother/nature and everyday mores (*Sittlichkeit; moeurs*) is one of a constant oscillation between opposing ways of evaluating that behavior, dependent on context, it is still an overall finality that determines the relative morality or immorality of conduct. Decency, honesty, modesty, reserve in pre-bourgeois culture become easy discourse and flirtation in monogamous society: they amount to being clothes for a hidden purpose ("intention plus élevée, la conservation de l'espèce," Derrida, *Glas*, 145), – which is, of course, the perpetuation of the domestic household.

26 As Mathilde de la Mole's mourning in *The Red and the Black* for her

Renaissance aristocrat ancestor, supposed lover of Catharine de Medici, who ordered the St Bartholomew massacre.

27 Critics always hesitate on Stendhal. On the basis of his biography, they identify Stendhal with Don Juan; but as he suffers so much for the women whom he never had, Stendhal also appears a Werther type. See Robert Alter, *A Lion for Love*, New York, Basic Books, 1979, 153.

28 See my essay, "Stendhal's Woman" in H. Bloom, op. cit.

29 Freud, "Group psychology and the analysis of the ego," *SE XVIII*, 69.

30 "The distinction would have been more precise if I had cited Saint Preux, but he is such a dull character that I should be wronging the sensitive if I were to choose him as their champion" (*Love*, 204). But he never goes back to the name of Werther in the text.

31 He thus sought her in nomadic models, and in Matilde Dembowski, leader of an Italian revolutionary group.

32 This version of "desire" and "satisfaction" is alien not only to Lacan's vocabulary, but also to the philosophical tradition, which, apart from Rousseau, and from Hegel on, always sees desire as what is unsatisfied. Yet as I note in chapter 1, Rousseau's peculiar blend of desire and *jouissance* compares with Stendhal's. The point is to undo the opposition between satiety (fullness, gorging) and unsatisfiable longing (passion; suffering) as the full polarity of human feeling in relation to the other. To continue to desire, as Saint Preux desires Julie after he "has" her, is a different way of understanding "possession" in which desire remains a motivation within the relation, rather than for "the next." See my essay, "Oedipus wrecks: Lacan, Stendhal and the narrative form of the real," in *Lacan and Narration*, ed. R. Con Davis, Baltimore, Johns Hopkins University Press, 1985.

33 See note 22. Schreber's employment of the euphemism is his discourse of mastery over this power. By controlling the word's oppositions through euphemism Schreber "harnesses" or channels the potential energy of the word – and also borrows its prestige. God will couple with Schreber by means of his very distant rays and beams, just as words that are at extreme antipodes can be forced into pairings. So drawn is Schreber to antiphrastic witticism that he calls things exclusively by their opposites (reward is punishment, e.g., 124). He also starts expressing himself only in a very savory kind of highly euphemistic German which he terms his *Grundsprache*.

34 De Rougemont's harsh rejection of courtly love and the poetry of the troubadours is echoed by many in our time, from Ford's *The Good Soldier* to the feminists, as it was by Wollstonecraft. See Elaine Marks and Isabel de Courtivron's *New French Feminisms*, New York, Schocken, 1981, pp. 7 ff.: the woman on the pedestal, the cult of the virgin, the deferral of sexual gratification and the glorification of the questing knight as hero are the chief heritage of courtly romance in our culture – and it is definitely hostile to the woman. Interestingly, the early Juliet Mitchell is less harsh on the paradigm, because at some level, the woman is the object of a man who sings his passion, and this leads her to wonder about the possibility of woman's becoming her own subject. Ian Watt, in *The Rise of the Novel*, Los Angeles and Berkeley, University of California Press, 1965, 138 ff. has a serious treatment of courtly romance in relation to the shift from "conjugal" families to independent individuals in the Enlightenment.

35 Lacan claims it is still at work in Breton's *L'Amour fou*, i.e. the relation to the objectivity of chance.

36 Stendhal and Lacan's point seems to be to designate the "other" courtly love, the anamorphic one in which the lady occupied the subject position. Its apprehension is blocked by the secondary revision given it by Petrarch.

37 Marguerite Duras, *Hiroshima, mon amour*, Paris, Librairie Gallimard, 1960. English edition New York, Grove Press, 1961. Both hereafter cited as *Hir*.

38 Simone de Beauvoir, "Women in Stendhal," in Bloom (ed.), *Stendhal*.

39 In Deleuze and Guattari's *Mille plateaux* the warrior resists the state. *A Thousand Plateaux*, tr. Brian Massumi, Minneapolis, University of Minnesota Press, 1987 (orig. 1980).

40 In the "Group psychology and the analysis of the ego," *SE XVIII*, 140, note D, he tells us that "two people coming together for the purpose of sexual satisfaction, in so far as they seek for solitude, are making a demonstration against the herd instinct, the group feeling."

41 And always lose – Catherine and Heathcliff, Julie and Saint Preux.

42 *Hiroshima, mon amour*, New York, Grove Press, 1961.

43 *The War: A Memoir*, tr. Barbara Bray, New York, Pantheon Books, 1986.

44 That is why our governments are anxious to be able to calculate how many will die – and where. See Dean MacCannell, "Baltimore in the morning . . . after," *Diacritics*, 1984 (summer) 33–46.

45 Again Freud's "Group psychology" provides the proper subtext for *Hiroshima*, when it traces the affinities among hypnotic fixation (displayed by both heroine and hero), the importance of a central focus (the two walk around and around the city of Hiroshima), and the radical destruction of real otherness in the name of group love, a distortion of egomimetic desire.

46 "It is inside the city walls that I became his wife/woman."

47 The repressed familial relations under the nuclear unconscious are, here, of course, seen to be to the children (and to their father). Riva's "having children" is what cures her melancholy madness, but she has no place for them in her "love." The only other children that appear are two who act in the anti-bomb propaganda film and wrangle over an orange on the side of the set. The bigger of the two gets the orange, leaving the other bawling. Peace movements have not got to the root cause of interpersonal aggressiveness.

48 It is akin to that of Deleuze and Guattari principally in its opposition to the idea of the state: in *A Thousand Plateaux*, 374 ff. in the section of "Treatise on nomadology" that poses "*Problem II: Is there a way to extricate thought from the State model?*" they concentrate not on love but war, on the warrior and war-machine, and how they are transformed when they work for the state rather than against it: the proper role of the warrior, according to them.

49 Linda Williams, "Hiroshima and Marienbad: metaphor and metonomy" [*sic*], *Screen*, 17 (Spring 1976), 34–9, has seen the metaphoric structuring of *Hiroshima* and linked it to Jakobsonian analysis.

50 Félix Guattari's essay, "Like the echo of a collective melancholy," appeared in *Semiotexte*, V:2 (1982), 102–7; it "plunges one into social-democratic, humanist reappropriation and ends by condemning all violent acts in the name of a morality that accommodates itself to even greater acts of violence perpetrated in its own name! It promotes the idea that the only means of social transformation are those sanctioned by the law" (106).

51 ibid., 103.

52 ibid., 106. "Like it or not, politics today has become inseparable from the

collective affects molded and transmitted by the mass-media, which constitutes a means of subjection crossing over classes and nations, and at the heart of which it is very difficult to separate the manipulated fantasies from socio-economic realities."

53 Maria Torok and Nicholas Abraham, *Le verbier de l'homme aux loups*, Paris, Aubier Flammarion, 1976. In Freud's text, the incorporation of the unmournable dead is fantasized by the survivor as a ghost who haunts him for having wished his death, affecting, like Hamlet, the behavior of the survivor. In the cryptonomic extension of Freud's hints, this living dead becomes an active force in relation to the survivor's behavior, but in the later iteration, this operation works at the level of the ego, not the id, and the "ghost" which may appear to be the father is rather the same-generation "other" (a brother or sister) whose rival (oneself) is the survivor. Hélène Cixous in her *L'Histoire terrible mais pas encore achevée de Norodom Sihanouk, roi du Cambodge*, (Paris, Théâtre du Soleil, 1987) and Sarah Kofman, *Mélancolie de l'art*, Paris, Editions Galilée, 1985, have attempted such a positive reading to the "revenant" as relational. The most elaborate and well-thought through of these recent efforts appear in the work of Avital Ronell, *Dictations: On Haunted Writing*, Bloomington, Indiana University Press, 1986. Torok and Abraham diverge, close-range, from Freud.

54 Laurence Rickels, *Aberrations of Mourning: Writing on German Crypts*, Detroit, Wayne State University Press, 1988, 16. At times Rickels does seem to think that it is primarily the mother rather than the father who is melancholized (11–12). Rickels's book expresses its debt to the suggestion of Horkheimer and Adorno in *The Dialectic of Enlightenment* (tr. John Cumming, New York, Continuum, 1982) that a theory of ghosts is necessary for cultural analysis.

55 It is only if we read this image with Riva's "ultimate of horror and stupidity" that its significance is clear, and its use as a melancholic indulgence in horror can be prevented. Riva's shame is after all only shame, not real guilt: a kind of egoistic embarrassment, not a sense of responsibility toward the life of the other.

56 While it is clearly too soon to assess the politics of Derridean (not Lacanian) deconstruction, it is fair to say that until now it has been, for the most part, concerned with the traditional: it enacts the revival of the dead, simulates the ancestral cult, makes-believe in the world of fathers. This builds a somewhat shaky bridge to non-western cultures, "traditional" societies – providing they remain traditional. New ethnosemiotic formations which would address the cultural penetration and attempted hegemony of the west have not been a feature of this discourse. On the other hand, "deconstruction" has not been able to reach into and reform the roots of the contemporary west, getting "stuck" with the remembrance of some rather unlovable characters. To remember the father without his root relation to the mother-as-other is also, I argue, incomplete.

57 I have also been personally surprised by which television series are popular in the "third world": having been told that, rather predictably, "action" shows like *Night Rider* are "universally" appreciated, I nevertheless have witnessed the ceremonial viewing of *Sesame Street* at elegant teas given by high-status professionals in a Pakistani community in Africa, and I was congratulated for my culture's producing such excellence.

5 THE END(S) OF LOVE IN THE WESTERN WORLD

1 tr. H. Briffault, New York, Farrar, Straus & Giroux, 1952 (Fr. orig., 1950).
2 Edward Said, *Orientalism*, New York, Vintage Books, 1979.
3 Jean Rhys, *Wide Sargasso Sea*, New York & London, W. W. Norton & Company, 1982 [orig. pub 1966].
4 *Out of India*, New York, William Morrow & Company, Inc., 1986; and *Heat and Dust*, New York, Simon & Schuster, 1975.
5 Hannah Arendt makes the point that imperialism is from top to bottom the overthrow of the hard-won concept of the law and its replacement with raw power relations without accountability in *The Origins of Totalitarianism*, New York, Meridian Books, 1958. She regards totalitarianism as rooted in an imperial disregard for the rights and justice so hard fought for and partly achieved in the eighteenth century.
6 It is surprising – and not so surprising – too, that de Rougemont's *Love in the Western World*, which despises oriental influence on the west, is not cited in Said's text.
7 Gayatri Chakravorty Spivak, *In Other Worlds*, New York, Methuen, 1987.
8 Frantz Fanon, *The Wretched of the Earth*, New York, Grove Press, 1963, 249–316. This book is not, of course, centered on the woman, but the psychiatric case histories he provides have the status of high literary art in their economy of detail and attention to the sign. In them we read the range of sexual "relations" operating in a colonialism in retreat (the French in Algeria): the rape of a taxi-driver/courier's wife by a French police officer in the attempt to make her reveal her husband's hideout; the torture of his own wife and children by a French police officer; the revolt against her father by a French university student when he enthusiastically takes to fighting the "terrorists." In the case of the taxi-driver, traditional norms within his social traditions demand he reject a wife who has been dishonored, and, psychologically, he does so, becoming impotent with other women and hallucinating that his daughter is covered with filth. But morally he cannot reconcile himself to her rejection: "She did this for me" (*Wretched of the Earth*, 257–8). Their traditional, arranged marriage is thus cast on a new foundation. The police inspector who ties up his wife and beats his children asks to be "cured" just enough so he can keep on doing his job: his superiors do not consider him sick enough to be given leave for treatment (ibid., 269). The young university student, who has "morally rejected" her father, and (mentally) sides with the terrorists, can nevertheless be seen to reject him essentially out of fear of his death, which shortly occurs: it is after he dies that the daughter's symptoms (anxiety, sweaty palms) appear (ibid., 277). Fanon, ironically, follows her case history with that of Algerian children under ten whose parents have been killed by the French and who show (in contrast to her) a marked love "for parental images" (ibid., 278).
9 They may be the same thing, actually, for Orwell's "policeman" in Burma is, of course, autobiographical: but the narrator is cast as the very "type" delineated in Orwell's depiction of Kipling in "Shooting an elephant," in *A Collection of Essays by George Orwell*, San Diego, New York and London, Harcourt, Brace Jovanovich, 1953 (orig. 1946). "He could not understand what was happening, because he had never had any grasp of the economic forces underlying imperial expansion. It is notable that Kipling does not seem to realise, any more than the average soldier or colonial administrator, that an empire is primarily a money-making concern.

Imperialism as he sees it is a sort of forcible evangelizing. You turn a Gatling gun on a mob of unarmed 'natives,' and then you establish 'the Law,' which includes roads, railways and a courthouse. He could not foresee, therefore, that the same motives which brought the Empire into existence would end by destroying it'' (119).

10 "The Colonel's Lady and Judy O'Grady,'' in Byron Farwell, *Mr Kipling's Army: All the Queen's Men*, New York and London, W. W. Norton and Company, 1981, 225–44.

11 Dread of venereal disease encoded this desire: "Lord Kitchener . . . tried terrifying his troops. In a long memorandum on the subject, the commander-in-chief, who, as far as is known, never had sexual relations with a woman and had no interest in having any, wrote: "Syphilis contracted by Europeans from Asiatic women is much more severe than that contracted in England. It assumes a horrible, loathsome, and often fatal form through which in time, as years pass by, the sufferer finds his hair falling off, his skin and the flesh of his body rot, and . . . his breath to stink'' (quoted in Farwell, op. cit., 224).

12 One of the most "reactionary'' of the Euro-women authors who treat the colonial situation, Isak Dinesen, also failed to enrich herself in the colonies. Hers is a pre-capitalist, aristocratic perspective, blaming the commercial middle classes for the ruin of her farm and for the degradation of life at home as in the colonies.

13 F. Fanon, op. cit., 296 ff.

14 See also Orwell's "Marrakech'' in *A Collection of Essays*, 184 ff. "All people who work with their hands are partly invisible, and the more important the work they do, the less visible they are. Still, a white skin is always fairly conspicuous. In northern Europe, when you see a labourer ploughing a field, you probably give him a second glance. In a hot country, anywhere south of Gibraltar or east of Suez, the chances are that you don't even see him. I have noticed this again and again. In a tropical landscape one's eye takes in everything except the human beings. It takes in the dried up soil, the prickly pear, the palm tree and the distant mountain, but it always misses the peasant hoeing at his patch. He is the same colour as the earth and a great deal less interesting to look at'' (183–4).

15 "In that epoch – the early twenties – the white districts of all the Colonial cities of the world were always of an impeccable cleanliness, so were the white inhabitants. As soon as the whites arrived in the Colonies, they learned to take a bath every day, learned to be clean as children do. They also learned to wear the Colonial uniform, suits of spotless white, the color of immunity and innocence'' (Duras, *The Seawall*, 135).

16 J. Rhys, op. cit., 42.

17 "She start first with Sandi'' (125), her colored cousin, the boy she apparently loved or made love to, Daniel Cosway writes Rochester. The letter serves as "moralistic'' excuse for Rochester's viciousness toward her, that and the revelation of her mother's madness.

18 In "Myself in India,'' *Out of India* (13–21) Prawer Jhabvala makes clear how the western paradigms (individual versus mass; duty versus pleasure; body versus mind, etc.) fail to fathom her experience of and *in* India, so that the optimum the self-conscious western mind can hope for is oscillation among the poles of settling into the bottomless depth of familial relations or sociability ("enjoying being with each other'') and the

constant urge to "do" something, to "work" to shake off the lethargy and do something difficult, "like read Kant's *Critique of Pure Reason*" (18).

19 There is a wonderful turn around, where the guru, "Master," a "dynamo" of unbound libidinal energies, who like the unconscious, never says no to anyone, reunites the couple the Countess has separated, couples them. The English girl must then be accommodated by the Countess if she wants to exploit the young Indian swami's talents: so the girl, a lower-class London type, is made over into a "Holy Mother," and sits on stage in the west.

20 Edmund Husserl, "The crisis of European man," in *Phenomenology and the Crisis of European Philosophy*, tr. Quentin Lauer, New York, Harper & Row, 1965, 157.

6 THE RECONSTRUCTION OF MOTHERING

1 Sigmund Freud, "The sexual life of human beings," *Introductory Lectures on Psychoanalysis*, SE XIX, 312.

2 Metaphor always has it both ways, because it also protects the ego from overly identifying with the father/other: we act "as" the father, etc.

3   Civilized education may only attempt to suppress the instinct temporarily, till marriage, intending to give it free rein afterwards with the idea of then making use of it. . . . It is clear that education is far from underestimating the task of suppressing a girl's sensuality till her marriage, for it makes use of the most drastic measures. Not only does it forbid sexual intercourse and set a high premium on the preservation of female chastity, but it also protects the young woman from temptations as she grows up, by keeping her ignorant of all the facts of the part she is to play and by not tolerating any impulse of love in her which cannot lead to marriage. The result is that when the girl's parental authorities suddenly allow her to fall in love, she is unequal to this psychical achievement and enters marriage uncertain of her own feelings. In consequence of this artificial retardation in her function of love, she has nothing but disappointments to offer the man who has saved up all his desire for her. (*SE IX*, 197–8).

4 I prefer the translations in the Collier edition, 1963 ("Sexuality and modern nervousness," *Sexuality and the Psychology of Love*, New York, Collier Books, 1963):

The uninitiated can hardly believe how rarely normal potency is to be found in the men, and how often frigidity in the women, among those married couples living under the sway of our civilized sexual morality . . . . Neurosis is the most obvious way of escape from these conditions. I would, however, further point out how such a marriage will increasingly affect the only child – or the limited number of children – which spring from it. On appearance it looks as if we then had an inherited condition to deal with, but closer inspection shows the effect of powerful infantile impressions. As a mother, the neurotic woman who is unsatisfied by her husband is over-tender and over-anxious in regard to the child, to whom she transfers her need for love, thus awakening in it sexual precocity. The bad relations between the parents then stimulate the emotional life of the child, and cause it to experience intensities of love, hate and jealousy while yet in its infancy. The strict training which tolerates no sort of expression of this precocious sexual state lends support to the forces of suppression, and the conflict at this age contains all the elements needed to cause lifelong neurosis. (38)

"'Civilized' sexual morality and modern nervous illness," *SE IX*, 1959, 34–5:

> Civilized education attempts . . . only a temporary suppression of [sexuality] up to the period of matrimony, intending then to give it free rein in order to make use of it. . . . Clearly, education does not look lightly on the task of suppressing the sensuality of the girl until marriage, for it employs the most drastic measures. It not only forbids sexual intercourse and sets a high premium upon the preservation of sexual chastity, but it also protects the developing young woman from temptation by keeping her in ignorance of all the facts concerning the part she is ordained to play, and tolerates in her no love-impulse which cannot lead to marriage. The result is that when the girl is suddenly allowed by parental authority to fall in love, she cannot accomplish this mental operation and enters the state of marriage uncertain of her own feelings. As a result, the artificial retardation in the development of the lover-function provides nothing but disappointments for the husband.

5 Henry James, *What Maisie Knew*, Harmondsworth, Penguin, 1984.
6 Marguerite Duras, *The Lover*, tr. Barbara Bray, New York, Harper & Row, 1985.
7 Marguerite Duras, *The Ravishing of Lol V. Stein*, tr. Richard Seaver, New York, Grove Press, tr. of *Le ravissement de Lol V. Stein*, 1966.
8 Marguerite Duras, *Théâtre III*, Paris, NRF Gallimard, 1984.
9 Mrs Wix explains that her adoration for Maisie is based on equating her with own deceased child: she makes Maisie the dead girl's "sister." Visiting the grave of the "little dead Clara Matilda" with Mrs Wix, Maisie learns that the lost daughter "was in heaven and yet, embarrassingly, also in Kensal Green, where they had been together to see her little huddled grave" (*Maisie*, 32).
10 To suggest as one reader (Granville Jones, *Henry James's Psychology of Experience*, The Hague and Paris, Mouton, 1975, 9) has, that "Maisie's education is remarkably, successfully complete: from Sir Claude has come the sense of honor, from Mrs Wix, the sense of goodness, from Mrs Beale the sense of beauty," betrays how ambiguous the "moral value" of the signifier always is, flip-flopping from negative to positive. It is this value Maisie never subscribes to, making her deficient in the moral sense.
11 Critics make much of her "innocence" (Jones, op. cit., 5; Malcolm Mackenzie, *Communities of Love and Honor in Henry James*, Cambridge, Mass. and London, Harvard University Press, 1976, 15; and Dennis Foster, "Maisie supposed to know: amo[u]ral analysis," *The Henry James Review* V:3, 207–16, 1984, p. 207), implying that the reader (and the adults and their bedroom farce antics in the novel) "know" what she does not: Juliet Mitchell in *Women: The Longest Revolution*, New York, Pantheon Books, 1966, points out that "we must share [the adults'] knowledge of adultery and betrayal if we are to make sense of the book." Dennis Foster's interesting article attacks the notion that anyone "knows" in the text (215). In a stunning act of misprision, however, he equates Maisie with James, accusing James of "mastery," of trying to be the subject who is presumed to know – Lacan's "*sujet supposé savoir.*" James is perfectly

aware that "knowledge" – of sexual difference, of relation to the other, is impossible for the linguistic, symbolically positioned subject, but like the "other" Lacan who is little known to American critics, James reminds us that something has been left out or cut off – recognition, consciousness, connection. Remainder, leftover, scrap, or excrement are always destined to be misrecognized.

12 As one critic puts it, "Maisie appears to satisfy the formal conditions of knowing" (D. Foster, op. cit., 208).

13 James lets us know that while Mrs Beale professes unbounded love for the child, Maisie is ill-dressed, ill-fed, and uneducated while under her care. Mrs Wix (her frumpish old governess) "cares" for Maisie, but does so because she is obviously in love with Sir Claude. Her biological parents reject her completely. Though several employ the imagery of love, and idealize the family for the sake of the child, it is a mere rhetorical family, used to conceal their own affairs.

14 Maisie's gaffe rather spoils her entrance into the symbolic order. Responding to the signifiers of her identity (name) and address (category of young lady), Maisie goes too far, taking them as license to speak about relationships, instead of merely accepting them as the pure ambiguities they are intended to remain. It should be clear enough by now that I think criticism has given insufficient attention to what James knew about the positive side of her exclusion from the symbolic order.

15 What Maisie knew, basically, is what Erving Goffman knew, that there are two sorts of "sign-vehicles" and that signs given can never fully prevent the reading – otherwise – of signs given off (whether these be parapraxes or seemingly insignificant details. See "Introduction" to *The Presentation of Self in Everyday Life*, Garden City, Doubleday Anchor, 1959, 1–3.

16 Merla Wolk, "Nature and nurture in *What Maisie Knew*," *The Henry James Review* IV:3 (1983), 196–206. Wolk makes a great deal out of the missing mother, in Maisie, assigning to the maternal breast the entire burden of the "interhuman relation" (196) that language severs: "Separation refers on its most basic psychic level to the separation from the mother's breast" (198). For Wolk, Maisie's problems stem from a "failure in the maternal care necessary to provide conditions for the healthy growth of an individual" (195), though her assumptions about the "healthy individual" are what the novel is designed to question.

17 Interestingly this is echoed by Claude a few pages later when he tells Maisie, "I want to see *you*" (*Maisie*, 220) and "I want to see you alone" (ibid., 221). Maisie replies, "That's the way I want to see *you*!"

18 She tells this to her Chinese lover, and she follows it with the remark, "That's how I came to be here with you."

19 Stretter reappears in *India Song*, where her cardboard character is even more pronounced. In one scene she lies completely limp on the floor between her two lovers, the men have to move her arms and legs for her. She is "desirable." She has no more life and depth than a photo in *Vogue*. Even her love triangles are flat: she has as much libido as a cadaver and the only action that occurs when she is with her two lovers together comes from a fan whirling on the ceiling.

20 Anne-Marie Stretter dies the most nondescript death in *India Song* after being no more than the figure of a woman all her life.

21 This is reminiscent of "Marguerite" in *The Lover*, who explains that her greatest pleasure comes by imagining her Chinese lover making love to

the body of Hélène Lagonelle, her school chum – but only on the proviso that her girlfriend's body is at the same time her *own*: "I want her to do it as I wish, I want her to give herself where I give myself. It's via Hélène Lagonelle's body, through it, that the ultimate pleasure would pass from him to me. A pleasure unto death" (*The Lover*, 74).

22 See Dean MacCannell, "Negative solidarity," *Human Organization*, vol. 36, no. 3 (Fall), 1977, 301–4.

7 AFTER THE NEW REGIME

1 In Barthes's terms in "Myth today." Even here it does not function the way traditional myth does according to Lévi-Strauss, where it reflects but also organizes the critical ties and relations in society. In modern, historical society, myths can respond only to limited factions, which does not prevent their being promulgated as totalizing.

2 Those who are egotists and latent monarchists cannot forgive democracy the realization of this ideal.

3 See chapter 1, above, and Lacan *Séminaire 1961–62: L'Identification*, vol. I, 6–7 (unpublished). I offer this paraphrase, in my own translation: "Experience suggests we seek the meaning of any identity in the heart of what designates itself by a sort of redoubling of itself, this my-self being . . . already this *metipsissismum* . . . which we do not notice, but which is there in the my-self."

4 "Democracy" as a political form is based on "representation" – our votes represent our desires, and added together, constitute "the will of the people." In terms of the figuration one trope dominates *representation* – metaphor. It seems the most economical means of representing collective life as a collection of such plural wills.

5 Thus, though the modern, democratic model appears to be formed as a "symbolic" we should not forget that, for Lacan, exclusion of the metonymic function (transfer of "name" from "mother" to "father") makes it a "symbolic order" in name only.

6 In "La fonction du bien," *Séminaire VII*, Paris, Seuil, 1986, 264.

7 This is "historical drama" *à la* Shakespeare, a kind of "epic" that makes its hero out of a near contemporary, not a mythical past figure.

8 Often of doubtful political acumen.

9 *Physics and Philosophy: The Revolution in Modern Science*, New York, Harper Torchbooks, 1958, p. 202. Heisenberg continued to teach in Berlin until 1945. Edward Said, criticizing Marx for being blinded by the myth of "Orientalism" offers a citation that is too familiar. Marx lauded the British imperialism in India for unwittingly giving birth to a more progressive society, since it disrupted small patriarchal structures which, though charming, were, for him, "backward" (*Orientalism*, New York, Vintage Books, 1979, 153–5). Gayatri Spivak, in *In Other Worlds* (New York, Methuen, 1987), also points out the problematic dialectic for the western feminist's belief in the need for woman to be taken out of the patriarchal system, even though it may cost her all her local value.

10 Lévi-Strauss's alternative calls for a *symbolic* modeling and re-modeling – a "science of the concrete" – instead of the imposition of modern rationality upon traditional societies. Yet the weight has been on the side of those – both pro- and anti-modernists, from Heisenberg to Heidegger, who assume the inexorability of the march of western rationalism and its

technological arms. (See Benjamin, *Illuminations*, New York, Schocken Books, 1969, 258.) Can even technology develop without the desiring subject? Or to put it another way, is lack lacking or merely hiding in modern technology?

11 Lacan has it that Melanie Klein's substitution of the mythic body of the mother for the centrality of *das Ding* participates in covering up this structure. See above, Chapter 3, note 10, and Lacan, *Séminaire VII*, 127.

12 F. Tönnies, *Custom: An Essay on Social Codes*, tr. A. F. Borenstein, Chicago, Gateway/Henry Regnery Books, 1961, p. 47.

13 This sublimation is the transference of the natural relation to an artificial form. As Lacan put it in *Séminaire VII* (171), it is on the basis of a visible, tangible apprehension of the mother as she who engenders that paternal primordiality "sublimates" her: It does not "sublate" her.

14 Tönnies, *Custom*, 47. Festivals, where those usually separated come together, are supposed to be a "convening of the clan," an exaltation – hilarity or the totem feast – differing from the continuously reverential and mourning-like priestly demeanor toward the gods. All changes with the advent of the modern polity, according to Tönnies.

15 Hélène Cixous' Sihanouk makes much out of America's continuing and unconscious reference to his Cambodia as "tiny."

16 Included among the phantasmatic are, for me, the "fundamentalist" types of regimes whose ruler's face is oriented less toward his or her own people than toward a modernity it opposes on principle.

17 Bear in mind, of course, that Sihanouk is not a natural but a completely artificial king and father: he reigns because of French imperialism. Nevertheless, it is his selection of the paternal function as a model that matters here: he is not, like Lon Nol, emulating a modern western general (while making decisions according to astrology), nor acting out the role of puritan revolutionary like Pol Pot.

18 Interestingly, it is when he has been "elected" Prince that he becomes most egotistical – and most blind.

19 One historian believes the version of communism installed by the Pol Pot regime was less a great leap forward than a step back into a feudal structure. David P. Chandler, *A History of Cambodia*, Boulder, Colo., Westview Press, 1983, 191 ff.

20 Denis Diderot, *Rameau's Nephew*, tr. W. Tancock, Harmondsworth, Penguin, 1966, 121. (I have modified the translations.) Orig. *Le Neveu de Rameau*, Paris, Garnier Flammarion, 1967.

Passages translated

3 Egomimesis

a. "L'amour est impuissant, quoiqu'il soit réciproque, parce qu'il ignore qu'il n'est que le désire d'être Un, ce qui nous conduit à l'impossible d'établir la relation d'eux. La relation *d'eux* qui? *deux* sexes" ("Encore," 12).

b. "Quoique ses semblables ne fussent pas pour lui ce qu'ils sont pour nous, et qu'il n'eût gueres plus de commerce avec eux qu'avec les autres animaux, ils ne furent pas oubliés das ces observations. Les conformités que le temps put lui faire appercevoir entre eux, sa femelle et lui-même, le firent juger de celles qu'ils n'appercevoient pas, et voyant qu'ils se conduisoient tous, comme il auroit fait en de pareilles circonstances, il conclut que leur maniere de penser et de sentir étoit entirerement conforme à la sienne, et cette importante vérité, bien établie dans son esprit, lui fit suivre, par un pressentiment aussi sûr et plus prompt que la Dialectique, les meilleures régles de conduite que pour son avantage et sa sûreté il lui convint de garder avec eux" (*IIe Discours*, 169).

c. "Instruit par l'expérience que l'amour du bien-être est le seul mobile des actions humaines, il se trouva en état de distinguer les occasions rares où l'intérêt commun devoit le faire compter sur l'assistance de ses semblables, et celles plus rares encore où le concurrence devoit le faire défier d'eux" (*IIe Discours*, 169).

d. "Les premiers développemens du coeur furent l'effet d'une situation nouvelle qui réunissoit dans une habitation commune les maris et les Femmes, les Peres et les Enfans; l'habitude de vivre ensemble fit naître les plus doux sentimens qui soient connus des hommes, l'amour conjugal, et l'amour paternel" (*IIe Discours*, 168).

e. "Un voisinage permanent ne peut manquer d'engendrer enfin quelque liaison entre diverses familles. De jeunes gens de differens séxes habitent des Cabanes voisines, le commerce passager que demande la Nature en améne bientôt un autre, non moins doux et plus permanent par la fréquentation mutuelle'' (*IIe Discours*, 168).

f.   ''Très souvent l'avantage de l'un fait le préjudice de l'autre, l'intérest particulier est presque toujours en opposition avec l'intérest public'' (*IVe Promenade, Rêveries, OC I*, 1028).

g.   ''J'allois presque tous les dimanches passer la journée aux Paquis chez M. Fazy, qui avoit épousé une de mes tantes et qui avoit là une fabrique d'indiennes. Un jour j'étois à l'etendage dans la chambre de la calandre et j'en regardais les rouleaux de fonte: leur luisant flattoit ma vue, je fus tenté d'y poser mes doigts et je les promenais avec plaisir sur le licé [lissé] du cylindre'' (*Rêveries*, 1036).

h.   ''Quand le jeune Fazy s'étant mis dans la roue lui donna un demiquart de tour si adroitement qu'il n'y prit que le bout de mes deux plus longs doigts; mais c'en fut assez pour qu'ils y fussent écrasés par le bout et que les deux ongles y restassent.'' (*Rêveries*, 1036).

i.   ''Fazy consterné s'écrie, sort de la roue, m'embrasse et me conjure d'appaiser mes cris, ajoutant qu'il étoit perdu. Au fort de ma douleur la sienne me toucha, je me tus, nous fumes à la carpière où il m'aida à laver mes doigts et à étancher mon sang avec de la mousse'' (*Rêveries*, 1036).

j.   ''Il me supplia avec larmes de ne point l'accuser; je le lui promis et le tins si bien, que plus de vingt ans après personne ne savoit par quelle avanture j'avois deux de mes doigts cicatrisés, car il le sont demeurés toujours'' (*Rêveries*, 1036–7).

k.   ''où l'on faisoit manoeuvrer la bourgeoisie'' (*Rêveries*, 1036).

l.   ''Mon autre histoire est toute semblable, mais d'un âge plus avancé'' (*Rêveries*, 1037).

m.   ''Je jouois au mail à Plain-palais avec un de mes camarades appellé Pleince. Nous primes querelle au jeu, nous nous battimes et durant le combat il me donna sur la tête nue un coup de mail si bien appliqué que d'une main plus forte il m'eut fait sauter la cervelle. Je tombe à l'instant. Je ne vis de ma vie une agitation pareille à celle de ce pauvre garçon voyant mon sang ruisseler dans mes cheveux. Il crut m'avoir tué. Il se précipite sur moi, m'embrasse, me serre étroitement en fondant en larmes et poussant des cris perçants. Je l'embrassois aussi de toute ma force en pleurant comme lui dans une émotion confuse qui n'étoit pas sans quelque douceur. Enfin il se mit en devoir d'étancher mon sang qui continuoit de couler, et voyant que nos deux mouchoirs n'y pouvoient suffire, il m'entraîna chez sa mére qui avoit un petit jardin près de là'' (*Rêveries*, 1037).

n.   ''Cette bonne Dame faillit à se trouver mal en me voyant dans cet état. Mais elle sut conserver des forces pour me panser, et après avoir bien bassiné ma playe elle y appliqua des fleurs de lis macerées dans l'eau-de-vie, vulneraire excellent et très usité dans notre pays.

Ses larmes et celles de son fils pénétrerent mon coeur au point que longtemps je la regardai comme ma mére et son fils comme mon frére, jusqu'à ce qu'ayant perdu l'un et l'autre de vue, je les oubliai peu à peu'' (*Rêveries*, 1037).

o. ''Sans m'en appercevoir, j'y décrivis ma situation actuelle, j'y peignis Grimm, Mad^e d'Epinay, Mad^e d'Houdetot, St. Lambert, moi-même . . . . Hélas, on y sent trop l'amour, cet amour fatal . . .'' (*Confessions* X, *OC I*, 495–6).

p. ''Ma simplicité fut telle que quoique la Merceret ne fut pas desagréable il ne me vint pas même à l'esprit durant tout le voyage, je ne dis pas la moindre tentation galante, mais même la moindre idée qui s'y rapportât, et quand cette idée me seroit venue, j'étois trop sot pour en savoir profitter. Je n'imaginois pas comment une fille et un garcon venoient à coucher ensemble; je croyois qu'il falloit des siécles pour préparer ce terrible arrangement. Si la pauvre Merceret en me défrayant comptoit sur quelque équivalent, elle en fut la dupe, et nous arrivames à Fribourg exactement comme nous étions partis d'Annecy'' (*Confessions*, 143–5).

q. ''La Merceret, plus jeune et moins déniaisée que la Giraud ne m'a jamais fait des agaceries aussi vives; mais elle imitoit mes tons, mes accens, redisoit me mots, avoit pour moi les attentions que j'aurois dû avoir pour elle, et prenoit toujours grand soin, comme elle étoit fort peureuse, que nous couchassions dans la même chambre: identité que se borne rarement là dans un voyage, entre un garçon de vingt ans et une fille de vingt-cinq'' (*Confessions*, 144).

r. ''Je vis ma Julie en Mad^e d'Houdetot, et bientot je ne vis plus que Mad^e d'Houdetot, mais revêtue de toutes les perfections dont je venois d'orner l'idole de mon coeur'' (*Confessions*, 440).

s. ''Pour m'achever, elle me parla de St. Lambert en amante passionnée. Force contagieuse de l'amour! en l'écoutant, en me sentant auprès d'elle, j'étois saisi d'un fremissement délicieux que je n'avois éprouvé auprès de personne. Elle parloit et je me sentois ému; je croyois ne faire que m'interesser à ses sentiments quand j'en prenois de semblables; j'avalois à longs traits la coupe empoisonnée dont je ne sentois encore que la douceur. Enfin, sans que je m'en apperçûsse et sans qu'elle s'en apperceut qu'elle m'inspira pour elle-même tout ce qu'elle exprimoit pour son amant'' (*Confessions*, 440).

t. ''Mais j'ai tort de dire un amour non partagé; le mien l'étois en quelque sorte; il étoit égal des deux côtés, quoiqu'il ne fut pas réciproque'' (*Confessions*, 443).

u. ''Elle étoit bien aise de conserver à son amant et à elle-même un ami dont elle faisoit cas: elle ne parloit de rien avec plus de plaisir que de l'intime et douce societé que nous pouvions former entre nous trois, quand je serois devenu raisonnable" (*Confessions*, 441).

4 Feminine eros: from the bourgeois state to the nuclear state

a. "Henriette, fière de représenter sa petite maman, joua parfaitement son rôle, et si parfaitement que je vis pleurer les domestiques.
Cependant elle donnait toujours à sa mére le nom de maman, et lui
parlait avec le respect convenable; mais enhardie par le succès, et par
mon approbation, qu'elle remarquait fort bien, elle s'avisa de porter
la main sur une cuiller, et de dire dans une saillie: «Claire, veux-tu
de cela?» Le geste et le ton de voix furent imités au point que sa
mère en tressaillit. Un moment après, elle part d'un grand éclat de
rire, tend son assiette en disant: «Oui, mon enfant, donne; tu es
charmante.» Et puis elle se mit à manger avec une avidité qui me
surprit" (*La Nouvelle Héloïse*, 727).
b. "c'est sous la tente noirâtre de l'Arabe-Bédouin qu'il faut
chercher le modèle et la patrie du véritable amour" (*De l'amour*,
197).
c. "celle qui, en l'occasion, domine" ("L'Amour courtois en
anamorphose," 188).
d. "caractère foncièrement narcissique" ("L'Amour courtois," 181).
e. "les volontés du plus puissant seigneur" ("L'Amour courtois,"
176).
f. "remplit un autre rôle – un rôle de limite" ("L'Amour courtois,"
181).
g. "grades les plus élevés de l'initiation cathare" ("L'Amour courtois," 182).
h. "La femme idéalisée, la Dame, qui est dans la position de
l'Autre et de l'objet, se trouve soudain, brutalement, à la place
savamment construite par des signifiants raffinés, mettre dans sa
crudité le vide d'une chose, qui s'avère dans sa nudité être la chose,
la sienne, celle qui se trouve au coeur d''elle-même dans son vide
cruel . . . dévoilée avec une puissance insistante et cruelle"
("L'Amour courtois," 193).
i. "C'est dans les murs de la ville que je suis devenue sa femme"
(*Hir.*, 127).
j. "Nevers, où je suis née, dans mon souvenir, est indistinct de
moi-même. C'est une ville dont un enfant peut faire le tour" (*Hir.*,
128).
k. "quelqu'un me saisit par les épaules . . . c'était l'ennemi" (*Hir.*,
147); "ses mains me donnaient très vite l'envie de les punir" (128).
Her aggression against these seizing hands is repeated – "Je mords
ses mains après l'amour" (*Hir.*, 127).
l. "Je n'arrivais pas à trouver la moindre différence entre ce corps et

le mien . . . je ne pouvais trouver entre ce corps et le mien que des ressemblances hurlantes, tu comprends, c'était mon premier amour" (*Hir.*, 100).

m. "Ma famille, elle, était à Hiroshima. Je faisais la guerre" (*Hir.*, 39).

n. "Je vois ma vie. Ta mort" (*Hir.*, 98).

o. "On dirait qu'elle aide à mourir" (*Hir.*, 125).

p. "Tu me tues. Tu me fais du bien. . . . Dévore-moi. . . . Déforme-moi à ton image afin qu'aucun autre, après toi ne comprenne plus du tout le pourquoi de tant de désir" (*Hir.*, 115).

q. "Je ne pouvais plus entrevoir la moindre différence entre son corps et le mien" (*Hir.*, 147).

r. "J'aimais le sang depuis que j'avais goûté au tien" (*Hir.*, 89; "ton corps était devenu le mien" (*Hir.*, 147)).

s. "Faite à la taille de l'amour" (*Hir.*, 115).

t. "Alors Nevers s'est fermée sur elle-même. Elle a grandi comme on a grandi" (*Hir.*, 129).

u. "La faute, à Nevers, est le bonheur. L'ennui y est un vertu toléré. Fous, bohémiens, chiens, l'amour circulent dans les faubourgs" (*Hir.*, 129).

v. "Je vais rester à Hiroshima"; "Reste à Hiroshima" (*Hir.*, 112).

w. "Leur absence de l'un à l'autre a commencé" (*Hir.*, 112).

x. "Je désire ne plus avoir de patrie. A mes enfants j'enseignerai la méchanceté et l'indifférence et l'amour de la patrie des autres jusqu'à la mort" (*Hir.*, 114).

y. "Ils s'appelleront encore. Quoi. Nevers. Hiroshima. Ils ne sont en effet encore personne à leurs yeux respectifs. Ils ont des noms de lieu, des noms qui n'en sont pas" (*Hir.*, 17).

z. "Entre ces deux êtres géographiquement, philosophiquement, historiquement, économiquement, racialement, etc., éloignés le plus qu'il est possible de l'être, HIROSHIMA sera le terrain commun (le seul au monde peut-être?) où les données universelles de l'érotisme, de l'amour, et du malheur apparaîtront sous une lumière implacable" (*Hir.*, 11–12).

aa. "Un halo particulier y auréole chaque geste, chaque parole, d'un sens supplémentaire à leur sens littéral. Et c'est là un des desseins majeures du film: en finir avec la description de l'horreur par l'horreur . . . ." (*Hir.*, 11).

bb. "Faire renaître cette horreur de ces cendres en la faisant s'inscrire en un amour qui sera forcément particulier et 'emerveillant'" (*Hir.*, 11).

7 After the new regime

a. "Il n'y a dans tout un royaume qu'un homme qui marche, c'est le souverain. Tout le reste prend des positions" (*Le neveu de Rameau*, 180).

b. "Il est dans la nature d'avoir d'appétit" (*Le neveu*, 177).

c. "Il est dans la nature d'avoir d'appétit . . . Je trouve qu'il n'est pas du bon ordre de n'avoir pas toujours de quoi manger. Que diable d'économie, des hommes qui regorgent de tout, tandis que d'autres qui ont un estomac importun comme eux, et pas de quoi mettre sous la dent" (*Le neveu*, 177–8).

Index